Our Schools Suck

Our
Schools
Suck

*Students Talk Back to a
Segregated Nation on the
Failures of Urban Education*

Gaston Alonso, Noel S. Anderson,
Celina Su, and Jeanne Theoharis

NEW YORK UNIVERSITY PRESS

New York and London

NEW YORK UNIVERSITY PRESS
New York and London
www.nyupress.org

Library of Congress Cataloging-in-Publication Data
Our schools suck : students talk back to a segregated nation on the
failures of urban education / Gaston Alonso . . . [et al.].
p.   cm.
Includes bibliographical references and index.
ISBN-13: 978-0-8147-8307-8 (cl : alk. paper)
ISBN-10: 0-8147-8307-4 (cl : alk. paper)
ISBN-13: 978-0-8147-8308-5 (pb : alk. paper)
ISBN-10: 0-8147-8308-2 (pb : alk. paper)
1. Education, Urban—United States. 2. De facto school segregation—
United States. 3. Minority teenagers—Education—United States. 4.
Minority teenagers—United States—Attitudes.   I. Alonso, Gaston.
LC5131.O87 2009
370.9173'20973—dc22   2008051337

New York University Press books are printed on acid-free paper,
and their binding materials are chosen for strength and durability.
We strive to use environmentally responsible suppliers and materials
to the greatest extent possible in publishing our books.

Manufactured in the United States of America
c   10 9 8 7 6 6 5 4 3 2 1
p   10 9 8 7 6 6 5 4 3 2

Contents

Acknowledgments

Over the years, my students at the University of California at Berkeley and at Brooklyn College of the City University of New York have provided me with daily inspiring reminders of young people's thirst for new knowledge. These reminders have shaped the commitment to a universal quality public education voiced in these pages. My special thanks to Samuel Farber, Alberto Ferreras, Anya Grant, Luisa Giulianetti, Jesse Goldhammer, Jacqueline McEvoy, Lorraine "Rainy" Rust, Francoise Verges, Lisa Wedeen, and my coauthors Noel, Celina, and Jeanne for their friendship and intellectual companionship over the years. I am indebted to Jason Schott, Brett Sullivan, Pamela Wolff, the students in my research methods seminar during the spring of 2008, and my coauthors for their editorial suggestions. I had the privilege of calling Michael Rogin my teacher, mentor, and friend for over a decade, and despite his untimely passing I remain deeply indebted to his intellectual and political insights. I have been fortunate to be surrounded by a family—*tias, tio,* brother, partner, mother—who encouraged me to believe in the power of my voice and to view the world of ideas, of books, of words, as an indispensable part of the struggle for social justice. I am forever grateful to my strongest supporter, Lloyd L. DesBrisay. These words would not be possible without his constant encouragement, editorial guidance, and intellectual, political, and personal companionship. My mother, Clara Mirta Donate, impressed upon me the importance of education, made that education possible through her sacrifice, and taught me the necessity of "talking back." These words would also not be possible without her. They are dedicated to her.

GASTON ALONSO

I want to acknowledge my coauthors and fellow activists Gaston, Celina, and Jeanne; Nadine Dolby, Colleen L. Larson, and Pedro A. Noguera for their time and support; and the courageous public school youth across the country who are trying to "make sense out of non-sense."

NOEL S. ANDERSON

My greatest thanks go to the leaders and organizers of Sistas and Brothas United, who shared with me their fears, aspirations, and incisive critiques of both themselves and the New York City school system. I cannot imagine engaging with a more thoughtful group of activists. Their clarity of vision and perseverance astounded me and continue to inspire me. Amid conditions of scarcity, they managed to help one another *and* struggle for educational justice with dignity and aplomb. I am not thanking these folks by name only because of our agreements of confidentiality. Besides, they deserve more credit than I can provide. Special gratitude goes to Jorman Nuñez for so generously telling and critically thinking about his story in the context of this book and for allowing us, in turn, to share it with readers. I am incredibly fortunate to have three colleagues who are equally moved and motivated by the dangerous cultural politics surrounding inner-city schools and who gave me the opportunity to work with them in response. It was a privilege to work with Gaston, Noel, and Jeanne on this book. The U.S. Department of Education's Jacob K. Javits Fellowship, the Whiting Award for Excellence in Teaching, and a Professional Staff Congress at the City University of New York grant allowed me to conduct months' worth of uninterrupted fieldwork and gave me the space and time to sift through students' testimonies and to work on this book. I also appreciate the help of James Mumm and Omar Wasow. My work on this book would not have been the same without the thoughtful critiques and indispensable support of Archon Fung, Barbara Green, Rufina Lee, Ceasar McDowell, Karen Miller, Carolina Bank Muñoz, Paul Osterman, J. Phillip Thompson, Joy Wang, and Althea Wasow. Thank you to Alexandre Su, Caleb Su, and Christina Su in all the ways I have yet to articulate. And then there's Peter Muennig—hardcore polymath, nonstop insight machine. Yeah, he's all right.

CELINA SU

This work owes its foremost debt to Steve Lang and Sarah Knopp for letting me into their classes and to the more than two hundred students whose lives, experiences, perspectives, and writings are the subject of this story. My deepest thanks go to Steve Lang for his tireless commitment to young people and for his friendship and unflagging encouragement throughout the research and writing of this book; to Alejandra Marchevsky for making it possible for me to imagine this project in all of its stages; and to LaVerne Brunt, Scott Dexter, Jason Elias, Claudia Gil, Jennifer McCormick, John Ramirez, John Rogers, Alfio Saitta, Pete Sigal, Sam Vong, and Mark Wild for all their help in enabling me to undertake this L.A.-based research. This research was made possible with a Rockefeller Humanities Fellowship through California State University, Los Angeles. It was also supported by a CUNY Scholar Incentive Grant and a Tow Travel Fellowship. I am also profoundly grateful to my coauthors Gaston, Noel, and Celina for modeling the kind of collaborative spirit that the academy often precludes and to Prudence Cumberbatch, Johanna Fernandez, Arnold Franklin, Dayo Gore, Robin Kelley, Karen Miller, Mojubaolu Okome, Komozi Woodard, and the Theoharis family (Nancy, Athan, George, Liz, Julie, Chris, Ella, and Sam) for their insights, feedback, and support of this work.

JEANNE THEOHARIS

Collectively, we thank Terri Bennet and Sofia Mussa for their research assistance; Pedro A. Noguera and Nadine Dolby for their generosity in reading and commenting on an early draft of the manuscript; and the anonymous reviewers of NYU Press for their critical reading of our manuscript, their insightful and detailed suggestions, and their support of our project. A special note of gratitude goes to NYU Press, in particular to Gabrielle Begue and Despina Papazoglou Gimbel for their attention to the project and to Aiden Amos for her careful reading of the manuscript and her assistance in bringing the book to publication. Last, this book would not have been possible without the work of our editor, Ilene Kalish, who understood from the beginning the importance of the project and who enthusiastically encouraged and guided us each step of the way.

GASTON, NOEL, CELINA, AND JEANNE

Introduction

CELINA SU

In 2003, Jorman Nuñez looked like a troublemaker. At four-teen years old, he should have been learning about American history, performing his first dissection in science class, and tackling algebra. Instead, by March of his freshman year at DeWitt Clinton High School in the Bronx, he began to routinely cut classes. Knowing his mother would be disappointed in him, he stayed clear of his apartment during school hours. Each morning, he dragged himself out of bed by 7:00 and tried to entertain himself outdoors until it was time to go home. He started hanging out with older teenagers and other dropouts. Although they did not engage in illicit activities, they occasionally did stupid things. "We were bored out of our minds," he said. Jorman remembered one day, for instance, when they hand-slapped a New York Police Department van. The van chased them. They got away that time, but any day now, he felt, he might land himself in big trouble.

At first glance, Jorman's story corresponds well with a narrative trope that abounds in the popular media these days—that of the wayward, perhaps even thuggish, inner-city youth. It looked as if Jorman was up to no good.

Just two months after Jorman dropped out of school, our nation celebrated the fiftieth anniversary of the 1954 *Brown v. Board of Education* Supreme Court decision that outlawed racial segregation in public education. The anniversary prompted a national reflection on the legacy of the ruling and the state of U.S. schooling. Educators, politicians, civil rights veterans, scholars, and even celebrities weighed in on the impact of *Brown*. They debated whether the historic case had lived up to its promise to create racially integrated and equal schools, or whether it had instead fallen short of its ambitious goals, particularly in view of the hypersegregated and dramatically unequal conditions in urban school systems around the country.

Since then, however, what started out as a public conversation has turned into a public spanking. At a May 2004 NAACP gala commemorating the fiftieth anniversary of *Brown*, Bill Cosby declared that "lower . . . and lower-middle economic [African American] people are not holding their end in this deal" on education. He asserted that the opportunities were there for the taking and that cultural values and norms explained the academic and economic success or failure of different racial groups. Cosby turned scrutiny away from the role of the courts, the political process, and school systems in perpetuating "still separate and un-equal conditions," to chastising poor and working-class students of color for their supposed deficient values, lack of motivation, and troubling behavior. "We cannot blame white people," he proclaimed. "It's not what they're doing to us. It's what we're not doing. 50 percent drop out."[1] This finger-pointing was coupled with a convoluted argument that since legal segregation of schools is no longer permitted, the failures of *Brown* can no longer be a failure of the "system." Instead, the responsibility for poor achievement in urban schools falls squarely on the shoulders of inner-city young people.

Cosby stumbles over the hard facts, which demonstrate that urban schools of all kinds (i.e., traditional schools, charter schools, magnet programs) are racially segregated and receive fewer resources than suburban school systems. From 1991 to 2004, the percentage of African American students attending majority-nonwhite schools steadily *rose* from 66 to 73 percent. By that time, 77 percent of Latino students attended majority nonwhite schools. The percentages of African American and Latino students attending *intensely* segregated schools (with 0–10 percent white students) have also risen since 1991. The flip side of the racial coin holds true as well: only 12 percent of white students attend majority-nonwhite schools.[2]

American schools continue to be plagued not only by racial segregation but also by unequal funding. Although some nonprofit organizations, parent groups, and state governments have attempted to reform school financing structures, the prevailing ethic is one of maintaining status quo inequalities.[3] Local property taxes continue to serve as primary revenue sources for school funding, and the Supreme Court's 1974 *Milliken v.*

Bradley decision rules out interdistrict desegregation programs. This provides a striking contrast to school systems in other industrialized nations, where more equitable funding is coordinated at the national level.[4]

Thus suburban school districts tend to be much better funded than inner-city ones. As Michael Rebell points out, "Students living in school districts with high-priced residential or commercial property [have] continued to have substantially greater resources available to support their education."[5] Linda Darling-Hammond notes that as of 2004, "The wealthiest U.S. public schools spend at least ten times more than the poorest schools—ranging from over $30,000 per pupil at the wealthy schools to only $3,000 at the poorest."[6]

Further, funding inequalities are not randomly distributed. Differences between city and suburb exacerbate differences between the schooling of white and nonwhite children, since most suburban schools are predominantly (if not nearly exclusively) white. Gary Orfield and Chungmei Lee explain that because of the ways in which racial and economic inequalities intersect in the United States, "the share of schools that are high poverty increases as minority population increases."[7] Such racial chasms and funding inequalities go hand in hand, even among schools in the same district. A 2003 study of eighty-nine elementary schools in Columbus, Ohio, found that "inequality in spending appears to correspond to the racial and class composition of schools" and that intradistrict per-pupil spending varied from $3,045 to $8,165.[8]

These funding differences have concrete consequences. For example, students attending California schools where racial minorities constitute the majority are ten times more likely to be instructed by uncertified teachers than students in majority-white schools. In Texas, students attending majority-nonwhite schools are more likely to have teachers with significantly fewer years of education than students at majority-white ones. A 1998 General Accounting Office report found that 67 percent of urban schools had structural problems, compared to only 52 percent of suburban ones.[9] Across the nation, high-minority and high-poverty schools have more crowded and physically decaying facilities; fewer qualified teachers; greater turnover in teaching staff and students; larger class sizes; more limited curricula; less challenging classes; lower quality and quantity of instructional materials, equipment, and books; fewer extracurricular activities; and, perhaps not surprisingly, lower achievement scores on standardized exams.[10] Thus schools with better funding provide their students with significantly different educational experiences than those schools, often just down the road, with less funding.

The lower levels of academic achievement and higher dropout rates found among segments of African American and Latino children relative to other groups—the so-called "racial achievement gap"—can be fully understood only in the context of an education system that maintains such highly segregated and unequal conditions.[11] Indeed, high dropout rates are concentrated in certain high-poverty and high-minority public schools.[12] A close look at the numbers reveals the questionable and unsavory nature of public discourses and academic literature that place African Americans and Latinos on one side and whites and Asian Americans on the other. (Native Americans are often ignored altogether.) For instance, even though many Asian Americans attend poorly resourced schools, they are subjected to another form of specious culture talk, one that anoints them the "model minority" and groups Cambodian refugees fleeing war atrocities in Long Beach, California, with well-to-do Chinese immigrants whose parents are attending graduate school in Palo Alto. Such essentialist stereotypes detract policy makers from the conditions at hand, dehumanize individual young people, and hinder students who need help—no matter what their racial or ethnic background.

Despite consistent and pervasive inequalities in the American educational system, Bill Cosby contends that inner-city youth have themselves to blame for their academic failure. After his infamous comment at the NAACP gala that "*Brown versus the Board of Education* is no longer the white person's problem," it seemed that every few days yet another high-profile pundit joined the bandwagon, announcing something like "Kids would do better if they just stopped listening to hip-hop" or "The real problem with urban schools is that kids no longer value education and disparage those who do." For instance, in August 2006, Juan Williams, a Fox News commentator, released *Enough: The Phony Leaders, Dead-End Movements, and Culture of Failure That Are Undermining Black America—and What We Can Do about It.* In the book, Williams draws heavily on Cosby's speech and announces that *Brown* did not fail Black youth; "Young people of color are failing *Brown* by failing in school or by dropping out."[13] Just a few weeks later, Bob Herbert of the *New York Times* joined the "culture of failure" fest, praising Williams and lamenting inner-city blacks who "wallow in the deepest depths of degradation their irresponsible selves can find."[14] Others shrilled that Latinos, too, were carriers of "the crucible of failure." A book by Puerto Rican–born congressman Herman Badillo that earned blurbs from both former New York City mayor Rudolph Giuliani and former New York State governor Mario

Cuomo lamented that "education is not a high priority in the Hispanic community"; it claimed that a five-hundred-year-old "cultural siesta" was the reason Latinos were reporting lower educational levels than "more economically and socially successful immigrant groups."[15]

Academics moved from sidelines to center stage in lambasting the "culture of failure." Harvard sociologist Orlando Patterson joined the fray by stating that young Black men would rather strike a "cool pose" of thuggery than pursue a meaningful education or seek a job.[16] Berkeley professor John McWhorter began to give fewer academic conference presentations on his field of expertise, the Saramaccan language, and more interviews on the "values" of Black and Latino students, proclaiming that "at Berkeley every third student is Asian. They're everywhere. . . . They're obsessed with doing well. . . . There's no reason for that in the black community, because if you do pretty darn well, you'll get into a school above and beyond what Suzie Wong could possibly get into. . . . With Latinos as well as black people, there's a sense that to be white is to be uptight and to sell out."[17]

These public intellectuals announce that we should not be focusing our attention on socioeconomic or school conditions; what nonwhite youth really need is not a librarian or experienced teachers but a moral flogging. While pundits imply that African American and Latino students *choose* to drop out because they lack educational values, those who seek to improve the educational performance of young people of color must not only grapple with grim statistics but also investigate what students themselves have to say about their aspirations and the realities of their education. What causal mechanisms do *students* assign to the racial achievement gap? A recent study, based on extensive surveys and focus groups, suggests that students drop out for a variety of reasons: for instance, 32 percent said that they needed to get a job, and 22 percent said that they needed to care for a family member. Quite a few had high grades before dropping out, and these students stated that their classes had failed to impart skills or interest them.[18]

Contrary to what Cosby et al. insinuate, former students did *not* dismiss high school as a worthless endeavor. In fact, two-thirds asserted that they would have worked harder if more had been demanded of them.[19]

Our Schools Suck: Students Talk Back to a Segregated Nation on the Failures of Urban Education highlights the voices of our nation's high school students. It is an intervention into the adult-driven debates on inner-city youth, providing needed voices of love, outrage, challenge, and hope. Gaston, Noel, Jeanne, and I started talking about this book project during the spring of 2006, when we realized that each of us had independently become alarmed by the absence of youth voices in the public discourse and the skewed nature of the public conversation around urban education. We had all spent quite a bit of time with low-income African American and Latino youth, the very "troublemakers" striking fear and eliciting disgust among pundits like Juan Williams and Herman Badillo. Somehow, our observations—which took place over years—never meshed with stereotypes about inner-city youth as dark menaces to society, shadowy figures lurking around corners who refused to attend school. Instead, students' stories simmered with complex analyses of the conditions in which they lived and the schools in which they tried to learn.

The youth spoke about the nuances of navigating the streets and the schools of inner cities. Hoping to succeed and make their families proud, most did not simply succumb to a pernicious "culture of failure." Indeed, signs of rebellion did not seem to loom any larger than they would among any teenage group—Black, Latino, white, or otherwise. Nor did those who triumphed over their circumstances accomplish this through sheer will and good parenting but often through the good fortune of encountering teachers, mentors, or special academic programs that shepherded them through the troubled schools they were attending.

By paying attention to what the students themselves have to say, this book serves two purposes. First, it refutes popular depictions of inner cities as homogenous cauldrons of a "culture of failure," or of *any* monolithic culture. The students' voices lead us to conclude, not that all urban youth are secretly angels, but that all of them, from the most successful to the most marginal students, are complex *persons* who deserve an excellent and challenging education. Second, the book demonstrates that to the extent that students express anger or commit foolish acts, these feelings and behaviors are largely born out of the conditions in which they live, work, and attend school rather than essentialized "cool pose" values. In doing so, it refocuses the public debate onto failed education as one of the causes, rather than one of the consequences, of the state of urban youth today.

In the remainder of this chapter, I contrast the popular news media's general portrayal of young African American and Latino people as a demographic group with their general portrayal of young white people as individuals facing specific circumstances. These media portrayals reinforce Cosby's thesis that if inner-city students reformed their cultural values, they would succeed.

I then discuss the approaches we took—the nagging questions we sought to answer and some of the lessons we learned—in each of the remaining chapters in the book. While I am the primary author of this introduction, as Jeanne Theoharis is the primary author of the book's conclusion, our arguments were developed and are owned by all four coauthors. Throughout, I include snippets of Jorman's story as a means of highlighting one young person's voice amid so many adult ones. The passages of poetry sprinkled throughout are all excerpts of spoken-word poems by Jorman.

> School didn't show me what it needed to show,
> And it wouldn't teach me what I needed to know.
> Bottom line: It didn't give me the tools I needed to grow.

Troublemaker? Are We Sure?

Did Jorman think staying in school was equivalent to "selling out"? When he dropped out of Clinton High that spring, he had a lot of company. Half of New York City's ninth-grade public high school students fail to graduate within four years.[20] Some educators fear that the real statistics are even grimmer, as those pushed into GED or alternative certificate programs are often counted as graduates, and the city's department of education fails to track students who "disappear" between eighth and ninth grades. Sometimes students "disappear" for no reason.

In speaking to the Advocates for Children of New York, Ruby Garcia, also a former student at Clinton High, noted that after she transferred to another school, Clinton High somehow "had no record of me and could not help me. After wasting about a year, I managed to graduate at the top of my class (and on time) at a different school."[21] Even Ruby Garcia's brief comment suggests that there is something amiss about Cosby et al.'s "culture of failure" theory. How come Ruby excelled academically as soon as she switched schools? According to her, "Classes [at Clinton High] were too full and teachers seemed more focused on their checks than the product of their teaching."[22] Approximately 4,600 students attend Clinton High, and there is not a single librarian to serve them.[23]

Students like Jorman do need help. However, it does not then follow, as Cosby intimates, that Jorman failed *Brown*. What if segregated schools failed Jorman?

Jorman first moved to the United States from the Dominican Republic when he was two years old, alone with his mother. Life in the United

States was difficult, so just a few months after their arrival, he was sent back to be with his grandparents in the Dominican Republic. Around age five, he came back to New York in order to live with his mother, this time for good.

According to Cosby, Jorman should have been one of the immigrants putting African Americans to shame with his work ethic. (After all, as Cosby declared at the NAACP gala, "Everybody knows it's important to speak English except these [working-class, African American] knuckleheads.") Yet according to Badillo and McWhorter, Latinos are as vulnerable to the insidious "culture of failure" as African Americans are. The pundits' conflicting claims show that their blanket caricatures of demographic groups lack nuance and substantive proof. Even as "model immigrant" stereotypes duel with those of Latinos as criminal gang members and social service leeches, Jorman's case tells a more complex story.

With the help of an ESL (English as a Second Language) class, Jorman learned to read before everyone else in his class. This was partly because his mother, like many immigrant parents, relied on her six-year-old son to act as translator in stores and offices, to read documents and basic instructions on household items, and to teach her English skills. As a result, teachers kept recommending that Jorman be placed in more advanced classes, and upon their recommendations he changed schools three or four times in as many years. By fourth grade, Jorman landed in an advanced program at P.S. 310 in the Bronx. He felt at home there. In sixth grade, he was admitted into AURORA, an advanced program for Latino youth. In addition, he spent most of his time outside class on educational projects of his own. For example, although he never owned a computer, he once came across an obsolete one sitting in the corner of a room in one of his wealthier friends' apartments. He jumped at the chance to take apart the computer and put it back together to see how it worked. When he watched television, he watched Discovery Channel shows. "I loved that channel. And I loved the fact that I knew the most in class," he noted. "If someone else got more right answers than me in class, I would go home and look up the answers for the next day. Yeah," he laughed. "I kind of had a competitive streak in me." Jorman was on a trajectory for success.

Unfortunately, this fortuitous trend did not last very long. The troubles started in middle school, when Jorman was exposed to a new pedagogical style.[24] In math class, he was not permitted to develop his own algorithms

for problem solving or to deconstruct formulas and put them back together in different ways. Instead, he was told to "solve and check, solve
and check" in the manner dictated by the teacher. Jorman was used to
being allowed to explore math. Now, he was still scoring 100s on tests,
but he sometimes received 70s on his report card. His questions in class
constituted "behavioral problems."

For the first time in his life, Jorman was told to attend summer school.
His teachers, even the ones who gave him lower grades for "behavioral
problems," balked. "You shouldn't be here," they kept repeating. They
would even break the rules and excuse him, telling him that he did not
need to show up every day to go over material he had in fact already
mastered.

On one hand, Jorman was told that he was too advanced for the classes
in which he was placed. On the other hand, he suffered the consequences
of being a "delinquent" student with "behavioral problems." In wealthier
school districts, he might have been considered gifted. It is unlikely that
Jorman would have been labeled as a "troublemaker" for asking questions
in class. These mixed messages surely did not help Jorman find his place
in the school system.

Unlike an eighth grader attending Springfield Middle School and assumed to attend Springfield High School, eighth graders in New York
City must take a standardized entrance exam to the city's specialized high
schools. Some high schools have minimum required scores; others require application essays and portfolios. Coveted seats at some of the magnet programs without stringent admissions criteria are allotted via lottery.
Although the bulk of New York's high schools have no specific criteria, all
students must research, consider, and list up to twelve high schools and
specific programs they wish to attend.

After some thought, Jorman came up with a list of schools. His first
choice was a selective program at DeWitt Clinton High School, the Macy
Honors Gifted Program. This program was known to be academically
challenging and to send students to Ivy League and top-tier liberal arts
colleges. It offered a variety of Advanced Placement courses, as well as
classes in specialized and advanced technology, law, philosophy, the "Great
Books," and other subjects.

If everything had gone along to plan, the city would have gone down
Jorman's list of preferred choices, placing him in the highest-ranked one
that both had space in it and accepted his academic record. Jorman was
fairly confident that he would end up in the Macy program.

When he got his assigned placement in the mail, however, he opened the document and saw . . . nothing. According to the document, he had no accepted placements and no rejected ones. It was as if he had never handed in a well-considered list—as if he did not exist. Jorman, once anointed a gifted child and precocious thinker by his teachers, would have to fight even to attend high school.

He made phone calls and told city administrators that something had gone terribly wrong with his application. Eventually he found a sympathetic ear, and administrators scrambled to find him a place, any place, in the Bronx. He landed at Clinton High, but no one had bothered to review his high standardized test scores and still impressive academic transcript. He was not placed in the Macy Honors Gifted Program. Nevertheless, Jorman hoped for the best.

He was in for a shock at Clinton High. He distinctly recalls the first day of his ninth-grade math class. He sat in silent horror as the teacher explained concepts he had learned three years before, in the sixth grade. He remembers thinking that surely this was a review. "I'll get to move on to new math concepts next week, right?" No, he would not.

Jorman began to panic. He went to the guidance counselors' office. When he arrived, he found three guidance counselors for the school of almost five thousand. The room overflowed with flustered students waiting to see the counselors. Jorman waited but never got to see one. Then he came back the next day and did the same thing.

After several attempts, Jorman got to see a guidance counselor, who reviewed his academic record and confirmed his suspicion that he should not be relearning math concepts from the sixth grade. Jorman asked to be placed in a higher-level class. The counselor stated that if he performed well in the first marking period she would transfer him.

To Jorman, this was suboptimal. Why should he have to lose the chance to attend months of challenging, level-appropriate classes? The counselor herself had stated that he should be transferred. Nevertheless, he agreed to the plan.

At the end of the marking period, Jorman took his report card to the counselor, showed her his good grades, and asked to be transferred. The counselor agreed that he had performed well in his classes but reneged on her promise. He could transfer to his appropriate level the next year.

By this time Jorman was "really frustrated." He could not imagine eight more months of showing up to classes with content he had learned years ago, and where teachers discouraged critical analysis or active student participation. Most of his classes took place "in the tower," where the heat was on way too high throughout the winter. In one room, the windows were always broken, so they could not be opened. (In other rooms, they could not be closed.) The classrooms were supposed to hold twenty students, but they usually held twice that number. Jorman had to race to class to get there in time, and there were often no seats left by the time he arrived. This meant that he would have to sit on the heater in order to take notes on his lap. "I burned my ass off," he dryly noted.

His other classes were not going well, either. For example, "History should have been engaging and fun." Jorman liked to debate how history could have transpired differently, how prominent movers and shakers navigated tricky situations, or what social forces or events shaped society. "I wanted challenging teachers," he declared. "I should have learned something, but it was really, really boring" because his teacher would pass out worksheets and then fall asleep in class.

Jorman muttered, "I cannot remember having fun." After making this statement, he paused for a moment. "When I said that I couldn't remember 'having fun,' I'm not saying anything about slacking. I mean that I don't ever remember learning something new." Besides history, science had been his favorite subject: "I loved it so much that I would spend all my time on it, even outside of class. I have younger twin sisters, and one of my teachers found out, and she told me that if I wanted to be a real scientist, I'd have to sharpen my observation skills. So I remember keeping a journal and logging in everything that they did. What time they were fed, what time they slept, what their moods were like, observing their behavior. I loved it!" Jorman laughed, clearly relishing memories of times when he was truly engaged with school.

Between classes, Jorman struggled to make his way through the crowds and to his next class. This was difficult, as Clinton High was (and is) an egregiously overcrowded school. At the time, the school was already running far beyond the building capacity of 3,363;[25] in 2003 it served 4,524, far outstripping citywide growth in student numbers.[26] Because of this severe overcrowding, the principal relinquished her office to be used for classes, and classes were organized according to three staggered schedules. The thousand or so Macy students, for instance, attended nine class periods each day instead of eight like everyone else in school. The growing presence of themed small schools in the same building added to the confusion. Further, multiple teachers were assigned to any given room. As a result, students could not put work up on the walls, and teachers had to carry their supplies from room to room. Even with the staggered schedules, hallways looked like rush hour subway trains during class change periods (though at least during rush hour one has the option to wait for a less crowded train).

The presence of armed police exacerbated matters. Between classes, they were constantly blowing their whistles and yelling in the students' ears. Every day, Jorman would feel the police officers' spit against his neck as he stood, shoulder to shoulder, with other students also trying to get to class. "It was tough going from that to boring teachers," he said. "I didn't have anything to look forward to."

Worst of all, Jorman was routinely harassed by the police. As he explained it, "You have to show your ID whenever the police want, and they pick on you. For anything. They always find something. Like me, for example. You see that I'm wearing a hoodie. I know that it's summer and kind of warm, and it looks funny that I'm wearing a hoodie. But it's my style! And it wasn't against the rules." When they could not think of anything else for which they could pick on Jorman, they would yell, "Take that off! Now! It's warm out! It's for your health. TAKE THAT OFF NOW OR I WON'T LET YOU IN!" Jorman complained but nevertheless complied and took off his sweatshirt.

Jorman had a friend who dressed as a goth, wearing lots of black. This friend had multiple piercings on his ears and on his face. The police kept calling him a metal "rack" and laughing, sometimes pushing the friend around as they did so. The friend kept quiet. "See?" the police would mockingly ask Jorman. "Your friend knows how to get pushed around and still stay quiet. You should learn to be more like him."

Every day Jorman arrived at school on time, only to barely sneak into class late because of the long lines he had to stand in while waiting to be inspected by the police. Every single day, he was harassed as he did so. One of his friends had been maced in the face. Female students regularly complained of inappropriate and humiliating touching and sexual harassment by male officers.[27] Teachers protested the police's tactics. (At other high schools in the city, teachers and principals had themselves been arrested when they stepped in to protect students.)[28] Occasionally, a police sanction or apology would be issued.

After months of this, Jorman began to lose his passion for school. Still, he is not sure whether he would have left school if the police had not given him the idea to do so. After all, one of their favorite refrains was "You don't have to be here! Get out of class! Get out of here! You won't do anything with your life, anyway! Don't come back! DON'T COME BACK! GET OUT OF HERE!"

One day, he took their advice and got out of there. Then Jorman started cutting class more often. Finally, by spring of his freshman year, he had dropped out of school completely.

The teachers can't engage me, so I just sit there, fighting off sleep
And they tell us we're all different, that our minds are unique at their best
But two minutes later, we suddenly have to take a "standardized" test
They tell me to think critically, "Don't just follow the mass"
But if I ask a challenging question, I get kicked out of class
And when I got my hat on, it shows that the discipline rules are not fair
'Cause Ms. O'Neill lets me slide, but Mr. Martinez suspends me right there
Screaming in my face so much, I could see his drool
He tells me delinquents like me shouldn't bother with school
But my mother tells me different, she wants me to obtain knowledge
She tells me to fulfill my dreams, be the first to reach college
I thought I was competent, I always thought I was smart
But these mixed messages have torn me apart.

The View Is So Much Prettier at the Top

Jorman's story highlights the disconnect between the prevailing public discourse on the lack of values among inner-city youth and the infinitely more complex realities these teenagers face. Somehow, the accounts of dropouts like Jorman rarely enter public discourse about them. Public declarations like those by Williams or Badillo are not neutral presentations of facts or motivational truth telling but polemics with captive audiences and dire consequences.

It is striking that the most prominent "culture of failure" pundits all happen to be Black or Latino men. Even as they claim to be the ultimate seers and spokesmen for the larger Black and Latino communities, there is an irony to this brand of tough love. In the intersection of class and race, these Black and Latino middle- and upper-class men elevate themselves while denigrating those "who are at the bottom" of the socioeconomic hierarchy. In so doing, they do not necessarily acknowledge existing inequalities in our schools, but they do help to maintain their own fragile mainstream acceptance and social sanction. Their sermons act like a magic password, one that allows them to join a private club of the elite.

By deflecting attention from the socioeconomic conditions in which students live and attend school, these "tough love" advocates diagnose the young as producers of their own disease. Their discourse may reflect a real and prominent split within communities of color, where leaders and everyday citizens legitimately engage in debates on what urban education policy should look like. However, in the larger national political context, it exacerbates binary "good versus criminal" conceptualizations of Blacks and Latinos. It renders inner-city youth a "not like us" alien species, one that does not quite have the same common sense, moral fiber, and mental faculties we do. That these aliens are resident ones does not render them any less foreign or inferior.

The prevailing discourse also helps policy makers keep racial and socioeconomic hierarchies intact. White Americans, who are more likely to fall at higher points along these hierarchies, are subject to an entirely different set of stereotypes. "Hip-hop, professional basketball and homeboy fashions are as American as cherry pie," Orlando Patterson intones in the *New York Times*. "Young white Americans are very much into these things, but selectively; they know when it is time to turn off Fifty Cent and get out the SAT prep book."[29]

Given such specious, sweeping characterizations, it is hard to imagine "cool pose" critiques sticking to wealthier, whiter, suburban counterparts,[30] even if students in neighboring Scarsdale also regularly mess up. When stashes of alcohol in white stretch limousines are considered a traditional part of their prom night experience,[31] policy makers do not suddenly deem these teenagers unworthy of a decent, and expensive, educational system. When eight students in suburban Montrose broke onto school grounds and planted covered clocks that were taken to be bombs, a *New York Times* columnist urged that administrators loosen up a little and let the "punishment fit the prank."[32] When high school seniors at elite New York City schools drank to excess on all-expenses-paid trips to the Caribbean over spring break, schools and parents responded not by taking privileges away but by making trips safer.[33] These parents took time off from work to go to the Caribbean as well, staying at adjacent resorts, so that they could be there to fix things at a moment's notice, just in case.

An important pattern emerges in the popular media's treatment of wealthier, white students. They are often quoted directly, and frequently at length. For instance, "Amazing +" profiled "perfect" female students at a public high school in Newton, Massachusetts, where the median house price in 2006 was \$730,000.[34] The most e-mailed article on the *New York Times* Web site for several weeks in April 2007, it featured the personal narratives and college application essays of Colby, Esther, and other "pretty, thin" girls who "are high achieving, ambitious, and confident. . . . [who] grew up learning they can do anything . . . they want to do." Although these students know how to be "good consumer(s)" with their own credit cards, don "cute lingerie" under the "latest North Face jacket," and reveal "expertise in designer jeans," they are not portrayed as morally bankrupt. When one of them struggled in school, this was not automatically seen as a reflection of her own shortcomings. Instead, her mother responded with, "Who gave you a B? I'm going to talk to them."

Indeed, the article focused on the pressures these young women faced to excel in school and still be popular and pretty—sympathetic to the balancing act they attempted and the flawed ways in which they sometimes handled it. With such fine-grained stories describing their views and struggles, it is easy for readers to see such young people as rebels with a cause. Those who buck the system are seen as insightful social critics rather than nihilistic troublemakers.

Even among youth accused of committing serious crimes, white teenagers are more likely to be pictured in a school instead of a criminal justice setting, to be quoted, to have their defense lawyer quoted, to have their family members quoted, and to be interviewed for biographical information such as their hobbies, aspirations, and concerns. They are also rarely identified in explicitly racial terms.[35] These young people are not reduced to statistics or quick generalizations.

By contrast, a meta-analysis of an entire decade's worth of studies on the media demonstrates that, viewed against actual crime rates, articles and editorials on crimes consistently overrepresent racial minorities as perpetrators and underrepresent them as victims. One study reported that although 80 percent of homicide victims in the Los Angeles area were African American or Latino, white victims were three times more likely to receive coverage in the *Los Angeles Times*.[36]

Just as they play a role in portraying white teenagers as well-rounded individuals, media outlets play a role in perpetuating stereotypes of Black and Latino inner-city youth as criminals. Although homicide rates decreased by 20 percent between 1992 and 1997, news coverage of youth homicides, especially in urban areas, on ABC, NBC, and CBS evening broadcasts increased by 721 percent over the same period. Partly because of this, even as the FBI and U.S. Department of Justice report a 33 percent decline in juvenile violence since 1994, two-thirds of Americans believe that youth crime is rising. According to polls, 82 percent of Americans admit that their perceptions of crime are based not on personal experiences but on the news.[37]

Without background stories as rich as those featuring the "Amazing +" girls, news reports lead to public misunderstanding not only of youth crime rates but also of their cause. Often nonwhite teenagers are portrayed not as individuals responding (in a whole range of positive and negative ways) to severe circumstances but as stereotypes of depravity. John Dilulio, then a Princeton professor and later the George W. Bush administration's first director of the Office of Faith-Based and Community Initiatives, put forth the "juvenile superpredator" theory in the early 1990s.[38] By 1998, former New York governor George Pataki declared that "the root causes of crime are the criminals who engage in it. And I've repeatedly made that point to the Legislature."[39]

It does not take long for hype to mutate into law. In the very same speech, Pataki urged that parole be abolished for all violent offenders, that multiple drug-related misdemeanors be charged as felonies, and that the death penalty be made easier to impose. Between 1992 and 1997, forty-seven states enacted laws allowing youth to be transferred from juvenile to criminal justice systems.[40] Nationwide, it has become more difficult for juvenile offenders, even so-called "status offenders" who are arrested for infractions such as running away from home, to seek help in public institutions rather than private prisons.[41] Some polls show that two-thirds of Americans believe that youth under the age of thirteen accused of murder should be tried as adults.[42] Some politicians have introduced legislation to apply the death penalty to children as young as eleven. As Henry Giroux writes, "The poor white, black, and brown kids at whom such laws are aimed do not live in a world in which the most serious problems they have to face include being asked to perform excessive school work. On the contrary, these kids live with the daily fear of being incarcerated and the ongoing experience of not having enough food to eat, proper housing, and medical care."[43] The stakes are highest for those with the least resources. Black youth with no prior record are six times more likely to be incarcerated than white defendants with similar backgrounds and the equivalent criminal charges.[44] These youth have little means to hire expensive counsel or to ask for psychiatric help or remediation.

The menacing line that "criminals cause crime" is a bit simplistic, and Pataki himself acknowledged this when he boldly stated that he was "not charged with carrying out a sociological study."[45] That might be because study after study demonstrates that delinquency, violence, depression, and high-risk behavior are strongly correlated with neighborhood, especially among teenagers.[46] Why do these behavioral responses tend to be clustered in neighborhoods? When individual-level characteristics are held constant or put aside, the actual primary culprits of high-crime neighborhoods—namely concentrated economic disadvantage and residential instability—become even easier to discern.[47]

Nevertheless, Cosby has focused on poor values, rather than concentrated poverty or lack of socioeconomic mobility, as the primary cause of high incarceration rates in the African American community: "Looking at the incarcerated, these are not political criminals. . . . People getting shot in the back of the head over a piece of pound cake! Then we all run out and are outraged. 'The cops shouldn't have shot him.' What the hell was he doing with the pound cake in his hand? I wanted a piece of pound cake just as bad . . . [but] something called parenting said [that] if you get caught with it, you're going to embarrass your mother."[48] Cosby suggests that in the pre–civil rights days of his childhood, parents instilled a set of moral values in youth that prevented them from acting in dysfunctional ways. He received widespread praise for implying that today fewer crimes would be committed if mothers reprimanded their children more. Such declarations detract the public's attention from the conditions in which teenagers like Jorman live. Indeed, these rebukes echo those of Pataki, even if Cosby chastises parents as well as the teenagers themselves.

Cosby's remarks also feed the popular perception that dropout rates in the inner cities do not partly stem from societal factors or root causes but instead result entirely from personal choices.[49] Policy makers then forward legislative bills for more surveillance and armed police in schools, even as the budgets for teachers, books, and classroom space continue to stagnate or dwindle. In these ways, how we are talked about becomes how we are treated.

If you were told that schools are equal then you were told the best lie
Because we have more stereotypes in our schools than Best Buy.
. . . .
We are not born criminals, we are created
We represent the youth destined to be incarcerated.

Jorman Sets New Goals

When Jorman dropped out of school, no one in his family found out for four months. How had Jorman gotten away with fooling them for so long? Well, despite Bush Sr.'s statement that "dollar bills don't educate students,"[50] Clinton High could have made good use of some. The calling system notifying parents of students' absences had stopped working long before. According to an administrator, it was "overwhelmed by the volume of calls because of the huge enrollment."[51]

What about Jorman's parents? Had they been paying attention? Why, yes. But when his mother and stepdad asked to see his grades, he put his computer skills to use, scanned real report cards, and generated incredibly well-crafted fake ones. Jorman spent his mornings hanging out with friends. In the afternoons, he went to the offices of a youth organizing group he had recently joined, Sistas and Brothas United (SBU). SBU worked with high school students on campaigns aimed at improving conditions in Bronx, especially in terms of alleviating overcrowding, improving teacher quality, and reducing police harassment.

Once the school year ended, Jorman spent more time at the SBU offices. He learned that many other students, at other Bronx high schools, also struggled in their classes. While not all of them excelled academically, and there was a wide range of reasons for this, lack of thirst for knowledge did not seem to be one. After all, they eagerly conducted research, attended and ran workshops, and worked on draft after draft of vision statements for campaigns. Jorman began to feel close to his peers and the organizers at SBU.

Finally, toward the end of the summer, he came clean. He told the organizers at SBU that he had dropped out of school. He was afraid of their reaction; he had heard that students who did not do well in school would not be allowed to continue working on SBU campaigns, which focused on school reform. But the way SBU organizers reacted caught Jorman off guard. They were disappointed in him, but they did not yell at him. Nor did they tell him that he could no longer participate in SBU. Instead, they said, "Whatever you want to do, we'll help you with."

Jorman had three major goals for the next year. He wanted to "read about youth movements and social movements in general, mess around with computers, and expand my vocabulary and improve my speaking and writing skills." He came to this last goal after attending school reform conferences around the country with SBU. "I had things to say, but they didn't come out the way it did when the other organizers—mostly older, white—talked. They could articulate their missions and what they were doing in a way I couldn't, even if I had similar thoughts. I decided that I needed to expand my vocabulary."

Jorman worked toward his three goals with the help of a former teacher and educator at SBU. He also regularly wrote spoken-word poems, like the ones sprinkled throughout this chapter, for rallies. (He looked embarrassed when I mentioned that I might include them in this introduction, however, because he constructs them as rhymes to be heard and to fulfill a very different purpose than written poetry.) It was during that year, 2004, that he realized that it was still possible for him to learn every day. He decided, "I want to go to college. I need to go to college. And in order to go to college, I'm going to have get through high school. I made that decision on my own."

Through a friend at SBU, Jorman found out about a program called CUNY Prep. The City University of New York program helps at-risk students to take challenging, college preparatory classes and acquire a GED. Jorman was deemed too young to be eligible. After turning sixteen, however, Jorman applied and was admitted. Once at CUNY Prep, he thrived. "The teachers were open to the students' opinions and super strict on me. The classes were really hard, but the teachers were down-to-earth and understood where I came from." As he described that year, Jorman became more animated: "You know what I especially liked? They were not condescending. And there was a cool school safety agent! The agent was there to help people! I didn't know that was possible!"

Jorman remembered that during his entire time at Clinton High he had seen the principal only once. At CUNY Prep, the principal greeted the students every day. To Jorman, that indicated that "he wanted to be with us. Hate him or like him, I knew he was there for me."

Under these circumstances, he rose to the top of his class and graduated with a GED in one year. He was ready for college. Jorman needed to stay in the city, where he had been living on his own and working as a community organizer, and could not pay high tuition costs. He chose Hunter College, within the CUNY system, because it was a reasonable commute away and featured strong political science and urban studies programs. He had visited the campus before, as a speaker on various panels about youth social movements or school reform, and Hunter College professors had encouraged him to apply.

In 2006, at the age of seventeen, Jorman became a Hunter College student. He loved it from the beginning. During his first semester, his favorite class was in political theory. For the class, he read Plato, Hobbes, Kant, Hegel, Marx, and Patricia Williams. At first, Jorman's favorite in the class was Nietzsche, but now he looks back at this with chagrin. "It might be kind of contradictory to my work for social justice," he said sheepishly. "Then my favorite was Foucault. When I read his description of the Panopticon, I thought, 'Wow, this guy is really onto something.'"

> They tell me there's no money for schools, but I think they're telling me
>   tales
> 'Cause Bloomberg funded our [surveillance] cameras, and they always got
>   money for jails.
> See what they fund schools with, and then times that by more than three
> You'll still get less than half of what they fund prisons—Huh! Wonder
>   where they want me to be.

Highlighting the Voices of Students on Their Own Education

It might be expected that media sound bites about anyone, let alone inner-city youth, would not offer full, complex portrayals of reality. Nevertheless, it is surprising to note just how pervasive and off-base many of the one-dimensional characterizations are and how far they go in shaping ill-informed public policy.

This book is borne out by the real-life experiences of inner-city students. Instead of presenting facile sound bites about "hip-hop" or "bling," it tells of students' persistent frustrations about inoperable school bathrooms and dirty homeless shelters at the end of the day; their awe at "beautiful" trailer parks and classes where they "really learned"; their complaints about being treated like "aliens" and "fxxx-up[s]" (written as if we needed to be protected from their coarse language); their self-flagellation over their inability to do better in school, even when assignments provided no meaningful lessons; and their fear of peer ridicule, not for "acting white," but for not being "smart" enough to read out loud in history class.

In response to these conditions, many students nonetheless held deep-seated beliefs, a religious faith even, in the promise of education to make them better people and to help them (and their families) move up in American society. Some students internalized stereotypes about their demographic group's moral failings. They, too, doubted whether they worked hard enough, even as they articulated the ways in which their efforts felt futile, given the few opportunities available to them. To the extent that these teenagers are sometimes ambivalent about school, they resemble other teenagers around the nation.

The following sections introduce the plan of the book, the ways in which *Our Schools Suck* traces the origins and the evolution of the "culture of failure" thesis in the social science literature and popular media, and what young people have to say in response. Foremost, they insist on their right to criticize aspects of their schooling—and for that to be seen as a measure not of their attitudes or determination to achieve but of the quality of their schooling itself.

What's Old Is New Again

In chapter 1 Gaston Alonso observes that the notion that African Americans are immersed in a drug- and crime-infested "culture of failure" is, in fact, just the latest riff off an old theme. The theme's lineage includes 1960s discussions of "the tangle of pathology" afflicting the "Negro family," early twentieth-century eugenicist tracts regarding the inferiority of the "Negro race," post-Reconstruction hysteria regarding the "sexual menace" posed by Black men, pre–Civil War cartoons and songs depicting free Blacks as dysfunctional "Zip Coons," and seventeenth-century associations in the European mind of "blackness" with savagery and violence.[52]

Pertinent to the consequences of the old-theme-in-new-clothing "culture of failure" thesis and its academic variations is James Baldwin's observation that popular representations of African Americans, and the myths we create about them, have historically allowed us to "victimize, as we do, children whose only crime is color and keep them, as we put it, in their place." According to Baldwin, their "place" was the material and symbolic "bottom" of American society. There, they are taken by other Americans as a touchstone against which they can measure their own social status. "In a way," Baldwin noted, "the Negro tells us where the bottom is: *because he is there*, and *where* he is, beneath us, we know where the limits are and how far we must not fall. We must not fall beneath him."[53]

The historical precedents of contemporary popular and academic characterizations of people of color are thus clear. However, the validity of those characterizations, and of the theoretical frameworks they serve, are less so. Gaston questions not just the validity of popular representations of urban teenagers but also the ways public intellectuals, journalists, and fellow academics have framed their discussions regarding the school performance of these youth.

Chapter 1 explores three strands of scholarship that have influenced current debates surrounding the "culture of failure" thesis: first, scholarship on the "cool pose" and "street culture" of inner-city residents and, for some, of African Americans and Latinos in general; second, scholarship on the "oppositional cultural identities" and the fear of "acting white" supposedly held by African American and Latino students; and third, "segmented assimilation" scholarship on how second-generation children who embrace the "oppositional outlooks" of urban youth risk being dragged down the social ladder with them.

Gaston argues that despite the much-heralded post-1960s "structural turn" in the social sciences, much of this scholarship remains trapped in the culturalist assumptions of earlier "culture of poverty" studies. Many of the authors depict the supposed dysfunctional norms and behaviors of African Americans and Latinos as "adaptations" to structural conditions found in the inner city but tend to give greater causal weight to cultural norms than to preceding structural conditions. Cultural norms thus become the fundamental emblem of the figurative "heart of darkness" of the inner city.

How many times are controversial academic hypotheses passed on, from person to person, before they are taken as fact? Chapter 1 suggests that the answer is disturbingly small. The questionable link between "cultural values" and educational performance is assumed to be not only strong but causal. The chapter traces how such hypotheses travel from the academic literature into the pages of national newspapers and best-selling books and how, in the process, historical representations of people of color as backward and inferior are given a new life and sold like hotcakes.

As a consequence of all this culture talk, the policy proposals with the most political traction are those that attempt to address the supposed cultural deficits of inner-city children and/or families rather than the real-life conditions plaguing schools in inner cities, those repeatedly highlighted by the students whose voices are heard in this book. Thus the chapter also articulates the ways in which current educational policies and trends, such as high-stakes testing and Bush's No Child Left Behind legislation, build upon characterizations of urban youth as pathological and anti-intellectual. As long as urban youth would rather strike a "cool pose" than study, the rationale goes, it is not incumbent on the government to provide them with a meaningful, challenging education.

If They Don't Care, Then We're Not Letting Them Down, Right?

The student journals in chapter 2 come from a class Jeanne Theoharis co-taught with Steve Lang, an African American veteran teacher at Fremont High School in South Los Angeles. Lang allowed Jeanne to co-teach his junior-level history classes twice a week during the 2003–4 school year, focusing on supplementing their regular American history lessons with additional material focused on African American and Latino history.

At first, Jeanne, used to midwestern winters and the tight spaces of Northeast cities, marveled at the fact that these students got to eat outside for lunch, on the courtyard and in the sun, every day. School looked so pleasant. It therefore took her weeks to realize that her first impression of carefree, pleasurable school conditions had been misleading. For one thing, lunch outside meant that there was not enough room inside. With only one half hour for lunch, many students did not make it through the lunch line. Further, students were not allowed to go to bathrooms or relieve themselves during lunch—or during class. The school sometimes had only one operable girls' bathroom. The bathroom problem constituted just one small detail among the many deplorable conditions the students faced every day. And the eight-hour school day left Jeanne mind-numbingly tired and overwhelmed. How adolescents could intellectually survive such a day was unclear to Jeanne.

In class, Jeanne encouraged the students to tell their own stories—to analyze the grand project of History with a capital "H" and to think about who gets to write the more familiar parts. Jeanne took pains to include in the case study presented in chapter 2 the wide range of students' writings about their own schooling. She did not want readers to dismiss a few highlighted students as somehow anomalous, representatives of some sort of "minority exceptionalism."[54] These teenagers, the very ones scraping by in school and derided by Cosby for "fighting hard to be ignorant," wrote about what they had done over the weekend, what music they loved, and whom they had crushes on. Without any prompting or any instructions, however, they also spent quite a bit of ink considering and astutely analyzing their schooling, imagining what they wanted for the future, and gauging their chances for socioeconomic mobility.

That even these students—a broad range of teenagers, including the ones assigned to a veteran teacher like Steve because they were viewed as troublemakers, the ones urinating outside on the sides of the school walls (because the bathrooms were not open)—argued to themselves and the world, again and again, that they wanted to prove people wrong about what they could do and about how badly they wanted to succeed should sound comforting. Heartwarming even. The ultimate effect, however, is one of troubling discomfort. If such students do care deeply about school, then how can we as a society allow poor schools like Fremont to carry on the status quo? Entranced by visions of dysfunction and criminality, we have found it all too easy to ignore the educational inequities that still flourish in this country. The focus on "poor values," then, seems more revealing of us as a society than of the character of young people. Most of these students believed in the power of education and the value of hard work, and they were quick to blame themselves, and often only themselves, when they did not succeed. How can we as adults insist that young people be held responsible for their educational outcomes when we have not demonstrated an equal level of responsibility toward them and their educational well-being?

Disbelief among the Believers

Noel Anderson's chapter highlights four of the African American and Latino high school students who, also during the 2003–4 school year, spoke extensively with him about navigating school and neighborhood conditions, financial and social pressures, and sometimes conflicting responsibilities. As young men in a selective New York City Upward Bound program, these students had to maintain high grades, write successful application essays, and balance their studies with family responsibilities, after-school jobs, and the Upward Bound program. They were purportedly among "the chosen," those on the track to success. Nevertheless, the details of their lives varied considerably, and the extent of the dangers they faced—attacks by gang members or bullies, eviction from their apartments if they did not quickly find a new job and help their families pay rent—sometimes astounded Noel.

One of the most salient themes for the interviewees was the large disconnect between what they wanted to achieve and what reality allowed them to accomplish. This disconnect occurred on many levels: some of the teenagers complained that the Upward Bound program, as well intentioned as it was, did not help them to help their families financially, ensure that they could afford college if they got in, get home safely, and avoid trouble. Others talked about the divide between their aspirations and the opportunities available. Those who needed to find after-school jobs were often unable to do so; they found that they had to compete against much older men for low-skilled jobs.

The teenagers also pinpointed ways in which their realities belied assumptions made about them in the media—and, in the end, by their neighbors, families, and themselves as well. One student spoke about being followed in the stores in which he shopped and about how this made him "feel guilty," even though he had done nothing wrong. As young Black and Latino young men, these star students were often treated as suspected criminals in their after-school jobs. They were often hired to execute special surveillance on their demographic peers. Despite living in an urban center with a small employment base for low-skilled young workers, attending under-resourced schools, and facing discrimination in their job searches, they were repeatedly told that success rested on their motivation.

The students' narratives were also strikingly *similar* to those in the student journals Jeanne describes in chapter 2. While these teenagers strove to succeed academically, they too expressed deep misgivings about the education they were receiving. One student said that he easily scored well in his English class, as he knew what the teacher wanted to read, but that he was not learning anything there. Like Jorman, this young man had developed a much more sophisticated analysis of teaching and learning than students like him are usually given credit for. When inner-city youth critique schools or when some complain that "our schools suck," proponents of the "culture of failure" thesis assume that the students' observations reflect a lack of values. In reality, many of these students are the clear-eyed truth tellers, those who are genuinely, deeply invested in our nation's public schools, have ideas for school reform, and pine for the opportunities and resources to do something about it.

Chapter 3 speaks to the sweeping assumptions that Black and Latino young men are sabotaging their education and subsequent employability by embracing a "culture of failure." As Noel listened to the students' stories, he came to grasp the ways in which these popular explanations ignored the political economy in which the students were attempting to study and work. Such discourse made them feel as if perseverance would grant them success when, in fact, they also needed physical protection, decent schools, and after-school jobs. He also concluded that the literature gave them little credit for their resilience, critical analysis, and creativity, especially in the ways in which they navigated tough situations and harsh conditions.

Speaking Truth to Deaf Power

In 2003–4 I spent a lot of time with several education organizing groups in the Bronx, studying the ways in which they encouraged the broad participation of everyday citizens, rather than elected representatives, in policy making. The groups I examined all aim to make the public school system more accountable to parents and students by forwarding policy proposals and engaging elected officials and civil servants through organized meetings, petitions, rallies, and protests. One of my case studies was SBU.[55]

The SBU leaders I present in chapter 4 were unabashedly activist and spoke of school reform as a vocation, not just a pragmatic goal. Partly because of this, I had thought that the SBU leadership might suffer from severe self-selection and "creaming," such that only the best students would show up and stay. What surprised me was that young people did not arrive at SBU as overachieving do-gooders; some excelled in school, but others were barely passing their classes, were failing in them, or, like Jorman, had dropped out of school altogether. I doubt that the SBU leaders are completely representative, as some members dropped out when they had to regularly baby-sit younger siblings, for instance. Still, I could not discern any specific patterns of bias except for one: most SBU leaders were recruited by peers, so those who were isolated in school were unlikely to join. As I listened to their stories, I came to understand that many came to SBU because it was a good place to hang out after school or because their friends had urged them to do so.

I learned that overall these leaders' testimonies reflected processes of personal transformation and empowerment, not self-selection. As teenagers became familiar with SBU's campaigns, they learned the statistical and political tools to better contextualize their educational experiences. They learned to read financing memos, scour School Construction Authority documents, and analyze high school building capacities and occupancy rates in order to craft their own proposals. As they engaged in meaningful political campaigns, research projects, and workshops, these teenagers thrived. It became obvious that those who had not always spoken this eloquently about school reform had always cared but had not had the opportunities or skills to express themselves before. They recalled dozens of incidents in which they had been demoralized by their abysmal school conditions, even in primary school. The difference was that now they were connecting the dots as they did so.

Just the fact that SBU existed, and that dozens of inner-city youth showed up to volunteer on campaigns each afternoon, upended stereotypes about these teenagers as disdainful of school. Nevertheless, they faced a constant, uphill battle in trying to get policy makers to pay attention. Again and again, the SBU leaders came face to face with adults who were well-meaning and claimed to care about social justice but who nevertheless refused to meet with the students or who dismissed the youth's critiques as insolent rather than constructive. Jorman stated that in such situations, he sometimes cautiously says, "I'm not trying to discredit your viewpoint. It's valid. But when it comes down to it, social justice for you is a hobby. For me, it's my life. For you, it's a good idea. For me, it's survival. I have a stake in these campaigns. If they don't work out for you, you have the privilege to go somewhere else."[56] These days, Jorman continues to attend Hunter College full time, work full time, and work on social justice campaigns, both at SBU and on his own.

As compared to the student narratives highlighted by Jeanne and Noel, those from SBU are more uplifting. What accounts for the difference? Is it that SBU leaders valued education more? Cosby's "culture of failure" thesis is partly appealing because it assigns agency to individuals living in inner cities; it says that by caring more as parents and students they will succeed. Indeed, Jorman is a gifted student, and his determination surely helped, but he also needed something to *meet* his determination partway. For SBU leaders, realizing one's agency requires articulating and naming injustices and visualizing something different.

> We want good schools, with a whole lotta class
> So that mommy can brag, & we can surpass
> the myth—to be leaders at last.

A Growing Chorus for a New Commonsense Vision of Public Education

The student voices in this book are not random or isolated. They bring to life the statistics about segregated communities, overcrowded classrooms, and low rates of educational achievement. By paying attention to what students have to say about their own education, we make it much more difficult for policy makers to ignore them, for two reasons. First, the American public can no longer dismiss these teenagers as thugs and whores or distance themselves from those "Other" people who live in the "dangerous inner cities." Second, the American public can and must make its policy makers accountable. As students attest, there are systemic problems in their inner-city schools, and these problems call for systemic solutions.

Together, these chapters are about more than eleventh graders at Fremont High School in Los Angeles, students in a New York City Upward Bound program, or activist leaders in SBU in the Bronx. After all, the case study settings of South Central Los Angeles, Harlem, and the Bronx loom large in the American public's imagination as iconic ghettos, often associated with images such as the Los Angeles unrest of 1992 or declarations like "The Bronx is burning."[57] Los Angeles and New York City also constitute the nation's two largest cities and school districts, together serving almost two million students each year. Further, the Los Angeles and New York public school systems are currently seen as laboratories of innovation and reform, trailblazers of mayoral control of schools, and immigrant gateways to the so-called Great Equalizer of American opportunity.[58] For all these reasons, what happens in these neighborhoods may not be representative, but it nevertheless affects the way in which local, state, and national education policies are framed and evaluated.

When Gaston, Noel, Jeanne, and I talked about the case studies, we noticed that they coalesced around common themes: the drive to do well under dreadful circumstances at school, the disconnect between school curricula and the real-life socioeconomic conditions students witnessed, and the difficulties youth faced in their attempts to empower themselves and to make a difference in their own schooling. Despite, or perhaps because of, the differences in our research methods and case study locations, the fact that the students *all* spoke of the importance of education is astounding. Sometimes, as Gertrude Stein said, "repetition in human expression" is "not repetition, but insistence."[59] Many of these students continuously and collectively insisted that they needed help and want a shot at a decent, meaningful education.

Of course, there are limitations in foregrounding young people's perspectives. These teenagers have not yet had the chance to "find themselves" in college or trips abroad, nor are most of them privileged enough to ever do so. Nevertheless, some of them are precocious, and some have already begun to analyze how their lives fit into larger social and historical trends. Further, in the debate on what inner-city youth really care about and want, it behooves us to ask them. As Gaston argues in this book's methodological appendix, young people have the authority and right to speak as the ultimate stakeholders in their own education. The contradictions, conflicts, and doubts they express are largely testaments to the complex circumstances in which they live and to their analyses of these conditions.

Drawing on students' insights, Jeanne formally presents our policy recommendations in the Conclusion. Her analysis centers on the policy issues that students raised the most: how their bodily experience of school is influenced by the quantity and quality of resources available in classrooms and the governance and organizational structures of their schools. Meanwhile, many of the most popular recent reforms—No Child Left Behind, mayoral control, and high-stakes testing—make students liable for their academic performance in standardized exams but fail to hold public officials and the government responsible for democratic accountability and adequate resources.

If we were to treat them like wealthy, mostly suburban teenagers (like those profiled in newspaper articles mentioned earlier in the Introduction), then inner-city youth would not have to constantly demonstrate to us that they deserve a decent education. They would just get it. These teenagers are like other teenagers; many are troublemakers, and many want to do well by their families and teachers, and for the most part, they do. Besides, what teenager faces no moral dilemmas or feels no sense of rebellion or alienation? These struggles are quintessential to American adolescence. In other settings, jaded comments render a teenager mature and introspective, the one who sees through all the plastic fakery of cheerleader-driven and materialistic Americana and eventually succeeds as the sensitive poet or screenwriter. Absurd as *that* stereotype sounds, an equally one-dimensional stereotype about the disillusioned kid in the inner city renders him or her as uncaring rather than sensitive, stupid rather than insightful, and undeserving of even a basic decent education rather than worthy of second chances.

Yet when it comes to specious stereotypes about youth in the inner city, so-called "experts" feel free to use them to build official public policy. The American public, and the policy makers who represent us, focus on how we struggle to put food on our tables, save up for homes in decent school districts, and pay taxes so that our children can take the classes necessary to get into good colleges. In other words, we will work for what is rightfully ours. But might such opportunities be rightfully those of *all* Americans? As long as we believe that *those people* do not particularly value education or make use of their schools, we will believe that our tax dollars should not be "wasted" on their kids.

Two recent court cases in particular, *Williams v. State of California* and *Campaign for Fiscal Equity v. State of New York*, highlight both the errors of current approaches and the efforts of continued movements, led by young people and their allies, toward an equal and excellent education for everyone. By examining these cases, Jeanne brings the discussion back full circle by reminding us that *Brown v. Board of Education* was about not just racial integration but equity. Thus the students' analyses of structural conditions presented in this book are not exercises in nihilism but quite the opposite: they are hopeful, substantive rallying cries for policy makers to listen to and partner with young people in school reform.

With help, urban youth can articulate what their aspirations are and what they need to succeed. For all the confusion about what to do with urban schools, policy makers seem to have ignored the best scientific proof out there: experimental design studies (where students with similar demographic backgrounds are randomly assigned to "control" classroom settings or to "experimental" ones with interventions) show that small classes, decent school services, and preschool programs have statistically significant and permanent effects on all major well-being outcomes: high school graduation, grades, crime reduction, even life expectancy.[60] Yet unquestioned, commonsense conditions in wealthier school districts are targeted as "unproven" and "wasteful" when implemented in poorer, primarily urban, districts—even when they are exactly what young people ask for. After all, students have ideas about what pedagogical styles work, where resources are really needed, and where bullies hang out. As one young woman, a member of the New York City–wide Urban Youth Collaborative, declared in a meeting with Department of Education officials: "Please. You keep staring at your piece of paper and referring to questionable 'data.' Please look up and listen to us. We're sitting in front of you. We are the data."

1

Culture Trap

Talking about Young People of Color and Their Education

Gaston Alonso

> Ideas never contain in themselves all the reasons for their influence and their historical role. Thought alone can never produce those reasons, for this influence derives not simply from what they are, but from what they do, or better still, from what they get done in society.
>
> —Maurice Godelier, *The Mental and the Material* (1986)

During the spring of 2006, Harvard sociologist Orlando Patterson took to the pages of the *New York Times* to decry the conditions of low academic achievement, persistent poverty, and violence plaguing Black communities. "The tragedy unfolding in our inner cities is a time-slice of a deep historical process that runs far back through the cataracts and deluge of our racist past," he wrote. "Most black Americans have by now miraculously escaped its consequences. The disconnected fifth languishing in the ghettos is the remains." Patterson focused his comments on those young men still "languishing in the ghettos" who fail to graduate from high school or to go to college because, according to him, they are immersed in the culture of the "cool pose." For them, he noted, this culture "was simply too gratifying to give up. . . . It was almost like a drug, hanging out on the street after school, shopping and dressing sharply, sexual conquests, party drugs, hip-hop music and culture, the fact that almost all the superstar athletes and a great many of the nation's best entertainers were black." Patterson argued that while young whites "know when it is time to turn off Fifty Cent and get out the SAT book," Blacks do not know. "Sadly, their complete engagement in this part of the American cultural mainstream, which they created and which feeds their pride and self-respect," he concluded, "is a major factor in their disconnection from the socioeconomic mainstream."[1]

Patterson's writing was occasioned by the Urban Institute's publication of a series of reports documenting the high percentage of Black and Latino young men who are "disconnected" from mainstream society. According to the reports, only half of Black men sixteen to twenty-four years old not attending school participate in the labor force, and close to 30 percent of this group are either on parole or probation or in jail or prison at any one time. Further, 10 percent of Black and 9 percent of Latino young men are "disconnected" from both school and work for over a year, with the rates of the incarcerated cohorts rising to 17 and 12 percent respectively. Moreover, despite the economic boom of the 1990s, Black young men without a high school diploma experienced a marked decline in labor force participation during the decade. The reports proposed various government-driven solutions to address the structural forces behind these indexes of "disconnection." These forces included the flight of manufacturing jobs from urban areas and the underfunding of government-sponsored employment training programs. As such, the reports shone a light on the structural forces that relegate many young men of color to the margins of our society and on the ways government intervention could lessen their marginalization.[2]

According to Patterson, however, these reports simply highlighted "the failure of social scientists to adequately explain the problem, and their inability to come up with any effective strategy to deal with it." The failure, Patterson argued, was rooted in "a deep-seated dogma that has prevailed in social science and policy circles since the mid-1960's: the rejection of any explanation that invokes a group's cultural attributes—its distinctive attitudes, values and predispositions, and the resulting behavior of its members—and the relentless preference for relying on structural factors like low incomes, joblessness, poor schools and bad housing." In addition to denouncing the way social scientists had become "allergic to cultural explanations," he also criticized the "recent rash of scholars with tape-recorders" busy collecting the "views and rationalizations" of Black young men. Whether running statistical regressions or conducting ethnographic fieldwork, Patterson argued, scholars need to recognize, once and for all, "what has long been obvious to anyone who takes culture seriously: socioeconomic factors are of limited explanatory power." Only then will they understand that the indexes of "disconnection" documented by the Urban Institute are primarily rooted in African Americans' cultural values and norms rather than in structural forces and that effective strategies to address such "disconnection" require the reform of those cultural values and norms rather than greater government intervention and spending.[3]

Patterson's editorial was followed by the publication, by National Public Radio correspondent and Fox News commentator Juan Williams, of *Enough*, a book that embraced his call for more culture talk in the analysis of social phenomena. The book was "sparked" by the extended and heated controversy that surrounded a speech the comedian Bill Cosby delivered at a May 2004 NAACP commemoration of the fiftieth anniversary of the Supreme Court's decision in *Brown v. Board of Education*.[4] Interestingly, given the occasion and the NAACP's own history, Cosby did not denounce the continued hypersegregation of the nation's schools, which violates the integrationist spirit of *Brown*. Instead, as discussed in this book's introduction, Cosby denounced those whom he referred to as "lower economic and lower middle economic people." These people, Cosby told the audience, had willfully failed to take advantage of the educational and economic opportunities brought about by *Brown* and the civil rights movement. Instead, they had created a cultural milieu in which it was acceptable to have a "50 percent [school] drop out rate," "people getting shot in the back of the head over a piece of pound cake," boys "wear[ing] their hats on backwards, pants down around the crack," and "knuckleheads" who "[didn't] know it's important to speak English" and who instead were "fighting hard to be ignorant."[5]

In *Enough* Williams defends what he calls Cosby's "love song to black America" by invoking the "cultural attributes" of his fellow African Americans. According to him, African Americans drop out of school and remain trapped in poverty because of their abandonment of the ideals of the civil rights movement and their embrace of a "culture of failure" that "celebrates [the] self-defeating behavior that keeps poor black people shackled in the twenty-first century." As such, Williams's book repeats Cosby's evasion of the structural conditions that continue to segregate African American students into unfit and resource-starved schools.[6]

Williams's reiteration of Cosby's thesis was followed by the publication of another editorial in the pages of the *New York Times*. This time, the writer was the *Times*'s Bob Herbert, and the man whose views were being defended was Juan Williams. While usually voicing more progressive political views than Williams, Herbert noted that Williams's *Enough* represented "a cry for a new generation of African-American leadership at all levels to fill the vacuum left by those who, for whatever reasons, abandoned the tradition of struggle, hard-won pride and self-determination." In a manner reminiscent of the arguments mounted by Patterson, Cosby, and Williams, Herbert argued that "a depressing cultural illness" was sapping away African Americans' willingness and ability to achieve educational success and move up the economic ladder. "The people who are laid low by this illness," Herbert explained, "don't snitch on criminals, seldom marry, frequently abandon their children, refer to themselves in the vilest terms (niggers, whores, etc.), spend extraordinary amounts of time kicking back in correctional institutions, and generally wallow in the deepest depths of degradation their irresponsible selves can find."[7]

The year ended with the publication of another book warning about the cultural dysfunction of people of color. This time, though, the focus of the book was not African American but Latino youth. *One Nation, One Standard: An Ex-liberal on How Hispanics Can Succeed Just Like Other Immigrant Groups* was written by Herman Badillo, repeatedly identified in the book as "the United States' first Puerto Rican-born Congressman." Badillo, who also served as Bronx borough president, deputy mayor of New York City, and chairman of the Board of the City University of New York, is currently a fellow at the Manhattan Institute, a conservative think tank. In the book, he argues that "the *primary* determinant of any immigrant group's success or failure in America is its attitude towards education." The problem, according to Badillo, is that "Hispanics, as a culture, do place less stress on the importance of education than do other, more economically and socially successful immigrant groups." Thus he contends that while Jewish and Asian immigrants have attained economic success because they place a "huge value on the importance of education," Latinos have not attained similar success because they "have simply failed to recognize the overriding importance of education."[8]

Latinos will succeed, Badillo cautions, only if they embrace "a total attitude adjustment regarding the importance of education." By altering their cultural values, Latinos will attain academic and economic success just "like other immigrant groups." Asian immigrants, after all, "have not been deterred by discrimination, language difficulties, ghettoization, or any other factor that supporters of the culture of dependency claim as excuses for a lack of progress among Hispanics."[9] This last passage may suggest that Badillo is more willing than the other voices surveyed above to acknowledge the structural barriers that remain in place in post–civil rights America. However, his suggestion that an "attitude adjustment" can overcome such barriers betrays the same culturalist perspective guiding those voices.

As 2006 came to an end, a chorus of voices lamented the presumed cultural values and norms of African Americans and Latinos. This chorus buried the structuralist explanations of the "disconnection" of young people of color—including their "disconnection" from the education system—and the policy solutions advanced by the Urban Institute earlier in the year. Like Patterson's editorial, these voices recommended greater discipline, hard work, and personal responsibility from African American and Latino parents and children. This culture talk told the public that since in our post–civil rights era any individual who values "strong families, education, and hard work" can succeed,[10] "socioeconomic factors are of limited explanatory power."[11] In this context, the "disconnection" that characterizes the lives of poor and working-class African Americans and Latinos is the result of a "depressing cultural illness."[12] This talk captures the prevailing common sense in American popular culture and social science regarding African American "culture" as deficient, dysfunctional, in need of explanation, and, at the same time, *itself* the explanation for all kinds of social ills. It also captures the increasing "ideological blackening"[13] of Latinos, the nation's fastest-growing nonwhite group, as part of the culturally pathological and racially coded "underclass" position usually associated in popular discourse with African Americans.

In the following chapters, African American and Latino students from public schools in Los Angeles and New York City testify against the way they are represented by this public discourse as well as against the conditions they encounter in their schools and communities. This chapter, however, focuses not on these students' stories but rather on the stories that others tell about them. While many of the scholars, journalists, and public intellectuals surveyed here claim to care deeply about the schooling of today's young people of color, in their talk one finds very little righteous denunciation of the conditions under which these young people receive an education. Rather, in their talk one finds well-crafted representations of these young people as immersed in a culture that undervalues and is often openly hostile to the educational process. Those representations, in turn, shape the way we as a society perceive and treat these young people. "Those texts that carry the weight of cultural authority as 'reliable knowledge' or 'objective information' (e.g. expert opinions or news reports)," communications scholar Mary Strine notes, "exert powerful influences on how common perceptions are formed and common sense is made."[14]

The common sense made by the experts discussed in this chapter has given currency to one-dimensional and devastating perceptions of young people of color as anti-intellectual. In doing so, this common sense draws the public's gaze away from the racially segregated, physically decaying, and crowded places where, as explained in the Introduction, instruction continues to occur. Instead, it draws the gaze toward students of color. It is the students, the expert voices emphasize, that are dysfunctional and in need of fixing rather than the school system or the social structures in which students find themselves.

In this chapter I place the culture talk that has burrowed itself into the pages of the *New York Times* and into the shelves of bookstores across the country in the context of the contemporary scholarship regarding the "racial achievement gap." I begin by surveying three of the prevailing schools of thought on the causes of this "gap," or the lower levels of academic achievement and higher dropout rates of African American and Latino youth relative to other groups. The first school of thought surveyed focuses on the social effects of the culture of the "cool pose" referenced by Patterson. According to this scholarship, the "cool pose" undermines the educational drive of those who embrace it. The second school of thought surveyed focuses directly on understanding the educational experiences of young people of color. African Americans, the scholarship tells us, have developed "oppositional identities" that lead them to view academic success as a form of "acting white." Afraid of being ostracized by their peers for "acting white," African American children choose not to succeed academically. The third school of thought surveyed is concerned that some children of immigrants are embracing these "oppositional identities" and fears of "acting white" and, by extension, also failing in school.[15]

I proceed to examine how the representation of African American and Latino youth popularized by this scholarly talk influences popular discussions regarding their education. These discussions have produced a political climate in which public policies increasingly focus on fixing the cultural values and norms that students are assumed to hold rather than on taking seriously young people's own perspectives and the decrepit conditions under which they continue to be made to learn. By tracing the scholarly and popular roots of the "culture of failure" narrative and of the contemporary political climate, the chapter provides a context for under-standing the popular representations, structural conditions, and public policies engaged by the students whose voices are presented in the ethno-graphic case studies that follow.

To understand the popularity of the "culture of failure" narrative, it is important to examine its academic roots as well as the relatively paltry ev-idence on which it is based. In doing so, in the next three sections I take issue with Patterson's claim that contemporary scholars are "allergic to cultural explanations." In fact, like the voices from 2006 discussed above, much of the scholarly talk regarding young people of color and their edu-cation remains either explicitly or implicitly trapped in long-standing as-sumptions and stereotypes about the cultures of communities of color.

On Poses and Codes

In his March 2006 *New York Times* editorial, Patterson blamed the "'cool pose' culture" for the problems facing African American young men. In deploying the concept, Patterson evoked Richard Majors and Janet Bill-son's 1992 book, *Cool Pose: The Dilemmas of Black Manhood in America*. Majors and Billson defined the "cool pose" as a "ritualized form of mascu-linity that entails behaviors, scripts, physical posturing, impression man-agement, and carefully crafted performance that delivers a single, criti-cal message: pride, strength, and control." They argue that this "ritualized form of masculinity" emerged as a "creative strategy" deployed by some African American men as a way to "counter the negative forces of their lives." These forces, Majors and Billson assert, left these men "psychologi-cally castrated—rendered impotent in the economic, political and social arenas that whites have historically dominated."[16]

As evidenced by Patterson's editorial, the language of the "cool pose" and Majors and Billson's characterization of the culture of African Ameri-can young men have entered academic and popular discussions regarding the schooling of African American teenagers. As such, Majors and Bill-son's description of African American masculinity has come to ostensibly represent contemporary African American culture and has emerged as an easy—perhaps *too* easy—explanation for why African Americans lag behind in terms of academic achievement.[17] Majors and Billson's original analysis pointed to socioeconomic factors as the source of the emergence of the "pose." Over time, however, the "pose" as an analytical category has gained a life of its own. It has allowed for the kind of culturalist analysis of social phenomena Patterson deployed in the pages of the *New York Times*. This analysis, of course, ignores the evidence of the scandalously substandard education that many African American youth obtain in the hypersegregated schools they attend.

The notion that socioeconomic factors create contexts that lead inner-city residents to affect certain poses is echoed in Elijah Anderson's influential 1999 *Code of the Street*, an elaboration of his 1994 *Atlantic Monthly* article.[18] Based on an ethnographic study of poor African Americans in Philadelphia, the article and the book seek to explain "why it is that so many inner-city young people are inclined to commit aggression and violence toward one another."[19]

In Anderson's writing, readers are cast as tourists or voyeuristic outsiders to the urban communities described. Thus the Editor's Introduction to the *Atlantic Monthly* article notes: "In this essay in urban anthropology *a social scientist takes us inside a world most of us glimpse only in headlines*—'Teen Killed in Drive-By Shooting'—to show us how a desperate search for respect governs social relations among African American young men."[20] Following a similar path, the book begins by taking the readers-cum-tourists/outsiders on a "tour down Germantown Avenue" from Chestnut Hill, a predominantly white and affluent neighborhood that is increasingly racially mixed and in which "everyone is polite and relaxed," to North Philadelphia, "the heart of inner-city Philadelphia," in which "businesses cater mostly to the criminal class," "the noise level is also much louder," and "public decency gets little respect."[21]

Anderson informs his readers that in inner-city communities such as North Philadelphia, everyday interactions among residents are governed by a "code of the street," or "a set of prescriptions and proscriptions or informal rules, of behavior organized around a desperate search for respect that governs public social relations, especially violence, among so many residents, particularly young men and women." Inner-city residents, readers learn, "shape their personal routines" to cultivate a public image of "respect" that can fend off the possibility of violence through the threat of potential retaliation. The "code" constitutes a "quite primitive form of social exchange that holds would-be perpetrators accountable by promising an 'eye for an eye,' or certain 'payback' for transgressions."[22] Part of the ensuing "campaign for respect" among both male and female residents of such communities involves their adaptation of public presentations of the self that echo Majors and Billson's notion of the "cool pose"—a calculated "street" appearance accompanied by an aggressive and defensive swagger.

Anderson's analysis of the "code of the street" also echoes Majors and Billson's analysis of the "cool pose" in the way it presents the "code" as a response to—or a "creative strategy" to deal with—the context of the ghetto. The "code of the street," Anderson explains, is "actually a *cultural adaptation* to a profound lack of faith in the police and the judicial system—and in others who would champion one's personal safety" and "a kind of *adaptation* to a lost sense of security of the local inner-city neighborhood."[23] In this "sociology of interpersonal public behavior"—rather than in the structural conditions documented by the discussion of school segregation and funding in the Introduction or by the Urban Institute studies on "disconnectedness" discussed above—Anderson finds the explanation for why so many inner-city young people are inclined to commit violence toward one another rather than, say, concentrating on achieving academic excellence.

In casting the "social exchanges" of poor and working-class African Americans and their "campaign for respect" as "quite primitive," the analysis by Anderson calls forth a long tradition of viewing Blacks as backward and more animalistic than other Americans. This tradition has its roots in early European associations of "blackness" with violence and savagery. These associations served as justifications for slavery and reached their apex in justifications offered for the defeat of Reconstruction and the violence of the Ku Klux Klan in the late 1800s and early 1900s.[24]

Anderson goes to great pains to highlight that not all inner-city residents are unemployed, violent, and lacking in decency. The book, in fact, is organized around the distinction between "street" and "decent" families. While Anderson refers to the categories "decent" and "street" as "two poles of value orientation, two contrasting conceptual categories," and spends some ink detailing the ways in which individuals "code-switch" to negotiate the often violent streets of the inner city, he also refers to distinct types of families ("decent families" and "street families") and distinct types of individuals ("the decent single mother," "the decent daddy," "decent kids," "street kids," and "the street element"—in which "the street is in the person, consuming his being") that inhabit the inner city. The conceptual fuzziness with which Anderson deploys the terms *decent* and *street* thus opens up the possibility for readers to view the struggle in the inner city not as a complex and ongoing struggle between contrasting orientations competing for the "heart and minds" of individuals but as a struggle between one-dimensional "types" of individuals who are fully defined—or, to borrow his language, "consumed"—by decency or by the street.[25]

The language that Anderson uses to describe decent and street families casts them as moral opposites and functional inversions of each other. Thus readers are told that while in decent families "the man takes pains to show he is in complete control—with the woman and the children following his lead," parents in street families tend to "have a limited understanding of priorities and consequences," "tend towards self-destructive behaviors," and have a short "fuse." As a result, while children in decent families are encouraged to "walk a straight moral line," children in street families learn "to be loud, boisterous, proudly crude, and uncouth—in short, street."[26]

In Anderson's telling, the inner-city school emerges as "a staging area for the campaign for respect" between the "street kids" and "decent kids":[27] "During their early years, most of the children accept the legitimacy of the school, and then eagerly approach the task of learning. . . . By the fourth grade, enough children have opted for the code of the street that it begins to compete effectively with the culture of the school, and the code begins to dominate their public culture—in school as well as out—becoming *a way of life* for many and eventually conflating with the culture of the school itself." In the resulting context, in which "the code" becomes "a way of life," teachers come to view all students as street kids. "Overwhelmed by clothes, the look, or the swagger," Anderson writes, "they [teachers] cannot discern the shy kid underneath, which may be why teachers classify the majority of young people as 'street.'" In turn, students begin to view authority figures as "alien" or "unreceptive," and the school loses legitimacy in their eyes. The danger, Anderson informs readers, is that "with each passing year the school loses ground as more and more students adopt a street orientation, if only for self-defense in the neighborhood."[28]

It is not clear from his writing exactly what kind of research Anderson conducted in inner-city schools and whether he actually interviewed students in these schools. In fact, there is an alarming lack of student voices cited in the book's section entitled "Schools as Staging Areas." The one voice of a young person reflecting at length on his or her schooling that Anderson quotes appears in an earlier chapter entitled "Decent and Street Families." He cites an interview with a young college student named Yvette who grew up in North Philadelphia and attended a private Christian school in which she excelled academically. "Whereas my cousins were going to public schools and getting in trouble, getting suspended, whatever," Yvette tells Anderson. "And I wasn't doing that, because I was in a private, Christian school." She also relates how her academic success was interpreted negatively by her aunts and cousins, who teased her for being "a nerd." Yvette blames public schools for her cousins' lack of academic success and accredits her private school for her own success. Yvette also attended a public magnet school. "The school had about six, seven hundred kids in it," Yvette recounts. "Not really big compared to most public schools. It was about 60 percent black. I was used to maybe two hundred people in the whole school—that's what my other school was. And I was seen as a nerd there, too. When people would try to fight me, I did not know what to do, because I was so sheltered I just never had that situation, so I talked my way out of it most of the time."

Anderson draws on Yvette's story not to examine the causes of academic failure but rather to point out "the difficulties that the decent family encounters when trying to live among so many people who are committed to the street, not only neighbors but relatives as well."[29] Beyond Yvette's words, Anderson gives readers precious little in terms of firsthand accounts from students (or teachers) regarding students' experiences in schools and their relative value of education. Despite the dearth of evidence, Anderson leaves readers with the impression that the low academic performance of many African Americans results from the predatory nature of the culture associated with "the code of the street" rather than from, say, the substandard conditions in which students struggle to learn.

In the book's concluding pages, Anderson lays out two potential solutions to the bleakness of inner-city communities. The first focuses on the political economy, which he argues creates the despair that "spawns" the "code of the street" culture. "Only by reestablishing a viable mainstream economy in the inner city, particularly one that provides access to jobs for inner-city men and women," he notes, "can we encourage a positive sense of the future." The second solution is proposed by "the old heads" that Anderson met in the course of conducting his research and centers on "build[ing] up the grit of the community through the return of the decent daddy and the support of the grandmother." The "decent daddy" accepts the patriarchal responsibility "to work, to support his family, to rule his household, to protect his daughters, and to raise his sons to be like him." The grandmother is the functional opposite of her daughters, whom Anderson represents as immersed in the street culture of drugs and welfare dependency; she "espouses abstinence," "does not drink or smoke," "takes religion seriously," "carefully manages her money," and views child rearing as a "religious obligation."[30] If decency is to win the struggle going on in the streets and the schools of the inner city, the "old heads" argue, decent daddies and grandmothers must, in a sense, take back the streets.

The first solution treats the community's supposed "oppositional" street culture as an "adaptation"—a "result"—of structural conditions. The second solution treats culture as independent of structural conditions. Thus, regardless of structural conditions in the neighborhood, one can expect the decent daddies and grandmothers to change the community's cultural values and norms. The first solution treats culture as a symptom of conditions that need to be addressed; the second treats it as the condition *itself*.

At times, Anderson appears to favor the first solution. He notes, for example, that "the condition of these communities was produced not by moral turpitude but by economic forces that have undermined black, urban, working-class life and by a neglect of their consequences on the part of the public." However, despite his repeated claims that the cultural values and norms he found in the inner city are largely adaptations to the deindustrialization of its economy, Anderson provides readers with little in terms of a detailed description of Philadelphia's political economy. He also provides few details of the conditions in the inner-city schools where, he tells readers, the "code of the street" destroys students' eagerness to learn. These failures, along with his conclusion in the book's final pages that "well-paying manufacturing jobs are unlikely to return,"[31] leave readers with little else to focus on but the "moral life of the inner city" that is highlighted by the book's subtitle and described and analyzed in minute detail throughout the book. In the end, readers searching for viable strategies to solve the problems of the inner city are left with only the possibility of moral redemption.

Thus, while Anderson—ostensibly the liberal social scientist—points to the structural roots of the "code" as a way to avoid being perceived as falling into the trap of neoconservative culturalist arguments, he positions readers in ways that nevertheless focus their attentions on moral economy, not political economy. As such, his argument remains embedded in the culturalist perspective that Patterson suggested social scientists became "allergic" to during the 1960s and that monopolizes contemporary public talk regarding young people of color.

Anderson's dissection of the "moral life of the inner city" voices the same anxiety regarding the behavior of poor Black people that Cosby voiced in his 2004 *Brown* speech. In *Is Bill Cosby Right?* Michael Eric Dyson locates Cosby's anxiety within a long tradition of well-off African Americans trying to distance themselves from poor and working-class African Americans. He notes that during the early twentieth century Black elites were "unnerved by the black poor—how they dressed, how they spoke, how they behaved—because they constantly felt the stares of white disapproval" and that as a result they "lectured, preached, cajoled, beseeched and condemned the black poor for the good of the race, or, rather, for the good of members of the race who were fatally obsessed with white approval."[32] While Cosby lectured the poor African American woman—as if she were a singular archetype—for wearing her "dress all the way up the crack" and having "five or six different children" with "eight, ten different husbands,"[33] Anderson critiques African American women for irresponsibly abandoning their children to the "grandmothers." Similarly, while Cosby lectured African American men for "beating up your women because you can't find a job, because you didn't want to get an education and you are [making] minimum wage,"[34] Anderson critiques them for failing to act as "decent daddies." In both cases, the message is clear: these two successful "decent daddies" tell those African Americans still "languishing in the ghettos"—to borrow Patterson's language—to get their act together and emulate the discipline and norms that in their view facilitate upward mobility. In the process, they leave the general public that is their audience with a one-dimensional image of African American youth as anti-intellectual, irresponsible, and violent.

On "Acting White"

Describing the negative effects of "the code of the street" on students' educational experience, Anderson notes that "for many alienated young black people, attending school and doing well becomes negatively associated with acting white."[35] Anderson's observation points to a second prevailing school of thought on the racial achievement gap. While the scholarship on "poses" and "codes" focuses on dynamics internal to the African American community, the scholarship on African Americans' supposed "oppositional outlooks" and fear of "acting white" focuses on distinguishing their cultural outlooks from the outlooks of other minority communities such as immigrants from Asia and the Caribbean. Despite this conceptual difference, both schools point to cultural outlooks as key determinants of students' academic performance.

During the last two decades, the work of anthropologist John Ogbu has deeply influenced the way many scholars, journalists, and policy makers talk about students of color.[36] Throughout his career, Ogbu dedicated himself to explaining low achievement rates among minority groups by pointing to "the relationship between their [groups'] cultures and the mainstream culture."[37] Ogbu's "cultural-ecological theory of academic achievement"[38] is organized around a typology of racial/ethnic groups. The relationship between mainstream society and "immigrant minorities," or groups such as Chinese and Punjabi Indians who migrated to the United States "more or less voluntarily," Ogbu argued, is characterized by "primary cultural differences," or "differences that existed before the groups came into contact." The relationship between mainstream society and "involuntary minorities," or groups such as African Americans, Native Americans, Native Hawaiians, and Mexican Americans, whose incorporation to American society resulted either through enslavement or conquest, however, is characterized by "secondary cultural differences," or differences that "develop as a response to a contact situation, especially one involving the domination of one group by another."[39]

These cultural differences, Ogbu argued, lead each group to hold very different "folk theories of getting ahead." Immigrants, according to him, take as their reference group "their former selves and their peers 'back home'" and thus encounter "much evidence to support their claim that they have more or better opportunities in the US." They hold a "folk theory" that places a high value on hard work and individual academic achievement. On the other hand, involuntary minorities take their ancestors as their reference group and thus "resent the loss of their former freedom, regard their past as their 'golden age,' and interpret the social, political, and economic barriers erected against them as undeserved oppression."[40] As a result, they view "the inadequate and unequal reward of education as a part of the institutionalized discrimination structure which getting an education cannot eliminate." Therefore, Ogbu concluded, the folk theories of involuntary minorities devalue academic achievement—which these minorities view as acting within a "white" frame of reference.[41]

In line with this conceptual framework, Signithia Fordham and Ogbu argue in an oft-cited 1986 article that the "cultural meaning of schooling" held by African Americans explains their low achievement levels. They claim that the "oppositional social identities" that African Americans have developed as a result of their historical experience lead them to "doubt their own intellectual ability, . . . define academic success as white people's prerogative, and . . . discourage their peers, perhaps unconsciously, from emulating white people's academic striving, i.e. 'acting white.'" In this context, they write, "one major reason black students do poorly in school is that they experience inordinate ambivalence and affective dissonance in regards to academic efforts and success."[42]

The last large-scale study Ogbu published before his death in 2003 focused on the educational experiences of middle-class African Americans. The study began at the request of a group of African American parents living in Shaker Heights, a well-off suburb of Cleveland, Ohio. They invited Ogbu to find an explanation for their children's relatively lower academic performance vis-à-vis the school districts' white students. In *Black Americans in an Affluent Suburb: A Study of Academic Disengagement*, Ogbu and his co-researchers report that even among well-off African Americans "oppositional identities" and the fear of "acting white" explain the low academic performance of children.[43] In this manner, Ogbu's last study gave weight to his long-standing argument that cultural outlooks rooted in the historical experiences of involuntary minorities, rather than their class background, accounted for their lower academic performance and the overall racial achievement gap.

To improve the achievement levels of students who think academic success means "acting white," Ogbu advocated initiatives that focused on changing the frames of reference such students brought to schools. For example, writing in *Educational Researcher*, Ogbu called on teachers and policy makers to design and implement "special counseling and related programs" that could be used to "a) help involuntary minority students learn to separate attitudes and behaviors that enhance school success from those that lead to linear acculturation or 'acting White' and b) to help the students to avoid interpreting the former as a threat to their social identity and sense of security." Ogbu concluded his discussion of "what can be done" by noting: "Finally, society can help reorient minority youths towards more academic striving for school credentials for future employment by (a) creating more jobs in general, (b) eliminating the job ceiling against minorities, and (c) providing better employment for minorities."[44]

Having determined that the racial achievement gap was primarily caused by the "oppositional identities" and outlooks of students rather than by the highly segregated and unequal conditions found in schools,

Ogbu's recommendations for fixing the problem focused on changing those identities and outlooks through specially designed counseling and mentoring programs rather than on fixing the schools. Even when he finally proposed structural solutions, those solutions focused on fixing the economy rather than the schools. As he told the *New York Times* on the eve of the publication of his last book, "No matter how you reform schools, it's not going to solve the problems."[45]

The validity of Ogbu's popular "acting white" hypothesis, as well as of the theory of "oppositional identities" on which it relies, depends on whether African American children actually hold the "folk theories of getting ahead" attributed to them. The evidence on this point is hotly debated among specialists. Numerous survey and ethnographic studies conducted in a variety of educational settings find that African American children are *more* likely than their white peers to hold proeducation/pro-school views, to value individual educational achievement as important for future job prospects, and to reward rather than punish high-achieving same-race peers.[46] In fact, Fordham and Ogbu's negative representation of "the cultural meaning of education" held by African Americans overlooks the well-documented historical struggle that African Americans have waged to gain access to equal educational opportunities.[47]

The validity of Ogbu's analysis also depends on whether voluntary immigrants hold the "folk theories of getting ahead" attributed to them. By counterposing African American and immigrant children, Ogbu's hypothesis draws on and reinscribes a long-standing discourse on "model minorities."[48] In this discourse, certain immigrants are called on to testify by way of their educational and/or economic success to the notion that in post–civil rights America any individual can make it if he or she simply "works hard and plays by the rules," to borrow Bill Clinton's popular refrain. This is a narrative that Patterson himself reinscribed in his 2006 *New York Times* editorial call for social scientists to embrace analyses that "invoke a group's cultural attributes." After critiquing African American young men for failing to "turn up to take" the opportunity created by the economic boom of the 1990s, he noted that "instead, the opportunity was seized in large part by immigrants—including many blacks—mainly from Latin America and the Caribbean."[49] However, the evidence here is once again *not* very clear. In fact, numerous studies have pointed to wide variations in the cultural outlooks and in the levels of academic and economic achievement found between and within national-origin immigrant groups.[50]

Further, there is always a potential for researchers to confuse general teenage outlooks with the specific outlooks of a racially or ethnically coded group of teenagers. Thus, as Karolyn Tyson has noted, "Tendencies toward disengagement from school and teasing 'nerds' are commonplace among all adolescents. However, when black high school students are studied, these tendencies are interpreted culturally and recommendations tend to center on 'fixing' black culture. When white students are studied, these same tendencies are interpreted as being characteristic of adolescence."[51] In making this observation, Tyson draws on Lawrence Steinberg's three-year study of twenty thousand high school students from different ethnic and racial groups, which found that "adolescent peer culture in contemporary America demeans academic success and scorns students who try to do well in school."[52] In a wider American context, such behavior is seen—and at times celebrated—as antielitist populism. Thus Tyson cautions that "when studying black students researchers must be careful to distinguish between a cultural burden of high achievement (such as acting white) and a more general burden of high achievement, because there is a difference."[53]

Ogbu's "acting white" hypothesis focused on what he referred to as "community forces" at the expense of what he referred to as "school forces": that is, the analytical gaze focused on students and parents rather than on the segregated and unequal conditions under which schooling takes place. For example, in their reviews of the Shakers Heights study, education specialists Margaret Gibson and Kevin Foster both point out that many students, parents, and teachers in the study suggested that the schools were plagued by a variety of institutional problems that research has shown can negatively affect students' academic performance. While one could read these voices as expressing legitimate criticisms of the conditions under which students attempt to gain an education, Ogbu's analytical framework led him to read them as signs of student "disengagement" that merely confirmed his decades-old hypothesis. Ogbu was then able to conclude that "school performance differences among minorities are *primarily* due to differences in the community forces of the community."[54] Such a totalizing framework, however, can lead to inaccurate readings of data, compromised conclusions, and misguided policy prescriptions.

Contrary to Ogbu's emphasis on the "cultural meaning of education," the causes of students' academic disengagement may be found in the quality of instruction they receive, the perceptions teachers hold of them, the nature of the instructional resources to which they have access, and the everyday bodily experiences they have in the nation's hypersegregated and unequal schools. Of course, addressing these causes of student disengagement necessitates very different public policies from those advocated by Ogbu. If this is the case, and as discussed in the next section much research suggests it is, then regardless of what Ogbu told the *New York Times* in 2002, reforming the schools—fixing the schools—might help solve the problem.

On Segmented Assimilation

Ogbu's "acting white" hypothesis has influenced how we understand the educational experiences not only of African Americans but also of the children of immigrants. In fact, some of the most influential scholarship on the "new second generation" is framed by the concern that these children will turn away from their parents' "folk ways of getting ahead" and adopt the oppositional outlooks that according to Ogbu undermine the academic achievement of involuntary minorities. This fear is manifested in the scholarship on "segmented assimilation" by Alejandro Portes, Rubén Rumbaut, and colleagues.[55] This work has been largely guided and informed by the results of the Children of Immigrants Longitudinal Study (CILS) that Portes and Rumbaut conducted between 1992 and 1996. The CILS surveyed 5,200 second-generation children and their parents in San Diego and Miami/Ft. Lauderdale. The study followed the children from junior high school to the end of high school.[56]

The theory of segmented assimilation is built around three "patterns of immigrant adaptation" that lead to divergent academic and economic outcomes. The first pattern, which Portes and Rumbaut refer to as "consonant acculturation," is mostly found among the children of professional and/or well-off immigrants. In these families, parents possess enough resources and human capital to keep pace with children's acculturation. As a result, children will probably have the support necessary for them to attain high levels of academic achievement and subsequently experience upward economic and social mobility. The problem, however, is that most immigrant parents do not possess such resources but rather confront serious structural obstacles to economic mobility. The three obstacles Portes and Rumbaut identify are (1) the flight of manufacturing jobs from urban areas, which limits employment opportunities for low-skilled workers; (2) the nonwhite identity of the majority of immigrants, which subjects them to discrimination in the workforce; and (3) the tendency among immigrants to settle in inner-city areas, which exposes their children to urban subcultures.

The last factor is particularly dangerous, Portes and Rumbaut argue, since it tends to "bring immigrant children into close contact with the urban underclass," which holds an "adversarial outlook towards middle class culture." Echoing Ogbu, they suggest that this outlook already stands in the way of the educational advancement of African American and Puerto Rican teenagers. Thus the fear is that if the children of contemporary immigrants come to associate too closely with those teenagers they will catch this outlook. As a consequence, they too will be trapped in a life of low academic achievement, poverty, and violence.[57]

According to Portes and Rumbaut, children who find themselves in this dangerous situation have two possible adaptation patterns available to them. The first—and preferred—pattern is "selective acculturation," and it occurs when children are able to learn American norms and English while simultaneously retaining strong cultural and linguistic bonds with their parents' ethnic community. These bonds protect children from the effects of outside discrimination and from exposure to the "adversarial outlooks" of their African American and Puerto Rican peers and, as such, promote their educational achievement. Portes and Rumbaut refer to the second—and most dangerous pattern—as "dissonant acculturation." This pattern occurs when children learn American norms and English at faster rates than their parents do and subsequently lose touch with their parents' ethnic community. "By depriving youths of privileged sources of material and moral support while leaving them exposed to all the challenges of outside society," Portes and Rumbaut argue, dissonant acculturation facilitates their "socialization into urban underclass roles" and their "adoption of an adversarial stance towards the mainstream." As a result, they come to believe that "school conformity is 'acting white.'" Thus, given the structural conditions in which immigrant families find themselves, parents interested in facilitating their children's academic success must help them maintain strong bonds of ethnic solidarity and, conversely, discourage them from identifying with "ghetto youth culture."[58]

The scholarship on segmented assimilation turns assimilation theories of the early twentieth century upside down. Those theories portrayed immigrants as mired in social pathologies similar to those associated in popular culture and academic literature with African Americans and prescribed that the way for immigrants to climb the ladder of success was to assimilate into the mainstream. Sociocultural assimilation, the theories held, led to structural and political assimilation. Portes and Rumbaut's work also portrays immigrants as mired in social pathologies similar to those associated with African Americans. However, the fear that contemporary sociocultural assimilation might not be to "the middle-class mainstream" but rather to "the attitudes and norms of the inner city"—read Black—leads them to suggest that immigrants and their children should resist such assimilation.

Despite turning classical theories upside down, Portes and Rumbaut's work voices the same racial logic that structured them. In both cases, immigrants must avoid and disavow identifications with those who inhabit what James Baldwin, as discussed in the Introduction, referred to as "the bottom," which is to say Blacks.[59] Becoming American in successful ways, social scientists told immigrants then and tell them again today, entails a deliberate process of social whitening rather than blackening. This is the racial logic that historically has upheld the varied privileges associated with whiteness in America.

As with Ogbu's "acting white" hypothesis, the validity of Portes and Rumbaut's segmented assimilation theory depends on whether African American and Puerto Rican children actually hold the "oppositional outlooks" and fear of "acting white" imputed to them. As discussed above, the evidence on this point is highly debated among education specialists. While Portes and Rumbaut do not significantly engage with this debate, it raises questions about their claims regarding young people of color's outlooks. Furthermore, as discussed above, researchers must be careful not to confuse young people's outlooks regarding schooling with the specific outlooks of an ethnic/racial group of young people. Doing so can lead researchers to present developmental responses as cultural essences.

Moreover, as suggested by Stacey Lee's ethnographic research of second-generation Hmong students, the oppositional outlooks adopted by second-generation children may be a response to "the racism of the school" rather than to contact with African American or Puerto Rican peers. For such students, Lee's findings suggest, "hip-hop style holds oppositional power. Their style and attitude represent an inchoate critique of an educational system that excludes them."[60] Thus such attitudes, rather than reflecting an embrace of academic failure as Portes and Rumbaut suggest, could serve as a strategy of resistance against school curriculums and teaching practices that devalue the experiences and voices of nonwhite students.

Because Portes and Rumbaut's conceptual model assumes that educational outcomes are influenced by students' perceptions, the CILS focuses on identifying students' perceptions through survey questions rather than on identifying the actual conditions found in the specific schools attended by students in the sample. As a result, the model does not take into consideration a number of important school-level factors that specialists have identified as influencing educational achievement. These factors include school funding; class size; quality of instruction; teachers' levels of certification, expertise, and experience; teachers' perceptions of students; and school physical conditions.[61] As discussed in the Introduction, these factors are unequally distributed between and within school districts in ways that tend to place poor and nonwhite children—including many second-generation children—at a disadvantage.

In their well-received book *Legacies*,[62] Portes and Rumbaut report the findings of their School Conditions Index, which measured students' responses to questions regarding school safety, and the presence of interethnic/racial conflicts, gangs, and drugs in their schools, and of their Teaching Quality Index, which measured responses to questions regarding quality of instruction, teachers' interest in students, and the fairness of grading and disciplinary actions in schools. The two indexes provide readers with a treasure trove of important data on how students perceive their school environment and how these perceptions might influence their educational ambitions and expectations. However, the indexes do not provide readers with much data regarding objective conditions in those schools and how those conditions might also influence students' performance. That is, the indexes measure variations in students' *perceptions* of school conditions, not variations in the actual *conditions*. Moreover, Portes and Rumbaut's typology of schools is based on a measurement of the average socioeconomic status (SES) of schools' student bodies.[63] Their findings, therefore, illuminate how average school SES levels influence educational outcomes but do not account for how other school-level factors identified in the literature as significant may influence educational outcomes.[64]

Portes and Rumbaut conclude both of their 2001 volumes, *Legacies* and *Ethnicities*, by laying out a policy agenda designed to promote the educational success of second-generation children. In *Legacies* they call on social scientists and policy makers to develop "a political constituency" for "selective acculturation." As a nation, they argue, we must give immigrant families the support and resources necessary for them to understand and pursue selective acculturation as "a strategy to preserve the original

achievement drive [of immigrants] and transmit it" to their children. Promoting selective acculturation requires two-parent families and tight ethnic communities. "Family solidarity can operate to pool the social and
economic resources necessary to escape dysfunctional neighborhoods or,
barring this, to limit the damage caused by external racism and deviant
subcultures," Rumbaut and Portes point out in *Ethnicities*. Because they
think that "public schools tend to discourage rather than support selective
acculturation," Portes and Rumbaut point to the system of private bilingual schools that Cuban exiles created in Miami as "the viable model for
the institutional promotion of selective acculturation."[65] In such schools,
second-generation children can be encouraged to hold on to their parents' cultural outlooks and can be surrounded by coethnic peers—and
segregated from the "deviant subcultures" of inner-city teenagers.

The policy recommendations advanced by Portes and Rumbaut reflect
two aspects of the post–civil rights agenda: our contemporary symbolic
celebration of bilingualism and ethnic cultures and, as in Anderson's and
Ogbu's respective recommendations, the current shift from a policy focus
on addressing structural barriers to socioeconomic mobility to a focus on
"moral economy" and "cultural outlooks." Since court decisions such as
Brown and civil rights laws dismantled structural barriers to equal opportunity, the argument goes, the persistence of poverty must be due to
the character of the poor. This argument, of course, obscures the ways in
which structural inequalities remain firmly in place.

In the ways each school of thought discussed above treats cultural values and norms as adaptations or responses to structural conditions, each
echoes 1960s "culture of poverty" studies associated with the work of
Oscar Lewis and Michael Harrington.[66] Reflecting the post–World War
II shift in the social sciences away from the eugenics-tinged language of
"race" to the anthropology-infused language of "culture," these studies
treated cultural values and norms not as genetic or biological features of
particular ethnic/racial groups but rather as adaptations by such groups
to environmental contexts. As such, these studies held that the environments in which the poor live lead them to develop subcultures quite distinct from the mainstream. Those subcultures are passed down from one
generation to another in ways that trap the poor in self-sustaining cycles
of economic dependency and poverty.

Studies focusing on the "culture of poverty" found in inner-city communities provided a useful challenge to scholarship that held that there were
genetic/biological differences among the racial groups. Such scholarship

had been used in pre–civil rights days to give intellectual support to Jim Crow segregation and discriminatory immigration policies. However, as Balibar points out, "Culture can also function like a nature, and it can, in particular, function as a way of locking individuals and groups a priori into a genealogy, into a determination that is immutable and intangible in origin."[67] As such, the language of "culture" found in "culture of poverty" studies, as well as in the contemporary scholarship surveyed above, allows us as a society to continue to talk about essential differences among racial groups without having to use the now-loaded language of biological "races."

"Culture of poverty" studies focused the attention of scholars and policy makers on the task of cataloguing the values and norms of the poor rather than on the task of dissecting the political economy and social structures—including unequal schools—that constrain the lives of the poor.[68] Similarly, contemporary scholarship on young people of color directs our attention toward the "moral life of the inner city" and the "oppositional outlooks" of its young residents and away from the kinds of educational inequalities documented in the Introduction. As such, these studies lend themselves to readings that focus, not on the environments that according to the studies provoke the cultural adaptations in the first place, but instead on the adaptations themselves.

On Scholarly Ideas in the Public Conversation

Despite concerns surrounding the conceptual frameworks and findings of much of the contemporary scholarship on young people of color and the racial achievement gap, much of it finds its way into public conversations on schooling. In this section, I explore how scholarly ideas enter the public realm. I do so through a discussion of how Ogbu's "acting white" hypothesis has become, in Dyson's words, "the academic equivalent of an urban legend."[69] In the process, the hypothesis's one-dimensional representation of African Americans as anti-intellectual has entered the writing of journalists and pundits and even the speeches of leading presidential contenders. Lost in the process, however, are the concerns scholars have raised regarding the hypothesis's validity.

Ogbu's dysfunctional portrayal of African Americans found its way into John McWhorter's 2000 *New York Times* bestseller *Losing the Race*, a book the *Wall Street Journal* characterized as "a sincere call to face the unpleasant truths behind black underachievement,"[70] and his 2005 follow-up book, *Winning the Race*, a book the *National Review* recommended for the way it "skewers the notion that racism remains ominous and oppressive."[71] At the time of the publication of *Losing the Race*, McWhorter was an associate professor of linguistics at the University of California, Berkeley, and he drew on his academic credentials to establish a public persona as an expert on the state of Black America.[72] The books, however, were published by commercial publishers and targeted to a general audience. Since then, McWhorter has become a senior fellow at the Manhattan Institute, the influential conservative think tank that is also home to Herman Badillo. With the motto of "turning intellect into influence," during the last two decades the institute has played an important role in shaping public conversations and policies regarding welfare, policing, and education. Thus McWhorter's writings afford a strategic avenue through which to follow the movement of ideas from the academy into the public realm.

Losing the Race is organized around McWhorter's claim that in post–civil rights America "acts of self-sabotage" by African Americans constitute a more serious barrier to their achievement than does "white racism."[73] Examining the racial achievement gap, McWhorter draws on the language of pathology to inform readers that "black students do so poorly in school decade after decade not because of racism, funding, class, parental education, etc., but because of a virus of Anti-intellectualism that infects the black community."[74] This virus, McWhorter holds, is "not foisted upon black Americans by whites" but rather self-generated from within the community as "a self-sustaining cultural trait" that is passed on through the lessons parents and peers give young African Americans.[75] In a passage that illustrates the ways in which, as Balibar points out, culture talk can "lock individuals and groups a priori into a genealogy," McWhorter asserts that "black people are taught from the cradle that books *are* not us."[76]

Writing in 2000, McWhorter acknowledges that his analysis of African American pathology is "not new" and cites Fordham and Ogbu's 1986 article. He notes, though, that since Fordham and Ogbu focused only on "rough urban schools" they failed to notice that the fear of "acting white" also depresses the academic achievement of middle-class suburban African Americans. "Growing up culturally black in America," he writes, "under *any* circumstances typically entails that children learn at an early age that 'black' and 'school' do not go together."[77] As evidence, McWhorter points to a 1998 *Washington Post* story on the performance of African American students in Shaker Heights, Ohio.

The reason black children underperform in school is that they belong to a culture that discourages them from applying themselves to books and learning—regardless of income or class, and regardless of intervention by even the best-intentioned people. The centrality of this factor is quite empirically evident: for example, a black student in Shaker Heights reported that she began as a good student, but that her black friends called her "acting white" and "an oreo" for doing so, and that in order to get back in their good graces she let her grades plummet; meanwhile a white student at the school felt nothing less than pressured by her peers to succeed.[78]

Three years after the publication of *Losing the Race*, Ogbu published his own Shaker Heights study reemphasizing his decades-old hypothesis that the cultural outlooks of African Americans, regardless of class, retard their academic achievements.[79]

Losing the Race also perpetuates Ogbu's counterposition of the cultural outlooks of African Americans and immigrants. "Asian immigrants' children," McWhorter writes, "take on school as a challenge. Learning English via immersion, helping one another in study groups, refusing to accept anything but their own best efforts. Black Americans, however, generally consider the particular challenges of schools utterly insurmountable without special set asides (be this in Watts or at Duke); black students are not considered to have even the potential for 'Success in Their Veins' when it comes to 'the books.'"[80] Drawing on his credentials as a university professor, McWhorter also notes that "in my teaching career thus far every black undergraduate I have ever taught who has been one of the best students in my class has been of Caribbean extraction." While celebrating the academic drive of Asian and Black Caribbean immigrants, McWhorter challenges "the equation between the initiative to immigrate and scholarly achievement" found in Ogbu's work. According to McWhorter, the problem with such an equation is demonstrated by the case of Latinos, who are "second only to blacks in lagging grades and test scores." He notes, "Few would disagree that culture is the decisive factor: a sense among Latinos, reinforced by the Civil Rights movement ideology, that school and other mainstream institutions are the 'gringo's' game. Latino students who excel report being teased by their Latino peers for 'acting white' just as their black equivalents do." Although McWhorter states that "few would disagree" with his claim that Latino culture is anti-intellectual, he cites no evidence for it. In fact, McWhorter's best-selling discussions of African American and Latino anti-intellectualism contain little in the form of evidence.[81]

The evidence McWhorter does provide consists largely of anecdotes from his personal experiences as an African American student and professor. In particular, he spends much ink regaling the reader with anecdotes of African American students at Berkeley, who, according to him, "tended to be among the worst students on campus, by any estimation."[82] In the Afterword to the 2001 edition of the book, McWhorter argues that he "use[s] anecdotes only to illustrate or bolster points defended with actual data or reportage."[83] The "actual data or reportage" he provides in support of the "acting white" hypothesis includes reports citing the racial achievement gap in SAT scores, high school test scores, and high school dropout rates. These, however, prove only that the gap exists, not that cultural outlooks are its cause. The only other data that he cites in support of his argument are passages from Fordham and Ogbu's 1986 article; the 1998 *Washington Post* story on Shaker Heights schools; stories from the *New York Times* and the *San Francisco Examiner;* discussions of the learning style of African American students found in a New York State Board of Regents manual and Eleanor Orr's *Twice as Less;* and data from studies by Lawrence Steinberg, Clifton Casteel, and Roslyn Mickelson.

In his follow-up 2005 book, *Winning the Race,* McWhorter dismisses the scholarship of education specialists (including Ainsworth-Darnell and Downey and Cook and Ludwig) who have challenged the validity of the "acting white" hypothesis.[84] "I am aware of no academic study claiming that the 'acting white' problem is a myth," he writes, "that even begins to address the issue with methods that withstand scrutiny."[85] To counter the conclusions reached by the social scientists he denounces for doing "flat-earther work,"[86] McWhorter provides readers with his own "data," which this time around consist of 1995 and 2003 *New York Times* editorial columns by Bob Herbert, a 2001 *New York Times* story by Tamar Lewin, comments made in 2004 by Harvard professor and *Cosby Show* adviser Alvin Pouissant to the Public Broadcasting Station's (PBS) *Newshour,* a comment by former National Urban League head Hugh Price quoted by William G. Bowen and Derek Bok in *The Shape of the River,* and a comment by Al Sharpton quoted in a 2002 *New York Times* story.

The rest of McWhorter's data consist of his report that "after *Losing the Race* was published, I received an avalanche of testimonials over years' time from people attesting to the reality of the 'acting white' problem and also have spoken to countless people on radio shows or in real life who

confirm the same." Specifically, he points to a file he compiled contain-
ing "more than a hundred entries" in which writers recall "being tarred
specifically as 'acting white' for doing well in school."[87] Since McWhorter
claims to have received "about four thousand letters and e-mails about
Losing the Race," the file appears to contain approximately 2.5 percent
of McWhorter's total fan mail.[88] Nonetheless, he asks readers to place
greater confidence on the testimonials in the file than on the scholarly
research he dismisses. This is because the letters "are not based just on
what subjects say [to researchers]" but on "simple, concrete memories of
experiencing or seeing the 'acting white' charge." Moreover, he notes, the
testimonials were "unsolicited."[89] While they were, technically speaking,
"unsolicited," they hardly reflect the quality of data social scientists garner
through random samples, careful surveys, or ethnographic methods. They
simply reflect the contents of a very small percentage of fan letters sent to
an author who proclaims the validity of the "acting white" hypothesis in
his books.

The "data" McWhorter presents in both books in support of the "acting white" hypothesis illustrate that all kinds of people are talking about
it. However, to treat those voices as proof of the hypothesis's validity,
as McWhorter asks readers to do, is to suggest that an idea becomes
valid simply if a lot of people talk about it—a rather "flat-earther" position from which to proclaim an idea's validity. Despite the heated debates
among researchers and the dearth of data he marshals, McWhorter tells
his readers that "it is quite simply, a fact that the psychological opera-
tions of 'oppositional culture' exert a decisive effect of black students'
performances."[90]

Toward the end of *Winning the Race*, McWhorter happily notes, "It is
my impression that the fact that culture plays a large part in the achievement gap is seeming less heretical to many concerned people than it
was ten years ago." As evidence of the increased currency that the "acting white" hypothesis has received, McWhorter cites the keynote address
Barack Obama delivered at the 2004 Democratic National Convention.[91]
The speech is accredited with bringing Obama, who at the time was running for the U.S. Senate, to national attention. In the passage referenced
by McWhorter, Obama told the nation: "Go into any inner city neighborhood, and folks will tell you that government alone can't teach kids to
learn. They know that parents have to parent, that children can't achieve
unless we raise their expectations and turn off the television sets and eradicate the slander that says a black youth with a book is acting white."[92]

Obama's speech was also picked up by columnist Clarence Page in a commentary for PBS's *The Newshour* in which he defended Bill Cosby's 2004 *Brown* speech. Page commended Cosby's willingness to remind African Americans that "our own self-defeating attitudes can take us out of the race before we even start." As evidence of these attitudes, Page cited the passage above from Obama's speech and followed it with the remark that "today's hip-hop generation [is] . . . eager to put you down for somehow acting white when you try to get ahead, as if blackness means you have to fail. Obama, the son of a black father from Kenya and a white mother from Kansas, has a more positive view of blackness. He wants the rest of us to pass that message on to our kids."[93] Page's defense of Cosby via Obama not only gave voice and legitimacy to Ogbu's "acting white" hypothesis but, like McWhorter's book, reinscribed the distinction between voluntary and involuntary minorities found at the heart of Ogbu's analysis. Obama's "more positive view of blackness," Page suggested, is tied up with the biographical—and *biological*—fact that he is the "son of a black father from Kenya and a white mother from Kansas," rather than just a Black kid from the American ghetto. In Page's televised commentary, Obama—the immigrant's child who drew national attention to Nigerian-born Ogbu's hypothesis about African American anti-intellectualism—emerged as *the* model minority that African Americans would do well to emulate.

In 2007, Obama, now a U.S. senator representing Illinois, was busy campaigning for the nomination of the Democratic Party to serve as its presidential candidate in 2008. As he criss-crossed the country, the idea that the fear of "acting white" keeps African Americans from doing well in school became part of his stump speech.[94] "Sen. Barack Obama (D-Ill.) is delivering pointed critiques of the African American community as he campaigns for its votes," the *Washington Post* proclaimed, ". . . lamenting that many of his generation are 'disenfranchising' themselves because they don't vote, taking rappers to task for their language, and decrying 'anti-intellectualism' in the black community, including black children telling peers who get good grades that they are 'acting white.'" The *Post* went on to note that "the concept of 'acting white' and worries that African Americans are not pushing their children enough to focus on education have been long-standing concerns of Obama—he has mentioned them in several speeches—and issues that many prominent members of the community, most notably comedian Bill Cosby, have focused on in recent years." The *Post* story complemented Obama for his message of "tough love" toward African Americans and noted that as a

Black politician he had "an ability to speak about issues that a nonblack candidate probably could not have."[95]

In this manner, academic ideas navigate from the confines of academic conferences and peer-reviewed journals through the pages of nationally circulated newspapers and best-selling books and into public conversations regarding young people of color—often without reference to the heated debates among researchers regarding the validity of those ideas. In the process, controversial academic hypotheses about the causes of the racial achievement gap gain currency and weight in the public mind as "quite simply" valid "facts"—to draw on McWhorter's words—and come to influence public policies.

Solving America's Education "Problem"

Through their descriptions and analyses, social scientists give voice to the consciousness and practices of their day and, in turn, shape such consciousness and practices.[96] As the scholarly literature surveyed above enters the public realm, it influences and reinforces representations of African American and Latino young people, popular understandings of their educational experiences, and policy debates regarding how to best solve America's education "problem." Through a reading of Williams's *Enough* and Badillo's *One Nation, One Standard*, this section explores how the culturalist assumptions that run through the scholarship on the racial achievement gap inform popular discourse and policy initiatives such as the federal No Child Left Behind Act of 2001.

On "Decent Daddies" to the Rescue

Williams casts *Enough*, which became a 2006 *New York Times* bestseller and was released in paperback in 2007, as a defense of Bill Cosby's 2004 *Brown* speech. The speech received a standing ovation and became a media sensation, well received by newspaper columnists and television talk-show pundits. Jonah Goldberg, for example, wrote in the *National Review* that Bill Cosby "should be congratulated for shaming those who deserve—and need—to be shamed."[97] However, despite the positive attention heaped upon Cosby's speech—or perhaps because of it—some African American leaders quickly denounced it. One of the strongest critiques was mounted in Michael Eric Dyson's *New York Times* best-selling book *Is Bill Cosby Right?* which denounced Cosby for "skewer[ing] the victims of educational neoapartheid, the very folk that *Brown v. Board* sought to help, instead of pointing to the social inequities and disparities in resources that continue to make American schools 'separate and unequal.'"[98]

In defending Cosby's views, *Enough* gives support and currency to the dysfunctional image of African Americans advanced by the culture talk of scholars such as Patterson, Anderson, Ogbu, Portes, and Rumbaut. Large segments of the African American community, the book suggests, are kept from performing well in school and from attaining economic mobility, not by the hypersegregated and unequal public education system documented in the Introduction, or by the structural economic forces discussed in the Urban Institute reports, but rather by the fact that—as Williams reports Cosby understands the problem—poor African Americans are "psychologically twisted."[99]

In a passage that explicitly evokes Ogbu's "acting white" hypothesis and echoes Clarence Page's defense of Cosby, Williams informs his readers that young African Americans have developed "a culture that openly demeans any black student who achieves academic excellence as inauthentic and acting white."[100] Williams cites Ogbu's Shaker Heights study to argue that even if *Brown*'s promise of integrated schools were fulfilled, African Americans' "culture of failure" and their fear of "acting white" would still keep them from succeeding academically. Williams's message to his readers is clear: the integration of public schools by itself will not help African American students succeed, since their fear of "acting white" will continue to make them think that it is "not cool to be successful."[101] Williams concludes his discussion of Ogbu's research by noting that "Professor Ogbu sounds a lot like Cosby. His analysis, like Cosby's, attracted hostile critics. And, like Cosby's critics, Ogbu's critics had no evidence to mount a legitimate challenge to the credibility of his work."[102] Of course, Williams is either betraying his lack of knowledge of the substantial research that has challenged Ogbu's hypothesis or is shielding Ogbu—and by extension Cosby and himself—from the damning conclusions reached by that research. Either way, like McWhorter, Williams positions readers to accept as established fact what the scholarly literature tells us is at best controversial and subject to debate.

Like Ogbu's work, *Enough* pairs criticism of the supposedly degraded culture of poor and working-class African Americans with celebration of the culture of "immigrants," as if they were a monolithic, homogenous mass of hard-working, high-achieving people. Williams cites a passage from a speech Cosby delivered in Houston that recalls the distinction

Ogbu drew between the "folk theories of getting ahead" held by involuntary minorities and immigrant minorities: "I am going to tell you that the Ethiopian knows the value of American education. The Nigerian knows the value of an American education. Drive a cab, all of them. Working at night, all of them. Living in the house, fourteen or fifteen people, but all of them are working, and got their books with them. They're at the community college, they are over at junior college working their way [to the university]. And they are going to become doctors, lawyers, engineers, and our people, born here, are standing around watching people go by."[103] The rhetorical move here and in similar passages in the book draws on the long-standing discourse on "model minorities" discussed above, in which the successes of some immigrants is taken as evidence that with the proper cultural outlook and work ethic anyone can succeed academically and attain economic mobility.

By insisting that a group's academic achievement and economic mobility are strongly influenced by its cultural values, Badillo's *One Nation, One Standard* also echoes the scholarly talk that explains academic achievement by "invoking a group's cultural characteristics"—to borrow Patterson's language. In invoking the "low status" that Latinos grant education, Badillo is careful to note that it is "a product not of genetics but of cultural values." These cultural values were "bestowed" on Latinos, Badillo claims, by Latin America's "five hundred year siesta—the three hundred years of colonial rule and the subsequent two hundred years of authoritarian leadership." As he explains, since neither the Spanish Empire nor the Roman Catholic Church had an interest in "creating democratic institutions or educating the masses," Latin America never developed the stable political institutions and universal public school system found in the United States. Instead, the region developed a culture characterized by "a disregard for the rule of law, an indifference to participatory democracy . . . and a lack of enthusiasm for education." This is the cultural baggage that Badillo argues Latinos carry with them as they migrate north and that ill equips them for success in the United States.[104]

Focusing public attention on the presumed culture of Latino students rather than on the structural conditions in which these students find themselves, Badillo gives public weight to a post–civil rights common sense that keeps the nation from directly confronting the segregated and unequal conditions of public schooling. Rather than courageously attacking the dominant common sense, the book reflects it. *One Nation, One Standard* constitutes another instance in which a community's self-appointed "decent daddy" demands the public's respect for daring to deliver a very public reprimand to a people that is already regularly reprimanded by others. In fact, the reason Williams and Badillo—like McWhorter—do not need to provide hard evidence for many of their claims to resonate with their readers is that their books reinscribe rather than challenge all-too-popular representations of the dysfunctionality of people of color.

On Tough Love

While Williams and Badillo spend most of their ink blaming cultural values and norms for the academic failures of African American or Latino children, another culprit rears its ugly head in their respective analyses: what Badillo refers to as the "educational establishment."[105] While each author acknowledges the inequalities that plague the nation's public school system, each criticizes schools primarily for being too willing to accommodate the supposed anti-intellectual culture of students of color.

Williams criticizes the silence he perceives on the part of civil rights leaders regarding the "horror show" of African American parents passing on to their children their "refusal to master standard English, a lack of interest in formal schooling, the acceptance of a culture of failure." He writes: "It is either the case that civil rights leaders believe that the one-third of black people who remain locked in poverty—despite all the new doors opened the fifty years since *Brown*—are beyond hope, or civil rights leaders are afraid to challenge black people who are profiting from the system, including members of teachers' unions, big-city school boards, and the political class of superintendents and city councils." Williams argues that "the key political concern" of the "alliance" formed between civil rights leaders and teachers' unions has been "creating teaching jobs, protecting those jobs, and increasing funding for schools, including money to pay teachers better." In this context, he claims, "what was happening to the students took a back seat." By "what has been happening to the students," Williams does not refer to the highly segregated and physically decaying schools that most students of color are forced to attend, or to the outdated and substandard curricula and poorly trained teachers that they often encounter in the classroom. He refers, instead, to the way schools fail to challenge students' oppositional outlooks and send them the message that "they'll be promoted to the next grade as long as they don't do drugs, fight, or bring guns to school."[106]

While much of *One Nation, One Standard* focuses on Badillo's argument that cultural values undermine the academic performance of Latinos, the book also attacks a "half century of misguided [U.S.] policy." Badillo goes after the "educational establishment," claiming that, "paralyzed by racially themed power struggles among teachers' unions, parents, politicians, and bureaucrats, our public schools have shunted Hispanics into low-intensity classes and asked too little of them, implicitly convinced of their inability to achieve." Using a broad brush, Badillo portrays bilingual education, academic tracking, social promotion practices, and special education classes negatively and suggests that they "undermine Hispanic achievement." While Badillo criticizes these programs, he reserves his harshest criticism for Latino parents who do not protect their children from the programs. "Whenever a child is left behind," he writes, "it is not the fault of the teachers, or the principals, or the school chancellor, or the mayor, or the president. It is their [parents'] fault."[107]

Efforts to address the racial achievement gap, Williams and Badillo suggest, must therefore target not only these children's anti-intellectual culture but also the educational system that rewards it. Schools need to hold all students to the same tough standards—the "one standard" evoked by Badillo's title—and to use mandatory high-stakes testing to measure students' ability to meet those standards. The "tough love" logic of this premise holds that such testing will force disrespectful students to change their attitude and their behavior and strive—at a bare minimum—to pass the tests. Tough standards and high-stakes tests can break the hold that the "culture of failure" has over African American kids and can wake Latino children up from their cultural "siesta." Of course, this "tough love" approach is legitimated by the one-dimensional representation of young people of color as dysfunctional that is crafted by the culture talk found in the scholarly literature cited above and in McWhorter's, Williams's, and Badillo's popular books.

On the Children We Are Leaving Behind

In January 2002, the federal No Child Left Behind Act of 2001 (NCLB) went into effect. The act's official name is "To Close the Achievement Gap with Accountability, Flexibility, and Choice, So That No Child Is Left Behind," and it seeks to use mechanisms of accountability, standardized testing, and school choice to improve academic outcomes.[108] With its rhetoric of holding public schools "accountable" and its mandatory standardized testing requirements, NCLB reflects the "tough love" approach advocated by Williams and Badillo. It mandates that to receive federal funds, schools must measure student proficiency in mathematics and English language arts (ELA) by administering statewide standardized tests to students in the third through eighth grades as well as once during high school.[109] To push schools to improve student scores, NCLB imposes penalties on schools that fail to show "adequate yearly progress" toward ensuring that all students will be proficient in both subjects by 2014. Under the logic of NCLB, as Deborah Meier points out, "A well-educated person is one who scores high on standardized math and reading tests. And ergo a good school is one that either has very high test scores or is moving towards them at the prescribed rate of improvement. Period."[110]

In *Enough*, Williams commends President Bush for supporting NCLB and for speaking truth to power—or at least to the "phony leaders" and the teacher unions that Williams blames for retarding the academic performance of African American children. In defense of Bush's education policies, he cites Bush's oft-repeated refrain: "Progress for African Americans and progress for all Americans requires good schools. . . . Look, the system tended to shuffle kids through. And you know what I'm talking about. You know, the hard-to-educate were labeled . . . and moved through. That's what was happening. . . .We can play like it wasn't happening—it was happening. . . . It's what I call the soft bigotry of low expectations."[111] This "soft bigotry" comes from school board members, principals, and teachers who, from Williams's and Bush's perspective, do not hold African American kids to tough standards. By holding schools accountable for students' standardized test scores, Williams suggests, NCLB will force principals and teachers to stop rewarding the "culture of failure" and to push those that Bush refers to as "the hard-to-educate" to get serious about studying and performing well academically.

While Badillo does not discuss NCLB in detail, he does argue that "one policy remedy for this state of affairs would be mandatory standardized testing," and he provides a spirited defense of such tests.[112] Moreover, in the foreword to *One Nation, One Standard*, former New York City mayor Rudy Giuliani credits Badillo with creating the political context in which NCLB arose. "I think Herman even deserves some credit for the federal No Child Left Behind Act," Giuliani writes. "It was Herman who put raising standards at the center of the education debate."[113]

No Child Left Behind also reflects the post–civil rights logic that guides much of the culture talk surveyed above. In support of the act, President

Bush noted that "the quality of our public schools directly affects us all as parents, as students, and as citizens. Yet too many children in America are segregated by low expectations, illiteracy, and self-doubt. In a constantly changing world that demands increasingly complex skills from its work force, children are being left behind."[114] As Katheryne Mitchell has noted, "The word 'segregation' in this speech no longer refers to racial and class separation caused by racism and poverty, but rather to 'cultural' values which are holding unspecified groups of children back."[115] Bush's words attempt to magically erase the structural inequalities that segregate poor students of color into overcrowded and underfunded schools. In post–civil rights America, the words tell us, the forces of segregation have been relegated to the cultural realm: students are "left behind" not by the educational inequalities documented in the Introduction but rather by other people's "low expectations" and, importantly, by their own "illiteracy" and "self-doubt."

The emphasis on mandatory standardized testing as a solution to America's education "problem" has shifted the policy discussion away from the goals of racial integration and equal schools that *Brown* represented. Lost in all the talk regarding how to stop schools from rewarding the "culture of failure" is the commitment to removing structural barriers to educational equity. Despite early expectations to the contrary, NCLB does not address funding inequalities between and within school districts,[116] variations in teacher preparation and salaries between and within school districts, the physical decay and overcrowded conditions of older urban schools, or the continued racial segregation of schools.

The Post–Civil Rights Language of Segregation

The stories scholars, journalists, and public intellectuals tell about young people of color influence public discussions about their education as well as policies such as NCLB aimed at addressing the "problems" with that education. The culture talk that permeates these stories casts these young people as one-dimensionally anti-intellectual; too consumed by the culture of the "cool pose" and "the street" to care about doing well in school; too fearful of being labeled "white" by their peers to try to excel academically; and too immersed in a "culture of failure" and a "cultural siesta" to aspire to academic success. Whichever way these writers frame it, the message is the same: African American and Latino kids simply do not care to do well in school.

The representations of African American and Latino young people advanced by the culture talk of the adult experts cited in this chapter draw on a long tradition of racialized images that have historically denied the complex and multidimensional humanity of people of color in the United States. Those representations evoked the language of nature to describe Blacks and Latinos—to fix their essence in the national imagination—as intellectually inferior and often dangerous and violent. As variations on an old theme, the current representations use the language of culture rather than nature. Nonetheless, they end up fixing the essence of Black and Latinos in similar terms. Of course, as Balibar suggests, culture talk can be another way to talk about people's nature. It does not take much to go from saying that the "cultural attributes"—to use Patterson's language—of young people of color are dysfunctional to saying that *they* are dysfunctional.

Despite the public currency that representations of African American and Latino youth as dysfunctional have attained, they are often built out little empirical evidence. Authors of best-selling books and popular press stories, as discussed above, craft such representations through vast generalizations based on first- and secondhand anecdotes but on a dearth of hard data. When these authors refer to scholarly research, they tend to present as "facts" what are—at best—controversial hypotheses around which there is substantial debate within academic circles. As these hypotheses—cloaked in the mantle of scholarly "expertise"—enter public discourse as established facts, they shape the common sense through which young people of color are perceived and treated.

Culture talk is what the language of segregation sounds like in our post–civil rights era. By denying the multidimensional humanity of poor and working-class young people of color, it allows us to segregate them into inferior schools even as we proclaim our nation's commitment to providing each and every person with "equal treatment under the law." A society publicly committed to treating all children as equal can justify confining some children to underfunded, overcrowded, physically dilapidated and substandard schools only if *those* children are viewed as essentially different from the kids attending the "good" schools. Why spend money and energy fixing the schools that large numbers of children of color attend if, as Ogbu told the *New York Times* in 2002, that will not "solve the problems"—the "problems" being defined as these children's culture?

While the stories collected in this chapter tell us much regarding how adults talk about and treat young people of color, they tell us little about what kids themselves think about their schooling and how they frame their own aspirations. What do African American and Latino students from today's segregated schools actually think about the value of their education, the conditions in their schools, their teachers, and their peers? What, in fact, do they think is the "problem" facing America's education system? And what do they think about the way adults talk about them as if *they* were the "problem"? In the following pages, African American and Latino students take on these and other questions. In doing so, they "talk back" to the racially segregated and unequal public schools they confront on a daily basis as well as to the one-dimensional and demeaning stories that adults tell about them.[117]

2

"I Hate It When People Treat Me Like a Fxxx-up"

Phony Theories, Segregated Schools, and the Culture of Aspiration among African American and Latino Teenagers

JEANNE THEOHARIS

A hailstorm hit South Central today, the national news reported. Hail in November in South L.A., a place that exists in the popular imagination as the stifling hot setting for two riots, gang violence, drive-by shootings, and West Coast hip-hop. Broadcast across the country, there was little mention that the weather anomaly had left tens of thousands of African American and Latino Angelenos without power for days. John C. Fremont High School, at Seventy-seventh and San Pedro, was one of those places that still had no power. But the principal lacked the authority to close the school herself, and the superintendent ordered that the school must be open the next day. Teachers were flabbergasted, some reporting rumors that the LAPD had pressured the district to keep the school open. Basically, each teacher was required to hold her first-period class for the entire day. There was not enough light in the school to do any effective work or to make it particularly safe for students to be changing classes. So students were essentially held in the school, neither educated nor sent home for their own safety. It is difficult to imagine that, in the tonier suburbs of Beverly Hills or Santa Monica across town, high schools would be open during a power outage and the district would think it appropriate to hold students for an entire day in a building without electricity.

—Fieldnote (November 2003)

It's not what they're doing to us. It's what we're not doing. 50 percent drop out. . . . What the hell good is *Brown v. the Board of Education* if nobody wants it?

—Bill Cosby, speech at NAACP
commemorative *Brown* gala (2004)

What's most interesting about the recent spate of studies [on Black males' underachievement] is that analysts seem at last to be recognizing what has long been obvious to anyone who takes culture seriously: socioeconomic factors are of limited explanatory power. . . . [These young men's] candid answer was that what sociologists call the "cool-pose" culture of young black men was simply too gratifying to give up.

—Harvard sociologist Orlando Patterson,
"A Poverty of the Mind" (2006)

It is time to acknowledge that *Brown*'s time has passed. . . . Racial malice is no longer the primary motive in shaping inferior schools for minority children.

—NPR/Fox journalist Juan Williams,
"Don't Mourn *Brown v. Board of Education*" (2007)

Public discourse on urban education has been overtaken by a discussion of values. As chapter 1 elaborated, it has become common sense to bemoan the declining value of education within urban Black and Latino communities, to assume a priori that students who value education succeed in school and that those with poor values drop out. This misinformed discussion about values not only takes the responsibility for schools away from the society that creates them and places it solely on students and their parents but distorts the regard for education held in the African American and Latino communities. Moreover, it caricatures criticism of the unequal structures of schooling as devaluing education itself.

Many commentators like those above, while purporting to speak authoritatively on urban teenagers, do not spend much time listening to how young people actually think about and frame issues of schooling. This chapter foregrounds the perspectives of a group of African American and

Latino high school students who attend a deeply segregated public high school in Los Angeles on the value and nature of their own educations. Using a set of journal writings students did for me over the course of the 2004 spring semester, I look at how young people write about their goals and aspirations, about good teaching and the use of testing, and about the structures of schooling today. Their writings demonstrate how profoundly students value education, how deeply they wish to be successful academically, and how much they hope to make their families proud.

Interweaving their beliefs and values with an analysis of the schooling they receive, I show how these young people are expected to be responsible (about attending school, doing their homework, making plans for college) while the school district does not have to demonstrate an equal level of responsibility in providing adequate classes and ample and excellent materials, clean bathrooms, sufficient college counselors, and a productive learning environment. Indeed, by showing the ways students hold up the promise of education, this chapter seeks to counter the incessant public lamentations that these students are unreachable and unteachable by demonstrating their hunger for substantive learning. While these students did not always choose to do their homework and attend class, this stemmed less from their devaluing of education than from a loss of confidence in themselves and the school to do right by them. Finally, this chapter demonstrates the ways this overwhelming focus on goals, hard work, and individualism is taken up by students themselves as over and over they are quick to blame themselves and narrate their talents through a frame that holds themselves—and often only themselves—responsible for the quality and success of their schooling.

The Case Study: Fremont High School

Considered one of the most troubled schools in Los Angeles and placed on the state list of failing schools, Fremont High School is not a flagship of Los Angeles Unified School District (LAUSD). In the bottom 10 percent of the state, Fremont was one of thirteen schools in LAUSD (a district with over six hundred schools) audited by the state in 2003. With approximately five thousand students, Fremont operates year round on three tracks. A response to severe overcrowding, year-round schooling maximizes the use—and thus capacity—of the building because the rooms are used every weekday of the year (and often at night and on the weekends).[1] On this three-track system, students go to school for four months and then are off for two months in scattered rotation.[2] The level of disruption caused by students and teachers coming on and off track, the shuffling of rooms and textbooks, and periodic interruptions to the daily schedule is treated as routine, though it actually regularly impedes instruction. B Track is perhaps the worst pedagogically: their May–September, November–March schedule means that midway through each semester (following the traditional calendar) students change courses. Attending school all summer, students are not eligible for any of the city's summer jobs/internships programs, and the yearly testing occurs just a couple of weeks after B Track has come back to school.

Because year-round schooling deprives students of seventeen class days per year, this instructional time is made up by lengthening the school day by seventy-one minutes. Thus school begins at 7:35 in the morning and does not end until 3:25 in the afternoon. With six sixty-one-minute periods a day, students and teachers are exhausted by the afternoon. Everyone looks forward to the one day each month when the day is shortened to a blissful six and a half hours to give time for a staff meeting. Perhaps what is most galling is that multitrack schedules are not customary throughout the city, according to the research of UCLA's Institute for Democracy, Education and Access (IDEA), but are used predominantly in public schools that educate Latino and African American students.[3] This disparity, never publicly accounted for, seemingly reflects an assumption that certain students' schooling is fungible; excellence is not essential in these schools, and other logistical considerations can take precedence. When Fremont student Akeishia McKnight raised the problems of overcrowding and year-round schooling at a town meeting with the superintendent, she received the following reply in a letter from then-superintendent Roy Romer: "It is the policy of this district that once a school becomes so over-crowded that more than 250 students are bused out to other schools, it must be put on the year-round calendar. That is the situation at Fremont . . . At this point, we don't expect there to be a change at Fremont in the foreseeable future. Thank you . . . for asking such an important question."

Not only the school but also the classes are overcrowded. Class size averages thirty-five students, with many class rosters climbing well into the mid-forties (or even fifties) in 2003–4. While no teacher or administrator would ever wish it, what makes this situation even moderately manageable is dropouts: if some students do not show up, the class is smaller and better for the rest of the students as well as for the teacher. Thus, for classes to function, the system banks on—indeed needs—truancy. Trying to get past the numbers games that districts like LAUSD often play to mask their dropout rates, IDEA has calculated what they term the "disappearance rate" in L.A.'s schools. At Fremont, they calculate, for every hundred students who start freshman year, only thirty-two finish four years later and a mere sixteen have had full access to and completed the A-G academic curriculum that makes a student eligible for admission to a four-year college.

At Fremont there are very limited spaces in the Advanced Placement classes (on average one section is typically offered per subject per track). Even though many teachers supplement their classes with college preparatory material and increasingly the school emphasizes preparing every student for college, not enough courses are offered to allow every student to become eligible for a four-year college. According to Fremont's own figures, only 10.3 percent of graduates in 2004–5 had completed all the requirements to be eligible for a California State University or University of California admission. Thus graduating from Fremont is not, by and large, a path to college. High-powered academic electives found across town at Beverly Hills High School are not available at Fremont.[4] Boasting a tremendous range of classes with 180 course offerings and 60 electives, Beverly Hills offers AP Spanish and AP French along with Hebrew and Latin; students can enroll in television production, broadcast studies, architecture, advanced computer graphics, physiology, and astronomy along with more vocational electives such as advanced robotics, entrepreneurship, hotel management, and sports medicine. Conversely, despite being a huge school, the variety of elective course offerings at Fremont is limited and tends toward vocational classes like sewing, cosmetology, and auto mechanics.

Fremont employs only one college counselor (separate from the other guidance counselors) for a student body of five thousand. She receives a teacher's salary, not a yearlong salary, even though she works year round—which means she is paid for 170 days over the course of the year. She is supposed to take days off to compensate for the time she is not getting paid, and she sometimes does. Thus one adult who is not at school every day of the year is responsible for the college prospects of the entire school—an impossible feat, despite how committed Fremont's counselor was to students. While the percentage of adults with college degrees in L.A. County has climbed to over 25 percent (from 4 percent in 1940), the percentage of college graduates among adults who have attended Fremont has remained largely *the same* over the past sixty years (hovering just under 5 percent in 2000).

School overcrowding also corresponds to limited classroom resources. In 2003–4 there were not enough textbooks for every student, only a classroom set, so the textbooks could never go home for homework. Indeed, the textbooks were collected at the end of each track semester so they could be juggled among the tracks. This often resulted in students going without books for the first week or two of each term, and teachers lost the first week or two of instructional time because they had not received their allocation of books. (This has recently been partially addressed through the out-of-court settling of the *Williams* case discussed below.)

While the original brick and courtyard structure built in the 1920s is quite lovely, the tremendous growth at Fremont in the 1980s and 1990s required the construction of a great deal more cheap classroom space now called "the bungalows." With its prefab gray architecture and few windows, its similarity to a juvenile detention facility is striking to visitors and does not create an inviting learning environment. Because the school is used all the time, it is rundown; roaches, ants, and rats make periodic appearances in class.[5] Since the school is always in session, repairs have to be done during classes, producing a tremendous amount of noise, dirt, and disruption. The bathrooms are often dirty, and students are not allowed to go to the bathroom during lunch or during class.

Police, both LAUSD and LAPD, are a constant and visible presence at Fremont, but no metal detectors greet students entering the school. Instead, a fence and locked gates surround the school, and a complex bureaucracy and surveillance system regulates anyone wishing to enter or leave the school. The school is entirely locked in during the school day; even the parking lots are gated shut. With students periodically paraded through the halls in handcuffs, the police presence at the school is palpable.

Fremont High School is a vivid example of the segregated nature of L.A.'s schools.[6] In 2003–4, approximately 87 percent of the student body at Fremont was Latino and the remaining 13 percent of the student population was African American. There were virtually no whites or Asians at the school. Many of Fremont's students are immigrants, and many more are children of immigrants. The vast majority of students at Fremont qualify for free lunch—and probably nearly all would if they had the documents with which to qualify.[7]

In May 2000, on the forty-sixth anniversary of the Supreme Court's *Brown v. Board of Education* decision, a group of students, parents, and rights groups led by the ACLU and MALDEF filed suit against the state of

California. *Williams v. State of California Education* charged that the state had failed to live up to its constitutional obligation to provide "basic educational equality" and ensure that schools were "kept up and supported."[8] Schools across the state that educated children of color and immigrant students (including Fremont High School), like those the NAACP documented in *Brown* five decades earlier, were separate and unequal. Cindy Diego, an AP student at Fremont who was one of the plaintiffs, provided a damning summation of the education she was receiving:

> We can't take books home, and in class two to three people share each book. Sharing doesn't work when we need to read to ourselves because we can't all read one at the same time. . . . A book would be better because you can read the information at home and learn. . . . I wanted to take health this semester, but my counselor said it was too full and I had to take a "service" class or AP Spanish, even though I have already taken AP Spanish. I got a 5, the top score, on the AP exam, so it seemed silly to take AP Spanish again. In my service class, I run errands for a U.S. History teacher. . . . The bathrooms at school are just horrible. There aren't enough for us to use. The school has closed five of the six bathrooms. The one open bathroom always has long lines and is on the first floor, which is too far to go from some classes. The bathroom only has five stalls, one of which is missing a toilet and a door . . . and usually there is no toilet paper. Sometimes even this bathroom is locked. . . . Many of my classes do not have air conditioning and are hot and stuffy. . . . The heat made me get really, really red. The teachers told us to just stay still and not move around too much. I saw a rat a couple of times in my AP Spanish class last year and I see cockroaches five to ten times a year around school.

Nineteen teachers, nine students, and one parent at Fremont, many of whom are quoted below, also provided declarations that helped form the basis of the plaintiffs' case.

In August 2004, Gov. Arnold Schwarzenegger agreed to settle the case out of court, leading to more textbooks, open bathrooms, and allegedly the end of year-round schooling. But at the time of this writing many aspects of the settlement have still not made their way to schools like Fremont, and other aspects, like teacher hiring, training, and promotion, have been deferred to be treated under federal NCLB guidelines.[9]

Los Angeles is a city of contrasts—great affluence and growing economic opportunities in parts of the city accompany deep poverty and high unemployment rates in other neighborhoods. Fremont High School sits in some of the city's poorest neighborhoods. In Los Angeles County, according to the 2000 census, 13.4 percent of families lived below the poverty level and the median household income was approximately $48,248 (with a per capita income of $20,683). In the neighborhoods around Fremont, the median household income is less than half that, $22,346 (with a per capita income of $7,804, which shows that many households have three people working). A staggering 38.8 percent of families in these neighborhoods live below the poverty line. In 2006, South Los Angeles boasted the highest infant mortality rates and the lowest percentage of children with health insurance in the county.[10]

The Class and the Assignment

The basis for this research is a set of journal writings collected from the four U.S. history classes I shared with social studies teacher Steve Lang during the school year 2003–4.[11] Our classes ran on A Track, and our students were juniors, ranging in age from approximately sixteen to nineteen. Mr. Lang is African American, a Fremont grad himself, and a former track star and now track coach. He had been teaching at Fremont for twenty-eight years. For a year, on a Rockefeller Fellowship, I spent two full days a week at Fremont teaching African American and Latino history as a supplement to the American history curriculum—with Steve Lang for the first four periods and another teacher, Sarah Knopp, for the last two.[12] The students in Mr. Lang's classes were a mix of African Americans, American-born Latinos, and more recent immigrants from Mexico and Central America. (Perhaps because Mr. Lang is African American, his classes had more Black students than most did at Fremont. For example, his second-period homeroom class was majority Black, and we often speculated that counselors were sending the Black students to him.) In the winter semester, students were required to do journals to begin to record their own histories. Due every Thursday, the assignment, as we explained, had a twofold purpose: to engage students in the act of telling and preserving their history and claiming their own voice and experience in the city and to prepare students to do the kind of personal writing found on college and scholarship applications.[13] Their writing—more than one hundred students' journals—forms the basis of this research.

This, then, is a story about inner-city students writing—about them filling up pages and pages about their dreams for the future and their plans for the weekend, their romances, and their deepest worries. It is about these young people getting to pick the topic but also the frame of that subject, about them controlling the nature and telling of the story— getting to be the narrators of their own history. Through this process, a number of students started to find writing helpful in sorting through their thoughts and lives. Because U.S. history is a required subject for every junior, these journals represent a cross section of Fremont's population from athletes to gang members to recent immigrants (to athletic immigrant gang members), from honors students to those students doing passable work to those who dropped out or got in trouble with the law (to the honors students who dropped out).

This chapter thus draws from the writings of more than one hundred students and, accordingly, will not provide an intimate portrait of these young people. I am choosing to organize the chapter this way this for two reasons. First, by including a large number and variety of students from a class required of all students at a comprehensive public high school like Fremont, I hope to make clear the representativeness of these students' perspectives. These are not simply the "good students" with "decent values" while another mass of "bad" ones with "poor values" lurk around the corner. This book focuses on young people's perspectives on and experiences with school; thus their writings highlighted here comment directly on education. To do this in a substantive way means this chapter does not have the space to detail their childhood experiences or immigration narratives or to examine their writings on work or church or violence, though these topics filled up many other journal pages.

Second, not telling long personal stories of these students means that they remain partly unknown. This is a conscious decision. These students need to be taken seriously and seen as worthy of a much finer education—not because we know a lot about them or because they are deemed individually deserving of a better education. One of the most pernicious aspects of post–civil rights racial politics is the holding up of certain meritorious people of color, who are then afforded certain opportunities, while making troubling generalizations about the rest, who are provided with very few. Part of the maintenance of school segregation fifty years after *Brown* derives from the ways certain students have to prove they deserve an excellent education while others are simply given one as a matter of course.

Mr. Lang and I continually pressed our students to do their journals, and they (like most self-respecting high school students) protested throughout the semester about having to do them. They constantly questioned our decision to make them do weekly journals, and we repeatedly told them that they had to do it. They often would argue about the length of the assignment and devise ways to write shorter pieces. Writing "The End" in huge letters about one-third of the way from the bottom of the page was a popular tactic—as were enormous margins and the use of smaller steno notebooks to get around the two-pages-per-week requirement. Chucky, for instance, devoted one journal to his critique. "I really don't understand why teachers make us write stupid journals. . . . I consider that harassment because I don't feel like doing the journals. Journals are also boring and take a lot of time to write like this one I'm writing right now." Chucky's criticism of the assignment and its "harassing" nature was brazen but also fair. Moreover, Chucky devoted the last two paragraphs of this particular journal to describing his favorite Japanese comic, *Dragon Ball Z*. He thus married his critique of the assignment with his control over its terms, willingly completing the task while contesting its nature.

The constant cajoling that was required to get students to write was sometimes frustrating, but it did result in our students doing a great deal of writing. Many days, we would simply shake our heads in delight at how well the class had gone, excited by the insight and work of our students. The appearance of their journals was often a testament to this effort. Many students had a specific notebook especially dedicated to their journal writings, often elaborately decorated with drawings and clippings from magazines. Some students would carry their journals around and write them when they got a chance. Many would perfect their journals over a number of days, often showing versions of them to their friends. Writing and learning were not clandestine or unimportant activities but public and often collective efforts.

Yet while the writing of a number of students improved tremendously, most of our students' skill levels were not where we wanted them. While we often had complex animated discussions during class, we were not always a community. Some students would cut class, our classroom often segregated along gender and ethnic lines, many students would be delighted to leave at the bell, and we struggled continually to maintain an orderly, productive classroom. At some level, it was a far cry from popular ideas about how good teaching works.

In popular teacher stories from *Dangerous Minds* to *Freedom Writers*, the narrative is largely the same: teachers struggle, students resist, teachers lay down the law, a miracle line is crossed, students are won over, and teaching works its wonders. At the heart of these stories lies the trope of conversion. In a society that holds fast to ideas of hard work, individual determination, and upward mobility, these teacher-savior stories have such resonance because they maintain the idea that young people need saving from the urban culture around them and that a good teacher is sufficient against the forces of injustice, poverty, and racism. They provide society with heroes, a shield from the glare of fundamental structural inequality, and reassurance about the opportunities available in the educational system. Triumphal teacher stories confirm, however wrongly, that a teacher's presence is enough: regardless of the scant resources, dilapidated school structures, lack of public support, and societal disregard for these young people, a good teacher can do the job because the problem largely stems from the students.

One of the recent archetypes of this popular teacher-savior tale is the celebration of the Black male teacher. Invested with almost godlike properties, men like Steve Lang—upstanding role models who work in the neighborhoods they grew up in and know students both inside and outside of school—are believed to be the key to turning schools around. If only we had more Black male teachers, people like Bill Cosby imagine, the schools would be a much different place. And indeed, men like Mr. Lang who know all the students and many of their personal situations and prod them to excel, who give students rides and buy young athletes the equipment they need, all the while insisting that schoolwork must come first, who come back year after year and do it again and again, perform an immense public service. Mr. Lang was strict about the conduct he expected from students. If students failed to meet the class standards (missing class, being tardy, chewing gum), they would be required to write the standards one hundred times. While this helped to maintain a respectful classroom, there is a danger in romanticizing this kind of male discipline as the solution to school problems. It was not. Committed teachers like Mr. Lang were still no match for the structure of a school like Fremont. Responsible for nearly two hundred kids a day, with inadequate resources and an overly long school day, Steve had cut back on the writing he assigned his classes and reserved his willingness to do extra things outside school for the track students he coached.

Indeed, having me in class (a part-time white teacher) meant we could assign multiple essay assignments along with the journals and other supplemental writing projects—which were impossible otherwise. Yet despite the presence of two teachers, many students still dropped out or failed the class. In one particularly extreme example, we spent the better part of the semester trying to get extra help for one young man who had a keen mind and motivation but who could barely read or write. Mr. Lang inquired and inquired, knowing the ins and outs of the Fremont bureaucracy, but never succeeded in securing any help for this young man. Thus, despite a hungry student and a persistent teacher, no services were forthcoming—and the student subsequently drifted out of school.

At the end of the year, Steve thanked me for helping him feel "like I was really teaching." Indeed, far from being saved by teachers like Steve Lang, this system of unequal schooling had worn him down. By concentrating his energy on a discrete group—his track students—he had managed to find a strategy to stave off the burnout that many teachers at Fremont experienced. It was having a second teacher in the classroom that allowed him, a dedicated teacher of thirty years, to feel again that he was really teaching and to give students the instruction he believed they deserved.

Being a committed teacher was not enough. For this was not the movies, and our students were not in need of some sort of conversion. Our classes were a microcosm of the successes and failings of many classrooms across the country. Tremendous amounts of learning took place. But we did not reach every student. It was sometimes easier to give in to a larger fatigue. Many of our students continued to struggle academically—and even with two teachers it was nearly impossible to provide consistent feedback on their writing or circulate through the class and get to every student. Many young people brought burdens from outside class that we never found ways to work past. Numerous students dropped out over the course of the year, and many of them we did not track down. Sometimes our attention was consumed by the ones who were the most disruptive, overlooking the ones who struggled silently.

My best explanation for these shortcomings as well as these successes is that we did as much as we could (and this was significantly more than most teachers are able to do, since there were two of us). We labored to get students to do better work than they had been doing before they came to our class. And the vast majority did. We did not treat students as if they needed to be converted—and this level of respect led most students to trust our expectations of them. We expected a lot from students, and they often fulfilled those expectations admirably. We contended with the tremendous problems many students brought to class (death and family sickness, economic troubles, family dislocation) that had often been created by larger social conditions and attempted as much as possible to enable them to do work while they were in class. And for many students we succeeded, in providing both a space to learn and someone to listen. We worked with the limited materials we had (we had only a classroom set of books, so students could never take the textbook home) and supplemented them daily with copies made on the ancient Duplo machine in the social studies office. We did this in the midst of an underfunded, year-round school where the lengthened school day was exhausting and teachers had little, if any, time to plan together or develop better teaching strategies. A number of teachers filled their classes with worksheets and bookwork, and students often arrived at our class tired and unchallenged. In sum, our class reflected the inequities that beset Fremont and LAUSD more generally. As will be seen in this chapter, the quality of instruction and the dedication of the student were not enough to guarantee a student a safe and fulfilling passage through school.

On Values and Peer Pressure

> In my government class I have 37 desks for 43 students. Some students have to sit at my desk. During the first 2 weeks of school, some students had to stand up because we didn't have enough desks and chairs for them. At that time there were over 50 students in the class. After that some students just stopped showing up because they felt like there was no room for them at school. . . . When at the beginning of the school year I ask my 10th grade students what they want to do in life, the majority say they want to go to college to become doctors, lawyers, engineers. . . . By the end of their four years at Fremont their hopes are gone, they feel underprepared and end up not applying.
> —Sarah Knopp, Fremont social studies teacher,
> declaration for the *Williams* case

As the previous chapter suggested, the connection between cultural values and educational success lacks empirical foundation. Relying heavily on the transcendent power of rugged individualism, this culture talk is remarkably detached from the kind of schooling many young people are receiving. Yet the current fixation with values makes it important to recognize these students' commitment to education. Their journals provide a new and revealing window on their cultural values with which the public is so concerned. Most students wrote about school as a way to get ahead in the world, and many saw it as a source of personal pleasure. When the second semester began in March, a number of students wrote about how "glad" and "excited" they were to be back in school after the two-month break. Over the course of the semester they wrote extensively about class and their education more generally, about teachers, college, and their plans for the future. Despite images of urban students being antischool, educational concerns abounded in their journals. Again and again, they wrote about hard work being the road to success, about the importance of a good attitude and sustained effort, about the centrality of education to achieve their goals. Berating themselves for not applying themselves enough, a number of students attributed their problems to their own motivation and vowed to adopt new and better attitudes. Overwhelmingly, these students believed that hard work was rewarded and that they could achieve whatever they put their minds to. They did not always make the choice to come to school or complete their work—but that reflected less a decline in their valuing of education than a declining confidence in themselves, in their teachers, or in the school to do right by them.

Discussions of their goals for the future or exhortations about the value of hard work and the importance of education filled up pages and pages of journals from the best to the most marginal students. While this might stem in part from the fact that this was a school assignment and that students felt they should give us what we wanted to hear, it is notable that nearly all of our students were willing to give us what we wanted (if this indeed was their goal). In most popular representations of inner-city schools, the majority of African American and Latino students demonstrate little patience with authority and certainly do not actively do things to please teachers. Yet here our students were, handing in journals week after week with a number of entries devoted to their educational goals. This preponderance demonstrates how much students were thinking about their aspirations and, perhaps, their attempts to impress their teachers—all of which points to the value of education among these Black and Latino students. Students were never instructed to write about their own ideas of education, though the list of suggested topics included their goals and plans for the future.[14] Moreover, the pages they wrote on education were juxtaposed with equally large numbers of pages on their romantic lives and weekend exploits as the most popular journal topics. Their romantic misadventures were certainly not a topic that they could be convinced that we were interested in hearing about; thus they exercised a large measure of autonomy in the form and nature of their journals.

What becomes clear from reading hundreds of pages of these Fremont students' writings is that scholars and journalists convinced of the indifference of urban students to school have not really listened to students. Popular talk of declining values does not reflect how real students explain their ambitions and fears, their thoughts on good teachers, their favorite classes, and their goals for the future. From student surveys in the National Educational Longitudinal Survey, Duke University scholars Phillip Cook and Jens Ludwig have found that Black students approach the educational system in much the same way as white students. Black students are as likely to believe they will get a college degree as white students, drop out at the same rates as whites after controlling for family circumstances, cut classes and miss school at the same rates as whites, and have parents who attend school meetings and inquire about their progress with the same frequency as whites.[15] More recently, sociologist Karolyn Tyson and economist William Darity, in an ethnographic study conducted in North Carolina, concluded that Black and white students are fundamentally similar in their desire to succeed academically and in their positive feelings about themselves when they do. When anti-intellectual attitudes appear among white students, they found, "it is seen as inevitable, but when the same dynamic is observed among black students it is pathologized as racial neurosis."[16] In sum, white teenagers are allowed to adopt poses, complain about school, and go through different emotional stages without a parade of sociologists and public figures lamenting a culture of failure—while these very same behaviors from Black and Latino teenagers are treated as a sign of cultural dysfunction and seen as intrinsic to their nature.

These findings are borne out in the Fremont student narratives. Reading these journals while trying to hold on to the idea that these students do not believe in education produces a bizarre disconnect. Rather than asserting that academic success was "white," students complained about how some teachers, counselors, and other adults did not believe they were capable of success. A reserved and talented Chicano student, Rodrigo wrote, "I hate it when people treat me like a fxxx-up. I'm not stupid and I'm not a little kid. If people give me time and space, I can do things at my own pace. . . . I do plan on going to college but with all this pressure how can I succeed." Indeed, Rodrigo challenged the disparagement at the heart of this discussion of declining values, highlighting the impact such negativity had on his ability to achieve his goal of going to college. Interestingly, "fxxx-up" is Rodrigo's own choice of spelling; it suggests that he wanted to make his point forcefully but did not want to be impolite and swear outright in his journal.[17]

If some journalists and academics have heard students make statements about educational success being "white" (as I never did), they need to reflect on why students might be saying this. Such an ideology seems to be coming more from adults and a larger society that often does not hold out much possibility for these young people. Most students were not resigned to such thinking and, at times, actively resisted it, believing they would succeed through education despite what others said about them. Moreover, students respond in different ways to being excluded from the rewards of the educational system—and these comments may be a way to shield themselves from the pain of that exclusion. To say that education is "white" reflects a critique of the ways that education actually operates in U.S. society. Our students were well aware of the much finer schools to be found in L.A.'s more exclusive (and whiter) neighborhoods across town, the kinds of college opportunities such schools opened for students, and the social meanings of the differences between Fremont and those more excellent schools. In the face of such differences, some students picked up on readily available explanations for their own self-protection—they "didn't really care about school anyway," since it was hard to be convinced that the school always cared about them.[18] In addition, when students say, "School sucks," analysts too often read it as an expression of these young people's "attitude" about school rather than a factual, if vernacular, description of the conditions of their schools.

Certainly, peer pressure exists. Peer pressure against doing well flares up in all high schools across this country (academic success never being a mechanism for teenage social success). Being a "nerd" carries a great social cost in the suburbs and the city. Teenagers across the country spend a great deal of energy trying to be part of the crowd, and succeeding academically is often stigmatized because it marks a student as different.[19] Still, the assertion that problems of urban schools stem from negative peer pressure fails to recognize that most students in these schools believe intensely in the worth of education and hope to succeed academically. Marion, a shy African American student, asserted her own intelligence as crucial to her identity, as "utmost important to me besides my family and friends." Rafael, a similarly reserved Latino student, wrote that one of his "proudest memories" was getting an award at his eighth-grade graduation for being one of the best students in math. Ayana, a tremendously outgoing and at times argumentative African American young woman, recalled fondly the beginning of her high school career at Inglewood High School: "I had great outstanding grades. I never ditched a class. I was always at school on time. I got along with my teachers great. I remember all my cool friends. I was the greatest back at Inglewood." Being "the greatest" for students like Ayana included academic *and* social success.

In fact, many students looked down on those who did not value the pursuit of knowledge. As Johanna, a similarly argumentative Latina who periodically cut class herself, explained, "People in school seem to come for the fuck of it. Like just to flash what they have, not to learn." Larry, a young African American man who described a fun day in class as "watching a video, class activity or a fine girl helps you out with your work," explained the importance of doing work alongside the romancing: "Really it's what ever you make of it. You could do your work and get good grades or you could chill play cool and then you won't get anything. . . . So what I'm saying is do your job and don't cheat yourself." Thus Larry saw school success and social success not as antithetical but as potentially mutually reinforcing.

Moreover, getting good grades or associating with the "smart kids" did not seem to automatically compromise students' popularity. As Trevor, an articulate African American young man, wrote about his old school: "I was semi popular . . . because I knew different people like the smart kids, a little [of the] rockers." Not a single student wrote about being laughed at for doing his or her work or excelling in class—though a number recalled incidents of being laughed at for how they dressed or for not being able to speak English well. Others recalled fondly the public recognition of doing well in school, often calling up memories from elementary school.

Many students worried that their classmates would think they were stupid or laugh at them for having difficulty reading or writing and thus often resisted reading aloud or turning in their essays because of these fears. Indeed, the fear of looking stupid was much more palpable than the fear of looking smart. Angel, who had immigrated from Mexico, often refused to read out loud in class, occasionally prompting a showdown between us where he unsuccessfully tried to insist that he "didn't have to read." Months later in his journal he wrote,

> I don't like to read out loud because that is just not for me. The other reason why I don't like to read papers out loud is because when you reading a paper all the people looking at you and that is when you get all the attention and that's the thing I don't like because sometimes I get nervous.

The thing that gets me nervous is when specially the class is quiet and I'm the only one talking in front of everyone. Sometimes when I get real real nervous I can't even read good enough and sometimes I also get red and I try to control my self but sometimes I can and sometimes I can't.

Arturo, also an immigrant from Mexico, struggled with writing, often turning in late the short analytical essays we required. "I just have problems putting my ideas together and separating them into paragraphs. Sometimes I get good grades on them but other times I do poorly and get me mad and makes me think what was the point in doing it if I wasn't going to get a good grade. But other times I say that at least I try and turned it in." Both of these young men, who were not native English speakers, articulated their fears and embarrassment about not being skilled enough and how this sometimes led to not wanting to do their work.

These fears of looking stupid extended to American-born students as well. One young man, whose older brother was attending Stanford, refused to hand in any written work because he never believed it was good enough. African American Naima also often refused to do work when she did not want to. Later, she wrote, "I was very disappointed in myself by how I have been behaving in school but you wouldn't be able to tell. It doesn't seem like I care but I really do care." Naima and a handful of other students identified their resistance in class as a construct put on for self-protection; they sought to camouflage their vulnerability and their fears of not doing well through stony silence, rudeness, or outright resistance.

Reading aloud in class prompted some of the fiercest showdowns and clearest vulnerabilities—the fear in some students' eyes, the ways they would count the students ahead of them and silently practice the sentence they were supposed to read, and the downright refusals to read from a handful of students (who were some of the poorest readers). Occasionally, these students were willing to be sent to the principal rather than to read aloud and be exposed as not good readers. In nearly every instance, the student claimed it was "stupid" and they "didn't have to read." In each case, they later returned to class and from then on summoned the courage to read out loud, growing prouder with each try.[20] As Naima pointed out, the attitude lambasted by commentators—acting like you "don't care"—in no way meant that she did not care.

Occasionally students were willing to explain their own attitudes of resistance as deriving from experiences they had had at school. Naima noted in another journal, "My first day in middle school was horrible. I didn't

want to go to that school, so I cried the whole day. When we w
office and I was getting ready to get my classes I was crying real lc
ing I didn't want to go to that school, because it was dirty and the p.
were dirty and I hated it there. . . . That's when I first started to hate scho.
Naima's description of middle school illustrates the ways that these young
people, from very early on, saw the condition of their school as a reflection
of their value to society and hated that debasement. But they found few
ways to have their critiques of school taken seriously. As a middle schooler,
Naima did not have many avenues to object to the dirtiness of her school.
The mistaken belief that a student like Naima simply does not hold the
proper value of education misses what she actually was doing: her sadness
and self-protective strategies of indifference were a form of objection to
the quality of her schooling and evidence of the ways "she does care."[21]

On Individualism and Hard Work

> Students tell me that overcrowding at Fremont makes them think that
> they are worthless because they rarely get any individualized attention
> or feedback from their teachers. . . . I have seen many of the brightest
> students at Fremont High become emotionally withdrawn because
> they have to spend long periods of time waiting to get their teachers'
> attention.
>
> —Mary Hoover, Fremont teacher and librarian,
> declaration for the *Williams* case

> When the current school year began, I had close to 50 students on
> my initial roster in my algebra II classes during period 1 and period
> 4. Those classes have both trickled down to about 46 students in each
> class now, but there are only 36 chairs with desks in my classroom.
> Several students sit at my desk. . . . Even with extra tables and chairs,
> some students have to stand and take notes on the tops of book-
> shelves or sit on other students' desks. It is nerve racking to say the
> least, and also tiring, to have more students than desks in my class.
> The problem has gotten so bad that I pray for days when not all my
> students will show up. I have asked my department co-chair for more
> seats, but the co-chair told me that if I got more seats in my class-
> room, I would be assigned more students.
>
> —Joel Vaca, Fremont math teacher,
> declaration for the *Williams* case

> My literacy students are frustrated because they don't have the
> materials they need to learn. One of my students gets so frustrated
> trying to learn to read without a book that he punches the walls in
> the classroom and at home.
>
> —Mario Becera, Fremont English and literacy teacher,
> declaration for the *Williams* case

The young people in our classes possessed a great deal of faith in the
fairness of the system. Their ideas about education correspond to
popular American ideologies about success through education. Hopeful and determined, they were informed by the messages the media
and society continually espouse: hard work and good attitude are what
it takes. They stressed the barriers to their success but also their determination to overcome them. They were simultaneously excited and
nervous about the prospects their future holds. In figuring out what
the future would bring, they consciously constructed themselves as
students who would go to college, who had the right to big dreams
and to imagine the possibilities for themselves. Aurelio wrote, "But I
am really proud of my self because I got an A on geometry and I have
never gotten an A in Math. I know one day I will be someone very
important in life. . . . I am so excited because in one year I would
be graduating during this time." Their excitement reveals these young
people not as indifferent or turned off to school but as curious, hopeful, and eager to learn and be recognized for good work. Their ner-
vousness shows them to be not hardened or nihilistic, as many commentators have suggested, but young, vulnerable, and uncertain about
their talents and what the future holds.

This belief in the possibilities their future holds is, in part, a conscious
and considered rejection of societal ideas that insist that urban Black and
Latino students have little future. Erica expounded in a later journal, "My
dream is to attend NYU and take up law. I want to move to New York and
fight big cases. . . . Ever since I was 7 years old, I dream of becoming an
attorney of law." Devon also refused to be dragged down by people's low
expectations of him: "The day my homeboy got out of jail people was saying that I was going to get in a lot of trouble but I proved them wrong. I
stayed in school." Indeed, the need to "prove people wrong" ran through
a number of students' journals and testifies to the ways students often had
to battle other people's low expectations of them.

Martin included a long description on the feeling of "happiness and accomplishment" that graduation meant for him and his tremendous determination to succeed:

> I have done the impossible to try to graduate. You may say why? Because when I was in the 9th grade, I hanged around the wrong people. My brother was one of them. Then they got in to some problems with another set of students. After that I had problems of my own because I got into a couple fights. Well I don't consider them fights because I got jumped by the other students. . . . My brother took the easy way out he dropped out and started working. I was left alone in Fremont, so the other set of kids decided to make my life a living hell. . . . This went on for about year or more, that made me lose my concentration and I eventually ended up failing a whole lot of classes.
>
> By the time I got to the eleventh grade I realized how far back I was. So I started making up classes by going to night school 4 days a week and even taking some college classes at East Los Angeles College. My schedule was very tight because I would go to normal school from 7:30 a.m.–3:30 p.m. Then I would go to night school from 3:30 p.m. to 6:30 p.m. Then after that my class at E.L.A.C. begun at 7:00 and ended at 10:00 p.m. those days I was very exhausted as you can imagine. . . .
>
> Unfortunately, although I did this all through the senior year, I didn't graduate because I was missing credits. At that point I was devastated because I thought that everything I working for had gone down the drain. I went back to school in July, I asked every single counselor and literally begged them for a extra year. I was "b" track so I wanted to stay in "b" track because of my friends but it looked hopeless. . . . So I spoke to the assistant principal and eventually made her understand how much this meant to me. So she gave me an extra year, and in that year, which is now, I managed to show every one what I'm capable of. For example, I made it to the honor roll with a G.P.A. of 3.0, something I would never expect from myself.

Martin's Herculean schedule in eleventh grade and his "begging" his counselors and principal to let him have an extra year do not square with popular images of young men who get into trouble for fighting at school. Nor does Martin's delight in making it to the honor roll and his pride in "showing people what he is capable of" square with these images. Indeed,

Martin's narrative challenges the moral typologies so prevalent in discussions of urban youth, since he is both a young man who fights in school and a committed student who had to convince numerous adults to let him have an extra year.

These Fremont students wrote repeatedly about subverting other people's assumptions by believing in their own potential. Such success through education begins to destabilize the power relationships students often find themselves in and disrupts the ways they are often seen. As Julio wrote, "My second goal is getting admitted to college . . . because I am the first child in my family and I want to put an example. I am going to college and nothing will stop me. I know it is going to be hard for me because they say in the U.S.A., I'm an alien. . . . I know a career in medicine is hard and takes a long period of time but I'm going to make it." These young people knew the odds, often describing them in their journals. Many students like Ayana wrote, "Life can be too much at 1 time." The pressure was enormous, and many students felt the weight of it. In explaining the difficulty of balancing school and work, Miguel describes himself as a "hard worker because I go to school and have a job. I think if I do not give up I will be the first person that will finish high school." They were also well aware of how they were often pictured by others, as "aliens" and "fxxx-ups," but many were determined that they would make it anyway.

Over and over, these students wrote about having a good attitude, about working hard and being able to accomplish anything they put their mind to—almost as if saying it many times would make it true. Julio explained, "Setting goals is very important to me because I set myself in something I want to do. I am so happy with all the goals that I set for me." Beti agreed, noting that having to struggle for something makes it more meaningful. "And up to now I have learned to fight any struggle or obstacle that life has for me. Because the good things never come free. You always have to work for it in order to feel more secure and proud of yourself and that's what I'll keep doing." Such statements, by their repetition, betray students' fears (and perhaps lived experiences) that this is not always the case. But they also reveal their profound hope—their deepest wish—that it will be so.

The anxiety in these journals was often palpable. Erica wrote,

> My life is ahead of me. I have to set a path. Good things come to those who wait. I think it is time for me to start to take control. I am going to college and law school to be a successful lawyer. . . . I will do all I can for the ones who need help. Ones who remind me of myself as I was growing

up. . . . So I believe I gave my all and all. So I will get paid in return. I'm not saying money. I'm saying a good life. . . . It's so important that I stay on tasks now. So, my future will be a success. I know I can't do anything in life without an education. My goals are huge ones because I want to be on top in my future. I know it can happen for me but I have to put certain things aside. My life is complicated but I am strong enough to get through it.

As Erica strings together a series of aphorisms, her journal reads like a cross between a prayer for help and a promise to be good. Implicit in these students' journals is the tacit recognition that, despite the love and encouragement of their families (as many students like Erica attest to), there is no safety net for them. If they mess up, there is no elaborate structure to catch them and return them on course. Promising to be good, to work hard, to do the right thing is an acknowledgment of the tremendous structural constraints working against them (along with the conditions at school, nearly all our students had some degree of family economic hardship, and many students were deeply poor). Many students thus clutched at a fervent wish for an American meritocracy. They wanted to believe that being good would lead to success.

Indeed, the number of journals written explicitly on goals, hard work, and motivation—and the constant exhortations of wanting to be someone when they grow up—may differentiate these Fremont students from their more affluent counterparts. It is hard to imagine students in Beverly Hills or Santa Monica feeling that they have to demonstrate over and over their determination to succeed in life and go on for pages about how hard they work. The number of journals on the subjects of hard work and motivation attests to the ways these students knew how they were viewed and attempted to write against these images. They objected, in W. E. B. Du Bois's words, to always being seen "as a problem."[22] An extremely talented student, Araceli devoted an entire journal to "Being Motivated" (as she titled it):

Things might not come out like we expect or want, but we always have to keep on trying. If one way doesn't work, we have to try it some other way. Some people don't motivate themselves, because they have tried so hard, and it seems the same, but really it's all about not giving up. For example, sometimes I want to ditch so badly and not want to go to my classes, but I keep telling myself, if I go good for me and I don't go bad for me. . . . If a person says to him or herself "no I'm not gonna make it" that person is just putting him or herself down and low. They don't care about anything, and that's what makes them not reach their goal. Sometimes there might be obstacles or things on the way, but really all you have to do is fight them, and go for the best.

One could argue, then, that these Fremont students had an abundance of educational values—that they had been forced, by their circumstances, to be more articulate about their values and more focused in their goals and motivation than middle-class high school students would have to be. But such articulateness offers little protection in a post–civil rights society where students like Araceli are expected to want to go to college but are not provided enough courses to do so and are expected to wait in line day after day to see a college counselor.

One of the greatest difficulties of teaching at a school like Fremont is this paradox. American society supports schools like Fremont that warehouse students but somehow expects young people not to act as if they are being warehoused. As teachers, we constantly exhorted students to work hard, aim high, and take responsibility for themselves while the school system treated them as undeserving of excellence and evaded responsibility for the parade of permanent subs, insufficient books, crowded conditions, and unbearable temperatures in many classrooms. We told them to set goals for themselves, not to let others define their worth, but in doing so, we risked being complicit in a system that works because students then blame themselves for their own failure.

We went off track for two months so I decided to volunteer my time to Claudia Gil, the college counselor. One of the most committed counselors I have ever met, she is swamped beyond belief, responsible for ushering every student at Fremont to college. Usually a long line of students wait patiently for her attention, and she juggles phone calls, requests from teachers, students, and administrators along with battalion of volunteers that she has commandeered to help staff her office. What she most wants me to do is to construct a database of seniors with their social security numbers and grade point averages; this information needs to be sent to the state via their online system for students to be eligible for state-based financial aid for college. Ms. Gil worried that if students had to do it on their own, they would have difficulty or not have access to a reliable computer to upload the information. To construct this spreadsheet required going class by class and asking students individually to fill out a form listing their social security number, if they have one; since many students are undocumented, this information is not collected formally by the school. From these small slips of paper, I made a list of which seniors had not turned them in so they could be tracked down; inputted all the names, social security numbers; looked up each student's grade point; triple-checked it for errors; and then uploaded the information through the state's online system.

Some of my university colleagues think this kind of data processing is a waste of time for a college professor—that my time in the college office could be better utilized. These same colleagues are deeply committed to diversity at the university. But who is supposed to do the work to make that possible?

—Fieldnote, January 2004

On Families and School Success

> I can't understand why my children's school does not have qualified and trained teachers when I know that other schools do.
>
> —Renee Carter, Fremont school site council parent,
> declaration for the *Williams* case

These students' ideas of success were not necessarily predicated on leaving the communities they grew up in or cast in terms of rejecting where they come from. For many students, their determination stemmed partly from wanting to make their families happy, having heard for years from their parents about how they needed to succeed in high school and go on to college. In writing about the pressure from their families to do well in school, they talked of wanting to make their families proud. Erica explained her plans to graduate and go on to college and law school by saying, "My family will be proud of me also. My momma will be so happy for me because I did something she never did." In a rather constant refrain, many students talked about how important it was to make their parents proud and how worried they were about disappointing them. While it is usually assumed that teenagers (and particularly teenagers of color) consciously reject what their parents and other authority figures think, the overwhelming majority of students who mentioned their families in their journals talked about how they did not want to let them down. Elena explained, "I just want the people that love me and care about me to be proud of having me. . . . Imagine that just if I don't get to graduate and get the opportunity to go to college and that I won't like it to happen because they I would let my parents and the people that care about me to be disappointed of me." The pressure Elena felt to make her family "proud of having me" resembles the pressure high school students of all economic backgrounds feel from their parents. Many students knew the sacrifices their parents and older siblings had made to ensure that they would receive a good education and felt a great deal of pressure not to let them down or squander these opportunities. Beti echoed these sentiments, saying she would "never give up on my education" because "I don't have to think just about myself but for my family also." Like Beti, some students saw their education as something they were doing not just for themselves but also for their families.

For many students, even brothers or sisters who had dropped out became invested in their younger siblings' success. Mercedes explained, "My older brother who is 19 years old had told me not to mess up right now cause he had been through all this. He actually didn't finish high school he's a drop-out, I appreciated him cause he gives me a lot of advice. He wants me to finish high school and get a career to be somebody in life. He wants to feel proud of his sisters." While Mercedes' brother had "messed up," he was not mired in "a culture of failure" and encouraging her to follow the same path. Rather, "making him proud" meant succeeding in school. Another student, Victor, talked about what he had learned from watching his brother "go through so much like having to work and go to school at the same time and also to drop out of college because he didn't have too much time to do both. This showed me that I can do things different and that I have to study first so I can get a good job." The example of his brother provided Victor a lesson of what *not* to do.

Many students also balanced their goals with wanting or needing to help out their families economically. Having a job often made finding time for schoolwork difficult but was also part of how they understood themselves as responsible young adults and what kept them motivated on their plan to go onto college. Michael, an African American young man, explained,

> I just hope my grade hasn't slipped too far but it's because I've been working more and by the time I get home from work it'll be almost 12:00 and I be too tired to even think about doing homework. That's why but anyway. Oh and my mom's birthday is coming up and I don't have any money I feel so bad because she always does stuff for me well she is my mom. I get paid June 11. Her birthday is June 9th I think she'll understand if I just tell her straight up that you are gonna have to wait until I get paid that's all I can do but I have like $4.

While working was having a detrimental impact on Michael's grades, it is difficult to convince a seventeen-year-old young man to stop working if he does not even have enough money to buy his mother a birthday present. Ruben, a recent immigrant from Guatemala, described his and his girl-friend's plans to go to college, first to community college and then to the University of Southern California. But then he wrote, "I planning to come just one more semester take the three classes I need and find a job and help my mom to pay the bills." Tomas, an immigrant from Mexico, wrote about helping out his little sister as he prepared to graduate from school: "I would help my little sister with anything she needs because when I was her age I [got] a lot of help from my big sister and my big brother. They were always there for me." A number of students felt responsible to help their families financially—and thus many had to balance school with work.

In revealing the pressure they feel to make their families proud, these students dismantle another popular construct of the "dysfunctional culture" of urban teenagers—namely that their parents are also not sufficiently committed to their children's education and contribute to a "culture of failure" among urban students. The vast majority of our students across racial and ethnic lines worried about disappointing their families and felt a desire and responsibility to make them proud by getting good grades, graduating from high school, and, for many, going to college. African American students, American-born Latino students, and recent immigrants all wrote on this topic. While popular notions suggest a deep divide between the family values of immigrants and those of Blacks and Chicanos, there was no clear difference in how fervently these students wrote about the importance of their educational success to their families.

On Personal Responsibility and Self-Blame

The classrooms at Fremont High are either way too hot or way too cold. Between 1990 and 1998, I taught in room C-5, which is a hot, windowless room with no ventilation . . . regularly as hot as 95 degrees some summer afternoons during the 1992–1993 school year, because I brought in my own thermometer to measure the temperature. When it got that hot, my students became lethargic and put their heads down on their desks. . . . I fainted several times because of the heat in that room, and I have developed permanent respiratory problems because of the lack of ventilation. Then, during the 1998–1999 school year, I was moved to classroom C-6, which also had no

windows. Room C-6 was frigid during the Winter. My students wore
hats and gloves inside the classroom in order to stay warm that year.
They told me that the extremely cold air made it difficult for them
to write, so they wrote with their gloves on. Because it was so cold, I
brought in extra sweatshirts and sweaters for my students to wear.

—Jillian Sargent, Fremont teacher,
declaration for *Williams* case

Ideologies of hard work and determination can easily turn on students
and become self-defeating. Almost none of these students were willing to
critique the limits of hard work—or to draw explicit lessons from the experiences of themselves or their families about how hard work might not
be enough to succeed in American society. While they maintained a profound critique of American racism and injustice at a larger level, at a personal level they saw themselves "as a problem" and as the cause of their
failure.[23] This self-blame came out in numerous journals in which students
would chastise themselves for their "badness" and "laziness"—for their
bad grades, attendance, attitudes, and work habits. Indeed, most students
wrote extensively in their journals about their own responsibility for their
educational success, placing very little responsibility on the school itself
for the quality of their education. Aida wrote, "I'm really trying my best
to not mess up in school but sometimes it's hard to stay focused. I really
hate that when . . . I start to daydream. I know I'm not doing really well
in all my classes. I'm gonna do anything I can to do all my best." They
attributed their problems to their own attitudes or lack of drive. Johanna
started one of her journals with the following declaration: "This is my second journal today and the reason is that I'm dumb. I've been messing up
lately but I already decided to act right. My grades are really getting low
and this is not a good thing. I'm going to stop ditching my 1st and 2nd
period because I really need good grades to keep my mom happy." These
students worried a great deal about their weaknesses. On one level, this
recourse to self-blame was a claim to agency, a way to assert their own
power to change their situations amidst the structural constraints of their
schooling or their family's economic situation. Johanna decided to "act
right" and posited that this choice would turn around her grades. Yet this
assumption of responsibility was accompanied by calling herself "dumb."
While Johanna may have said this to motivate herself, the repetition of
such a sentiment—let alone its internalization—could have significant
consequences on her sense of self.

Shimea's journal similarly elaborated on her own responsibility for her "bad" situation:

> Time is getting too close to graduation and I am messing up. So from now on I'm going to come to school and do my work. I'm only messing up in 2 or 3 classes but it is still bad. . . . I am not a dumb young lady. . . . I'm going to prove people wrong that I can graduate. I don't have any babies running around here. I don't go out having sex chasing boys. So I thought to my self why am I not going to school? Why am I not going to class? Well there is no reason. I just don't like this school but not coming to school is not going to solve it. So I'm just going to come to school.

Shimea felt she had to go through and reject an array of stereotypes about young Black women to distinguish her own behavior and "prove people wrong" about who she was. Yet she still felt bad. Her journal alluded to something being wrong with the school, but ultimately she was quick to castigate herself for her performance.

Such self-recrimination sometimes took on painful proportions. In a particularly poignant journal, Natalia, a Chicana student who had begun slipping in her winter classes, berated herself for her laziness.

> My life nowadays is getting the way it used to be. That is not so good. I'm falling apart in regards to school. I'm so lazy I don't even open my backpack to study or do homework. I'm so irresponsible that I'm sick of myself. No matter how much I try I can't seem to get my act straight. I really don't know what is up with me. With this kind of attitude I'm not going to make nowhere. . . . Sometimes I really hate myself. This is one of those times. . . . As I had mentioned before, when I first started high school I didn't think I would make it. Once again I feel that way again.

Natalia had struggled since the beginning of high school with a lack of confidence in her ability to succeed in school; this had eroded her commitment to completing her work in a timely fashion and sometimes led to her "hating" herself and having suicidal thoughts. But Natalia had not always lacked confidence in school. She wrote in an earlier journal, "School to me was great! At first, I loved elementary. I went everyday. . . . I enjoyed school, learning and having fun. . . . I graduated Middle School enter Fremont. School and work became more serious. In the beginning I was down. I believe and still sometimes do that I won't be able to graduate from high school." But is Natalia's recent lack of confidence and school performance simply "irresponsibility," as she terms it, and separable from her actual experiences in school?

Part of what is missing, then, in national discussions about the cultural values and norms of urban teenagers is any public acknowledgment of the fact that most young people take to heart that hard work and motivation are the keys to success. Most students come to school and do the work. They wait in line for counselors, cobble together schedules from classes that are available, and make do with the class materials on hand—and then blame themselves for not being good enough if they do not do well, grow tired, or drop out. This carries tremendous psychic costs. Young people under these conditions (and despite commentators who seek to portray them otherwise, they are impressionable *young* men and women) begin to take to heart that it is their own selves, their efforts, their goodness, that are the problem. So they blame themselves when they encounter difficulties, taking the pressure off the school system to do right by them.

What is notably absent in these public discussions is a public willingness among adults to take responsibility for this culture talk. If day after day young people are told that hard work and motivation will be justly rewarded and yet schools like Fremont are not designed for most students to excel, young people are being set up. Public figures, policy experts, journalists, and many ordinary citizens have sidestepped this obligation, with the pretense that "opportunities" exist if students are just motivated to try. But there is a cynicism to this language of "opportunities." No one—not Cosby or Patterson, Williams or Badillo—claims these are excellent schools, just that students should be able to rise above them. None of these "values" proponents is willing to commit to building the most magnificent schools, hiring enough well-paid teachers and counselors to make class sizes manageable and get the job done right, and guaranteeing a college education for every student who qualifies—and then seeing who has the will and determination to show up (perhaps because they know that a tremendous number of young people would show up). Curiously, in a society that calls on young people to be responsible, these commentators—and the public more broadly—do not demand of themselves an equal level of responsibility toward these students. The essence of the *Brown* decision was that segregation foreclosed equality, yet Americans today seem curiously comfortable with this abdication of the nation's commitment to an equal education for all children.

While much of the news coverage of Fremont has been negative, describing a "school in chaos," the school received a spate of good press when LaVerne Brunt assumed the principalship in 2002. She was getting students out of the halls and into class, the stories extolled. All it took was the right kind of forceful leadership, the stories implied. This media fanfare illuminates all too well how the structural inequities inherent in the city's schools can be ignored in favor of either a spectacle of marauding delinquency, as earlier articles on Fremont had highlighted, or moving human interest stories of saviors and tough love, as these new articles trumpeted. Yet Brunt, like the three principals who preceded her, was not long for the job. After two years, she too left Fremont to be principal at a middle school. Two principals, Larry Higgins and Rosa Denny, then ran the school. Denny left in 2006.

The media coverage of the school took a new negative turn with a flurry of stories on Black-Latino tensions in LAUSD, with one melee taking place at Fremont. These stories, while on the surface markedly different from the celebratory principal ones, actually operate from the same logic. The *Los Angeles Times* does not consider it a story that Fremont has insufficient AP courses, tremendously overcrowded classes, and closed bathrooms. It is a story, however, if small groups of Black and Latino young people take out their frustrations on each other and if the real problem in a school like Fremont can be cast as the hatreds between African Americans and Latinos. In one of the few articles in the alternative newspaper *L.A. City Beat* that gave space to students to talk freely about Black-Latino tensions in schools, what young people actually brought up was the overcrowded conditions at school and the difficulties they had finding a seat or securing adequate books in class.[24]

On Taking Responsibility

> This year, I do not have any textbooks for my life skills class, which is a course required by the State of California for graduation. One of my colleagues, Chuck Olynyk, who teaches Advanced Placement ("AP") social studies, did not receive his class books for last year until two weeks before the AP test.
>
> —Jenna Wiggenhorn, Fremont teacher,
> declaration for the *Williams* case

This is not to say that our students always acted responsibly or completed their work on time. Numerous journals contained admissions of slacking off and promises to do better in our class (if they were having trouble) or school more generally. Many students wrote openly about when they did their work and when they did not. Describing herself as "a hard head," Laura returned to school after multiple absences and after Mr. Lang had made clear to her that she would not otherwise be able to pass the class. Laura wrote, "I'm going to try [to do all my work] I know that I have said a lot of things and I never do what I say and that's why Mr. Lang don't believe me any more." Ayana, who had been doing well at Inglewood High School, transferred to Crenshaw High School (both comprehensive public high schools, though Inglewood was not part of LAUSD). "I started . . . being a follower, ditching class . . . not doing homework. . . . So of course I wasn't going so great. I had started cool, but started to fall off. So I realize I should turn myself around before it's too late. So I said that I wanted to check out and go back to Inglewood. But in order to go back I had to have a B or C average. And at that time, I have no average of anything. So I checked into Fremont." Her popularity at Crenshaw did not lead Ayana to decide that her bad grades were "too gratifying to give up," as Orlando Patterson suggests; rather, she transferred to Fremont to try to turn her situation around.

Craig gave a brief history of his high school career:

My time at Fremont has been alright. I have a lot of friends and my teachers have been cool. In the ninth grade I was doing pretty good. I was doing all my work and keeping up with everything. I think I had a B in English, an A in Biology, a B in Algebra, a B in History. I didn't have anything to worry about. After I finished the ninth grade and went to the tenth my grades started to get a little better. I was still on a roll doing all my work and staying on task. I was kicking my work butt. I was on the high-honor roll and I was feeling good. But all of a sudden my grades start falling. I stopped doing all my work and started getting Cs in my classes. In the 11th my grades were looking pretty bad. I don't know why I just started slipping in class not doing all my work, slacking off. I think I just started getting lazy and got tired of doing work. Now about in the middle of the semester before I graduate to the 11th, something hit me and I realize that if I went to do something with my life, I better stop messing around.

African American, basketball-playing Craig made no excuses for slipping; nor, contrary to what Orlando Patterson and Juan Williams allege, did he celebrate the "cool pose" of doing poorly in school. Rather, he highlighted "kicking my work butt." He attributed his lower grades to slacking off but then vowed to stop "messing around" because he wanted "to do something" with his life. Many other students referred to themselves as lazy— not as a badge of pride but as a painful admission or self-criticism.

Toni described her own route through school as one of slipping from success to her current "laziness":

> When I was growing up, I always wanted to be successful in life. . . . In elementary and junior high, many of my teachers seen the potential in me. Throughout my adolescent years I was reputable for making good grades and constantly awarded for my good grades and my good deeds. I wasn't a teacher's pet but I could say I was one teachers loved. . . . Throughout the years of receiving my education things changed. When I got in the [high] school, the first semester was fine and I received some okay grades which to me was B's and C's but them months went by and things began to change. . . . Now I'm in the 11th and I've messed up very bad. . . . I'm still competent of doing necessary work but it seems as if now I'm lazier. I'm still going to go to college and make sure I make it no matter what. It's hard being a teen mother but God makes anything possible. And as long as I have people by my side like Mr. Lang, my future will be delightful and successful.

While Toni put the burden on herself, her journal reveals the importance of teachers to students' confidence in themselves, since she talked proudly about her teachers' high opinions of her in elementary school. She did not use being a teenage mother as an excuse for her poor grades—and her current less-than-stellar school performance clearly sits painfully at odds with her own self-identity.

Students often explained their choices in opposition to friends or family who had made poor ones. Olivia, a recent immigrant, described the different route she had taken from her friends:

> What makes me happy that I am doing good in school so that mean that if I keep this good work that means I am going to graduate. Well what that mean is that most of the time people end up dropping out of school.

I don't want to do the same things they did because they are going to realize that it was better to go to school and graduate and have a better life. I have friends that they drop out of school and they had told me to never drop out of school because there is no future without an education.

Individualized notions of success and failure were well internalized by these students. While students could offer a critique of how some teachers, shop owners, employers, and police treated them shabbily, they simultaneously saw themselves—and often only themselves—as responsible for their path to adulthood. They valued education, but that was not always enough to ensure school success at a deeply inadequate school like Fremont. Some of the students whose journals are highlighted here did not pass or dropped out before the semester ended. But can this fairly be attributed to their poor values?

On Teachers

Last year in my 10th grade algebra honors class, my teacher left after the first month and we had about 20 different substitutes for the rest of the semester. Each of the substitute teachers lasted for a day or two before we would get a new one. At least seven times there was no substitute at all. When there was no substitute, the security guards would let us in the classroom, close the door, tell us not to open it and we would be left unsupervised for the whole class period. Because there was no teacher and no work we didn't learn any algebra and when I took the Stanford 9 algebra test I didn't recognize the questions and had no idea what was going on. When it was time to get grades, the substitute who was there on that day said to people "You are a nice person, you get an A." I complained to the administrators and teachers at Fremont about this class but nobody did anything.

Martha Daniel, Fremont student,
declaration for *Williams* case

Sarah Knopp interviewed for and took a job at one of LAUSD's continuation high schools. A last-stop high school for students who have been kicked out of or had difficulty in one of the city's traditional high schools, continuation schools have lower class sizes and Sarah, worrying that she was starting to burn out from the work of teaching so many students at Fremont, had decided to apply. She wanted the job but hoped—and requested—that she could finish out the school year at Fremont. Instead, in a matter of a week of receiving the job offer, Sarah had to pack her stuff and clear out of Fremont. Her students were given a permanent sub to finish out the school year. The substitute had a family tragedy and the students were given yet another sub.

—Fieldnote, March 2004

During my time at Fremont, the school faced a pervasive shortage of credentialed teachers. Only 54 percent of teachers there in 2003–4 were fully credentialed, compared to a districtwide a percentage of 77.6 percent (90.8 percent of the state's teachers were fully credentialed).[25] Further, most students had a permanent or semipermanent substitute teacher for at least one course each semester.

Contrary to much public opinion, the students we taught were not in need of some educational conversion; they understood the importance of education, whether they always acted upon it in the ways Mr. Lang and I wanted or not. They needed teachers who cared about them, challenged them, and moved them to do their best work. In talking with students about their favorite classes and teachers, across the board they would mention those who challenged them, believed in them, and inspired them to greater learning. Susana devoted an entire journal to her physics teacher and praised him for his ability to explain things and for "show[ing] every student the concepts and studies of physics." Susana's use of "every student" is telling—numerous students highlighted that good teachers made sure every student understood the concepts being presented. Stephanie described her American literature class, which was studying Native American writers. "I really feel that I'm learning. . . . Reading their literature give me an idea of how they thought and their experiences. I love this class."

The students' journals showed a special affection for teachers who had pushed them to reach for their potential. Young people like Justin respect teachers who respect them and explain things to them and do not appreciate teachers who let them coast. He wrote,

Some teachers are here to work and some are just here to get paid. Most of my teachers teach good and really trying to make me graduate. I think there should be someone from the district checking classes at least three times a week. I also think that they should give us more tests. The bad teachers at Fremont just sit their behind down all day and expects us to work without them helping us to work. I think Fremont has the hardest workers in the L.A.U.S.D. but some are just lazy. . . . This semester all my teachers are good and are definitely here to help us achieve. They pay lots of attention to the students and even call home if they have to.

Justin was not always the most polite or conscientious student, but this journal reveals how invested he was in school and his disappointment in certain teachers for not having helped him learn. (If we use the concept of the "cool pose," then, contrary to Patterson's claim, Justin did not find his own "gratifying." Rather, he wanted to be called out on it. He highlighted good teachers as those who gave lots of work, helped him complete it, and called home if they needed to.) At some level, Justin's praise for teachers who "pay lots of attention" seems like a low bar to set, but at a school where many teachers have 150 to 200 students a day, this certainly is not a given.

These students came to school committed to education but still needing particular tools to succeed—particularly teachers who took the time to explain things to them and to push them to do their best. Johanna, who skipped a lot of school, explained in one of her first journals, "I have easy classes so I really don't care about coming." Johanna linked her truancy not to a lack of interest in school but to the fact that her classes were too easy. She continued in a later one, "Lately I've been noticing that Mr. Lang is a cool person. He just asks for a lot more than the usual person but that's a good thing." Both Justin and Johanna were students with a lot of attitude. They did not always show that they appreciated teachers who pushed them and on occasion responded sarcastically and angrily to direction. Both demonstrate the danger of making a quick judgment of what young people think and desire based on a few interactions. Certainly a journalist like Juan Williams could come to class for a day, see a student like Johanna or Justin be rude, and jump to a hasty conclusion that these young people had poor values. (Yet would evidence of similar rudeness encountered at Beverly Hills High be proof to Williams of a "culture of failure" among the upper class?) Teenagers—regardless of race—often cop an attitude of disdain or indifference. To interpret this as the core of their person misses the self-protection and disappointment at the heart of this strategy. Underneath the attitude of indifference often lies an appreciation for those who "[ask] for a lot more than the usual person."

Numerous students mentioned teachers they particularly liked in their journals, teachers who took the time to explain new concepts, presented engaging material, and made sure everyone understood. Michael, a gregarious African American young man, wrote, "They switched my math teacher with a way better one Ms K. She explains everything and she's really young so young we could have went to the same middle school. Ha Ha. I'm serious she really knows how to teach." Marisol, a self-possessed Latina, wrote in her journal shortly after we had done a unit on the civil rights movement: "I like all my classes. My first class is history. We learn many new things, that we don't know. Like about we are learning about the civil rights movement. How it was started. None of my other teachers and school we have never learn that much. In other classes, we just read but we don't really understand." Affirming the importance not just of reading but understanding, Marisol continued, "I like my second period too is English. We read and write a lot. Although my teacher never comes, we still have to do all of work. The only thing I don't like is that my teacher is never here, but when she's here we do a lot of work." Marisol's description of having to do a lot of work even though her English teacher was "never here" highlights one of the contradictions of being a student at a school like Fremont. Students were supposed to stay motivated about their coursework even when their teachers did not show up.

Some students were willing to point out some of the problems at school. Paloma was critical of the lack of discipline and character of some teachers: "If I were principal of this school I would change many things. First of all I would change the staff. Specially, the teachers since most . . . have lost their interest in teaching. The teachers will be replaced with younger teachers that have graduated and took the extra classes that are required by the state. This will give the school a better learning environment straight from the textbooks. Not like the previous teachers that get stuck with a single worksheet and students don't even learn about the subject." Paloma's characterization of being "stuck with a single worksheet" speaks both to the lack of materials found in many Fremont classrooms and to her desire for intellectually challenging and rigorous material. Indeed, *every* description of teachers that appeared in these students' journals demonstrates students' desire not to "get by" but to "learn"; they were frustrated by easy teachers and longed for and appreciated teachers who drove them hard and ensured that they were learning and understanding. One of the cruelest distortions in this current public hysteria around the declining values of urban students is that it completely misses—and perhaps intentionally erases—these students' desires for rigorous, intellectually rich classes and their joy in classes and teachers that fulfilled these higher standards.

On Testing

> The school is so overcrowded that I had to proctor an AP Spanish
> exam in the auditorium, where approximately 200 students took the
> test in auditorium seats without desks. The exam had an oral com-
> prehension section that was intended to be administered by playing
> Spanish on a tape recorder. Unfortunately, we only had a dozen tape
> recorders for all the students taking the test, so many students were
> not able to complete this section of the exam. I believe that many stu-
> dents failed the test as a result.
>
> —Jenna Wiggenhorn, teacher,
> declaration for *Williams* case

> No room . . . is big enough . . . so the students must take the exams
> in the school auditorium. Because there are no tables or desks in the
> auditorium, students have to write their exams on lap boards they
> bring into the auditorium with them.
>
> —Mary Hoover, librarian,
> declaration for *Williams* case

With No Child Left Behind as well as various laws on the state level, high-
stakes testing has become a regular event of the school year. In June, we
lost an entire week of instructional time because of various forms of statewide testing. The school itself made a huge effort to turn students out for
the test and was offering a "food surprise" for students at the end of the
week for good participation. Students were bombarded with reminders of
the importance of the test, posters telling them to "turn the heat up," and
continual exhortations to "make the school proud." Particularly because of
the state audit, tensions were running high at Fremont. Students who had
not been to class in months showed for the tests; when I asked them why,
they explained that the school had called their house and stressed the importance of the test. (This suggested that if resources had been available
all year to find truant students, these students might have come to class
consistently.) As we sat for the test, our students grew increasingly fidgety,
unconvinced that these tests were being administered in their best interest.

   In their journals, during and after the week of testing, our students
questioned the fairness and purpose behind the tests—and the equation
of how well they did on the test with their intelligence. They saw testing
not as a way to evaluate what they had learned but rather as an arbitrary

form of discipline and, too often, humiliation. Calling it a "waste of time," they criticized the length of the test, the amount of school time devoted to testing, and the structure and content of the test. Since NCLB's passage, a rich academic literature on the use of high-stakes testing has begun to flower—yet very little of it includes the theorizing by students themselves.

Some students challenged the ways these tests were used as a measure of their intelligence; as Amy observed, "The state think that what ever score you get that's how smart you are." They pointed out that ultimately these tests were used as proof of something innately wrong with them. Amy complained about the length of the test and how much class time it took up, noting, "This just causes students to miss school," drawing a sharp distinction between what she saw as the academic purpose of school and what seemed to be the antilearning diversion of the test. Chucky elaborated on the anti-intellectual nature of the test: "I don't know why I have to take the stupid CAT-6 test. I don't like taking tests because they waste lots of time. I really don't like to say any thing about tests but this one sucks is like I was in a room, but it's all empty from the inside." His description of tests—a room "empty from the inside"— highlighted what he saw as the test's vapidity. He continued, "I would normally not take them but the school staff said that this test is really important to us. This test is crap because it's supposed to show us how smart we really are but I don't need to know how smart I am because I try hard and that is how I get far in my classes." Chucky called the test "crap" because it would be used to show "how smart we really are," not what he had done in school. Moreover, he implied that he did not believe it would actually show how smart he really was; instead it would be used against him to claim that he was not smart.

Others tried to be more upbeat about the test but then descended into self-blame. Angelina wrote,

> The first one we did was pretty good and I think that it wasn't really that hard. I like reading maybe that is why I liked it. . . . Yeah I'm going to be honest there were a couple kind of confusing but I hope I did alright. I really put everything I could to pass this test. The one that I did today was hard. It was Geometry. In geometry I'm kind of having problems. I mean I do understand some things but there are some other things that I really don't get and have some trouble dealing with them. My teacher tries to help me and for the first hours I do understand but then I get confused with all the numbers and don't know what to do. My aunty says that, that is really weird because when I was in middle school I used to

love math. In fact she says that was my favorite class and would always get a good grade in that class.

Angelina struggled with the ways that the test reinforced her own anxiety about her abilities in math, all the more troubling because she "used to love math."

Students noted, and at times criticized, the ways the teachers became complicit in the regime of testing. Alejandro, a very articulate Chicano student, wrote about getting tired during the test and then getting in trouble for not staying focused: "My testing instructor made me literally get up and 'jog in place.' What kind of crap is that? If I don't want to don't make me do it. It might get ugly. She had the nerve to call my parents and tell them I didn't want to get up and was defiant. Since my dad doesn't speak real good English but he hung up on her after he told her she was crazy." Indeed, there were few avenues for students to object to the tests without getting in trouble (as Alejandro had). And there were few good outcomes for this testing. If all the students scored high, this would serve as proof that the lack of books, AP courses, and tremendous overcrowding did not need to be addressed. If some of them scored high, it would be used as proof that their classmates did not try as hard, and again these resource shortages would not be met. And if the majority of them scored low (or they blew off the test), the school would be kept on the state blacklist, and they and their younger siblings would be further deprived in the process.

However students scored, it became the choice and thus the fault of the individual: the individual student for excelling or failing, the individual teacher for preparing her students, the individual principal for the test scores of her school. High-stakes testing personalizes the problems of schooling. By rendering all performance individual, it obscures collective responsibility for the nature and content of the curriculum, the resources available for instruction, and the kind of anti-intellectual and punitive schooling this testing climate creates.[26]

The day testing begins I open the California Standards Test booklet and read a question that asks for the main reason the United States entered the Vietnam War. The choices include protecting U.S. business interests in South Vietnam; ensuring that France maintained its control over the colony; stopping the spread of communism in Southeast Asia; and supporting the humanitarian mission of UN peacekeepers. Three of the four answers are true. I read farther. A question on the aims of the Montgomery bus boycott includes choices for ending racial segregation and stopping the exclusion of

Blacks from transportation jobs—both of which were goals of the boycott. I am unsure of why Lord Baltimore established the Maryland colony. I believe the Know Nothing Party gained popularity because it focused on people's fears regarding foreign immigrants and industrial growth—that these fears were inseparable—and thus Answers A and D are both correct and both necessary for understanding this historical phenomenon. I begin to panic . . .

This test is extremely hard for me—and I have had access to some of the very best education this nation has to offer. As a meaningful measure of high school learning, it is grossly off the mark. These tests cultivate an abandonment of independent thinking and complex analysis. If I were testing my students on the Vietnam War, I would expect them to understand the cluster of reasons that drew and kept the United States involved in Vietnam for decades. I would require them to distinguish political rhetoric about the necessity of the war to prevent the spread of communism from long-term economic and geopolitical aims that the United States had in the region. Yet the California Standards Test rewards a young person who provides simple answers like "The United States went into the Vietnam War to stop the spread of communism." It asks students to reduce complex historical phenomenon to simplistic truisms, to dispose of what they have learned in favor of what others want them to believe.

Testing brings out the complex negotiation teachers face. In this era of increased accountability and high stakes testing, we are the ones who prepare students for the test, administer it, exhort them to concentrate, insist that they take it seriously—all the while knowing that we do not have the adequate resources to teach properly and that the test itself is a mockery of the kind of critical thinking we want our students to possess.

—Fieldnote, June 2004

Twenty-first Century Segregation

The bathrooms at my school are really dirty. Out of the four bathrooms for girls, one bathroom, the one of the first floor of the main building is open, and the rest are locked. . . . Sometimes the bathrooms don't have toilet paper, and they always smell really bad. Sometimes I don't use the restrooms because they are so dirty.

—Cindy Barragan, student at Fremont,
declaration for the *Williams* case

God is tired of you. . .
—Bill Cosby, speech at NAACP commemorative *Brown* gala (2004)

The rhetoric of public figures like Bill Cosby, Juan Williams, Orlando Patterson, and Herman Badillo examined in the first chapter casts public disregard as tough love. *God is tired of you.* These are young people. *God is tired of you.* Whose sense of self is still being formed. *God is tired of you.* To be told by adults that you are not sacred or special; to be treated like a fxxx-up or an alien; to be given an education that, as often as not, reinforces your lack of social importance; to be schooled in overcrowded classrooms without adequate books and materials or clean bathrooms while the nation proclaims that segregation has ended; to wait in line day after day to meet with a college counselor, all the while being scolded for not holding the proper value of education; to have your beliefs and values publicly and loudly lied about and to have those lies be the justification for your inferior education—that is what segregation looks like in twenty-first-century America.

Part of the appeal of believing that urban students do not care about education is that the responsibility for change lies with them and not the rest of the nation. This culture talk works effectively to invalidate a call for social change, to cast socioeconomic factors as having "limited explanatory power," as Orlando Patterson suggests, and to individualize the task of school failure and success. The conditions in schools like Fremont parallel the unequal conditions of Black schools pre-*Brown*. Yet if students are seen to be less committed to their education they can be cast as deserving of (or at least not particularly harmed by) the limited resources and personnel in urban schools like Fremont. If students are believed to be the problem with urban education, then the American public is not at fault in maintaining a segregated system of schooling that produces overcrowded, under-resourced high schools like Fremont where one counselor serves the entire student body, class sizes climb into the forties, the school day is made too long in order to accommodate a perverse three-track system, and there are not enough books and materials to go around. This ideology creates a Catch-22 for young people themselves. Criticized for not valuing education when they actually do, they too hold themselves, and often *only* themselves, accountable for the quality of their own education and are quick to engage in self-blame for the successes and failures of their own schooling.

In a political climate that increasingly scapegoats African American and Latino youth for the problems facing schools and attributes to them the decline of American values and decency, these young people's writings strikingly challenge this portrayal. They demonstrate, contrary to Juan Williams's earlier assertion, the racial malice that is at the heart of our present system of unequal schooling and in the claims that the problems with schools stem from the values of students. These young people insist on the right to represent their own humanity—on their entitlement to the rights and privileges of American society. By believing that hard work leads to opportunity and that society rewards those who try hard and play by its rules, they reveal the lie of this ideology and the cynicism behind its widespread trumpeting. And they celebrate—and long for—rigorous classes, committed teachers, decent, well-appointed classrooms, and the opportunity to go to college, to fulfill their dreams for the future and their aspirations of educational success.

I came back to visit and Steve took me to his classroom today. It is one of the worst I have seen at Fremont yet—old and cluttered, crowded with no windows, with a dark and dirty staircase leading up to it. The computer was working today but they have no printer. We went out by the track and kids are still urinating on the side of the gym because the bathroom is not open. There is no hot water for kids to shower after athletics. The *Williams* settlement has meant that now every student has a book to take home and Steve tells me that the bathrooms are open more often. They are looking to create two lunch periods to enable all students to actually eat lunch.

Looking around this classroom I am struck by how comfortable and comforting it is for people to believe that young people don't want *Brown*. It obscures a much harder truth. We as a society don't seem to want *Brown*—to summon the money, the vision, and the public will to transform schools like Fremont into cathedrals of academic excellence. I am reminded of a line at the end of Toni Morrison's *The Bluest Eye* where the narrator explains the community's abandonment of Pecola: "We tried to see her without looking at her and never, never went near. Not because she was absurd . . . but because we had failed her."

—Fieldnote, June 2006

3

"They Ain't Hiring Kids from My Neighborhood"

Young Men of Color Negotiating Poor Public Schools and Poor Work Options in New York City

NOEL S. ANDERSON

One afternoon as I sit on a crowded subway car en route to the campus of Eastern University, my fieldwork site,[1] the chatter of passengers is suddenly drowned by the amplified voices of two men. "Ladies and gentlemen, we are here to entertain you. If you enjoy our performance, we ask that you give what you can. It would be greatly appreciated." Two African American men, appearing to be no older than seventeen, stand in the middle of the train making this plea. One wears a baseball cap pulled low over his eyes and sports an oversized white T-shirt. The other wears a sweatshirt and holds a portable radio. They are dressed in popular teenage clothing but are obviously working the trains for cash.

With the flip of a switch, rap music blares from the radio, and the young men begin to dance, stunning the audience with awe-inspiring acrobatics. Many passengers who had nervously diverted their eyes to their newspapers, visibly afraid or cautious for their own safety when these young men entered the train with raised voices, are now grinning with relief and staring in wonderment as these young men somersault in the middle of a congested subway car, locking arms and feet, twirling their way down the aisle. As the young men perform, some spectators reach into their pockets, pulling out coins and dollar bills and smiling as they drop loose change into a hat.

—Fieldnote

In New York City, subway performers are a common sight, an ever-present feature of the cultural and commercial cityscape. These performers amuse strap-hangers and entertain camera-wielding tourists with song and dance, helping to both reinforce and sell an "authentic" New York City experience. In addition to getting the gratuitous applause from spectators, these performers make some money, collecting the spare change from people's pockets. However, while the street performance enhances an arts-rich image of the city, it also conceals realities of urban life. It casts a shadow on a world in which many people live, where street performance is one of a few viable (legal) ways for young people of color to make ends meet in an increasingly economically polarized and class-stratified city. When walking the streets of New York, I am often struck by the numbers of young men of color asking for money, particularly during school hours, whether by street performing, peddling stolen or expired candy, or outright panhandling. Given the inadequate, hypersegregated conditions of public schools and the limited (part-time and full-time) work options that young men of color have in many communities throughout New York City, these young men's performance on the subway exemplifies both the boundless creative energy and determination of urban youth and a harsh reminder of the quality of life for many Black and Latino young men. Behind the performance, is this surge in various forms of peddling and panhandling by young men of color an indication of a larger decline in real opportunities? Is it growing increasingly difficult for poor and working-class young men to achieve lives that they have reason to value?

As these young men collect their hat full of bills and coins at the end of their performance, I wonder about their lives. Where do they live? Are they in school? In addition to performing, what are their other passions? Do they plan to attend or even want to go to college? I think about their lives and the lives of the young men I am going to interview at the College Access Initiative (CAI), a college preparation program on the campus at Eastern University. The young men attending CAI are generally viewed by the wider society as the "exceptions" because they are focused on college, navigating schools and tough communities to achieve an ambitious, admired goal. Yet are their lives that different from those of the young men performing on the train or the young men I often see peddling candy on these same subway cars? They all have passions and goals yet are surely equally vulnerable to the same conditions and treatment young men of color often face in urban communities. As one young man passes me, smiling and thanking the passengers-turned-audience for "giving what they can," I want to ask why they perform. But just as I muster the courage, the train screeches to a halt, the doors open, and the young men disappear into the crowd on the station platform.

—Fieldnote

The request from these young men to "give what you can" is still, to this day, on my mind. The plea sheds light on the larger concerns regarding the well-being of young men of color in New York City. The need for young men to perform for money on the subway when they could be in school, or to "hustle" candy when they could be engaged in jobs that provide meaningful pay and marketable work experience, is further evidence of the current crisis in our inner cities. In fact, we are seeing that our government and society at large is not "giving what it can" to those who need the most support: those economically and educationally marginalized in neighborhoods around the country.

This chapter focuses on the lives of four talented Black and Latino young men, Shawn, Miguel, Raymond, and Angelo, as they try to make sense of substandard schooling as well as of job options in New York City. Their narratives are taken from a larger interpretive case study I conducted over one year (2003–4) in an after-school college preparation program. The original focus of the study was to examine the college preparation experiences of young men of color. These four young men attended CAI, a thirty-year-old Upward Bound college preparation program.[2] CAI currently serves over 150 students from the Harlem and Washington Heights areas of the city. The young people who attend the CAI program at Eastern University mirror the diversity of the city. The goal of CAI is to strengthen the relationship between the university and neighborhood residents, to open the proverbial gates of the university to the community.

CAI students are recruited from public high schools in Manhattan, must have at least a C average, and must be low income or first-generation college-bound students. They attend the program three days a week and receive homework help and test preparation from college tutors. Given my broader interest in understanding how urban young men of color who attend public schools make sense of college access and preparation, I was invited to conduct a study at CAI.

Although a voluntary program, CAI has been struggling with high attrition of young men of color. For instance, according to a program report in 2003, young women made up the majority (over 65 percent) of CAI participants. It is also common for, on average, five young men to drop out of the program each year, and recruitment of men each year is still a great challenge. This has been causing great alarm in the program for two reasons: (1) the program is small and serves only 150 students, and (2) the precipitous rate of dropout (from a voluntary program) of young men of color seems to mirror what is occurring in public schools. Preliminary conversations with CAI administrators and faculty led me to believe that the young men who were dropping out either were engaged in sports or had part-time jobs. Many CAI staff members claimed that unlike the young women in the program, who tended to be more focused on academics and "disciplined toward school," the young men who left probably "wanted to work" or "have jobs after school that conflict with the program schedule."[3] Interestingly, this claim has been supported by several evaluative reports on Upward Bound in recent years.[4]

Subsequently, I was allowed access as a researcher to better understand from the young men who attended CAI how they made sense of their schooling, college preparation, and experiences in their communities. I also wanted to better understand how these young men negotiated the often discrepant worlds of school, college preparation, and urban life.

The findings from the original study reveal that the college preparation program's overemphasis on narrow academic preparation (e.g., high school tests, college entrance exams, skill building) left little to no room to address the young men's personal and family challenges, disappointments with school, and concerns with safety in their respective communities. Equally revealing was that the young men interviewed spoke insightfully about the lack of part-time jobs in their neighborhoods and their frequent experience with discrimination in the retail stores where they would potentially seek work.

Shawn, Miguel, Raymond, and Angelo appeared at first to be your "common" urban male teenagers, the one-dimensional characters often portrayed in popular media. Yet after spending a year with these young men, sharing their stories, their passions, their frustrations with school, relationships, their communities, their challenges accessing work, and their experiences of being followed in stores, I gained a deeper understanding of the complexity of their lives and, most importantly, their need to share their stories. Most striking of all, though, is that their narratives seemed to contradict the predominant notion in the program and in some Upward Bound Program evaluation reports that the young men had been leaving for work. Jobs for these young men were, in fact, a scarce commodity.

Although these young men were all attending the CAI program, for the purposes of this chapter I intentionally highlight their experiences in public school and the youth labor market.[5] I want the reader to gain greater insight into the complex lives of young men of color who attend poor schools and face poor employment options in inner-city communities. The chapter thus provides rich personal narratives that are absent from many studies and broader conversations on the "urban male youth problem."

Youth Speak Out: The Crisis in Urban Schools

Young people are disturbed by the deteriorating conditions in their schools.[6] By speaking out about inadequate resources and unhealthy school conditions, they are not only shedding light on the environment in which they are expected to learn but also voicing concerns about the level of their "readiness" for life after graduation. They wonder if their high school diploma will be valued in the labor market. They worry that their grades will not get them into a college of their choice. This anxiety echoes the concern among researchers about the growing influence of educational experiences among poor and working-class youth of color on their early labor market experiences.[7] Will inner-city young people be able to transfer the education they have garnered attending inadequate public schools into careers they find meaningful, or, equally important, jobs with livable wages? Unfortunately, for young people in places like New York City, drastic budget cuts to youth employment programs as well the decades-long underfunding of public schools by the state government have deeply affected their lives, foreclosing opportunities and reducing the quality of their preparedness for higher education and the world of work.[8]

In short, public policy decisions that have an impact on public schools as well as on the youth labor markets are responsible for the educational options and work choices of young people in urban communities. If schools are not adequately educating young people and jobs are not readily available, it is not a leap in logic to argue that a great many young people are being underserved in neighborhoods around the city. To illustrate, in a report by the Community Service Society, nearly one in six youth (ages sixteen through twenty-four), approximately 170,000 young people in New York City, are "disconnected"—meaning they are neither attending school nor participating in the labor force. Further, the "disconnection" rate for Black and Latino youth is double that of non-Hispanic whites and Asians. Most alarming is that for Black and Latino males in New York City there has been no long-term increase in the number either in school or in the labor market, with the total number of disconnected for this population at 16 percent, twice the rate nationally.[9]

From Dropout to "Disconnected"

National data highlight that in 2000 one out of every six young Black men was disconnected from both school and work.[10] In New York City, high school dropouts make up a high percentage of disconnected youth, with more than 50 percent of such youth lacking a high school diploma.[11] Yet a closer look at the "dropout-disconnection phenomenon" shows that from 1997 to 2001 over 160,000 students in New York City were discharged from or "pushed out" of public school.[12] For the class of 2001, the discharge rates were higher than the dropout rates, slightly over 55,000 students compared to 14,549.[13] This means that number of students who were discharged from public schools is higher than those who made the so-called "choice" to drop out. Equally disturbing is that the New York City Department of Education does not have the breakdown of discharge rates, including the demographics of the discharged students.[14]

Given that 80 percent of the 1.1 million students attending New York City schools are Black and Latino and that discharging is most readily applied in under-resourced schools where a disproportionate number of students of color attend, we can assume that those students being discharged are overwhelmingly Black and Latino. Moreover, given that the dropout rates for Black and Latino males in New York City are on average higher than for young women from the same racial group, we can also assume that young men are disproportionately represented among the discharged numbers. Hence we begin to see more influences shaping the larger disconnection phenomenon of Black and Latino male youth in New York City.

Jobless in New York

Although New York City has experienced an economic recovery since the events of September 11, 2001, the financial rebound has not incorporated Black and Latino young people. While unemployment rates have fallen for many New Yorkers, there has been a rise in joblessness for youth.[15] The virtual absence of manufacturing jobs since the 1960s, the subsequent rise of service sector jobs in urban centers, and budget cuts to youth employment programs have resulted in young people increasingly fending for themselves to find jobs and acquire the needed work-related skills. Stuart Tannock notes that when youth do find jobs, these are low-end or "dead end" service sector "McJobs" located in restaurants, malls, retail stores, and so on.[16] Researchers studying youth labor markets also highlight that persistent job discrimination continue to affect Black and Latino males disproportionately.[17] Michael Stoll's book *Race, Space and Youth Labor Markets* shows not only that a great many jobs have shifted to the suburbs from the central cities in the recent decades but that Black and Latino young men, even when they reside in suburbs where more jobs may be located, experience significant levels of job discrimination and are most often passed over for part-time and full-time work in favor of white male job candidates.[18] Interestingly, Stoll stresses that studies examining the high unemployment rate of Black and Latino young men often do not factor in the multiple times these individuals have actively pursued and failed to secure employment: the unemployment rate for Black males tends to be double the percentage for white males. Stoll warns that if youth are "unable to develop on-the-job skills and work experience while on a job precisely because they are unable to attain or maintain employment, they may be more likely than others to experience relatively lower wages and higher unemployment as they age in the labor market."[19] It appears that for young men of color the experience of trying to access work as well as on-the-job-training can greatly shape their own outlook and real prospects for future employment.[20]

The Voices of the Black and Latino Young Men

These compelling data shed some light on the relative living conditions and well-being of young Black and Latino men, particularly in New York City, and on the apparent "disconnection" of this population.[21] Although young men of color may value education and hard work, they are up against tremendous challenges, such as inadequate public schooling and persistent joblessness, that, as Stoll stresses, "may tend to produce scarring effects over time."[22] The social and psychological scars these young men may carry, resulting from insufficient academic preparation and skills after years of sitting in public school classrooms and hitting a virtual brick wall when attempting to access jobs that allow for a decent standard of living, influence the short- and long-term progress of communities.[23]

In the flurry of debate over "disconnected" male youth, the voices of young men of color who are actually negotiating the daily challenges of urban life, who are struggling to stay in school or to find even part-time work, are silenced or left out of the discussion altogether. Few qualitative studies explore how young men of color make sense of and navigate both public schools and youth labor markets in under-resourced urban communities and the impact of such experiences on their lives, particularly their educational, professional, and personal aspirations. Moreover, since these issues are very rarely explored together, we seldom receive a multidimensional view of lives of young men of color. In fact, young men of color are usually talked about as unidimensional caricatures and are very rarely encouraged to speak for themselves. They are overrepresented in images of street culture conveyed by music videos and urban-themed movies, yet they are rendered "nonpersons" (e.g., disenfranchised as felons, isolated in racially segregated urban communities, and represented among the unemployed and undereducated) in public discourse on social, political, and economic matters. Yet when young men of color attempt to "talk back" and challenge misconceptions about their values and behaviors (whether through essays, poetry, rap music, public debate, or other forms of expression) their words fall on deaf ears. Therefore, more expansive, qualitative research would advance the discourse on the complex dimensions of the so-called "disconnection" of young men of color in urban centers.

Ironically, what makes the stories of the young men in my study even more compelling is that they are not among the "disconnected" population. They attend public schools, are law abiding, and are preparing to attend college in the near future. In fact, on the surface, they exemplify the alternative category of people that Patterson and Cosby are promoting— the "inner-city exceptions." Like the idea of the "self-made (young) man," the "inner-city exception" is a trope in literature and a popular character in contemporary Hollywood films. A cinematic representation of the "inner-city exception" is the highly motivated, school-attending boy or young man who lives in the inner city but who escapes involvement in the danger and crime that are prevalent in his environment by pursuing his own course with the courage and tenacity of an Olympic contender and keeping an unwavering focus on attending college. To survive, this young male underdog combines his "raw" talents (academic, artistic, or athletic) with the requisite "street" skills. Eventually, through the guidance of stern but attentive mentors, he succeeds in transcending and distancing himself from his community or origin to achieve a better life.

At first glance, each young man in this study could be conveniently reduced to this image. Each comes from a poor or working-class family in New York City. While two are children of immigrants, all are first-generation college-focused students attending an after-school program designed to support college access. They could be singled out as the ones destined to "make it" out of the 'hood through impressive motivation, discipline, and channeled academic and social skills.

However, these young men's narratives illustrate the complexity of their lives. As readers, we quickly learn that they are not truly "inner-city exceptions" and that the determination they display often hides alarming despair and doubt. Although they value education and hard work, the inadequate conditions in their schools and frequent encounters with racism, discrimination, and disappointment in the labor market have greatly influenced their self-esteem, their interest in school, and their outlook on life. They nervously walk a fine line between success and failure, the promise of college and the threat of incarceration, not simply because of a lack of agency but because of the larger social, political, and economic factors that shape their present condition and life options. As talented as they are, as dedicated and disciplined as they appear, these young men are just as vulnerable as the young men I witnessed on the train that afternoon. Each young man's narrative illustrates that the "inner-city exception" is more myth than miracle.

"The Next Johnny Cochran": Shawn

At the time the study was conducted, Shawn, an African American, was a bespectacled sixteen-year-old. He lived in the Central Harlem neighborhood of New York City, a predominantly poor and working-class African American community, with his mother, Dorothy. Shawn was always well dressed, preferring white Oxford shirts and stylish dress shoes to the popular athletic jerseys and fashionable, expensive sneakers worn by his peers. He was also career oriented and wanted to become the next "Johnny Cochran." He admired the flamboyant attorney who had become internationally recognized during O.J. Simpson's murder trial and took him as a model for his own career aspirations because Cochran, he said, is "smooth, has money and can work the law." Like many African American kids from poor or working-class backgrounds, Shawn viewed being a lawyer as an avenue to financial security. Shawn, in fact, had joined CAI the previous year to gain support to enter college and to fulfill his dream of becoming a high-powered attorney. He traveled twenty minutes by bus at least three days a week after school and on Saturdays to attend the program and receive extra academic and test prep support. He spoke well of CAI and the faculty, stating: "People at CAI are cool. They help me with my work. Tests preparation for college. They look out for you here. It's a lot of work sometimes. Not that CAI is hard, but coming from school and then going to the program is a lot sometimes. Sometimes you just want to go home and go to sleep or watch TV and eat something." Shawn found value in the CAI program, though his comment that "it's a lot of work" shows that he felt the strain of juggling so many commitments. However, he described glaring weaknesses in his high school with regard to its ability to prepare him for college and his professional goals:

> I go to Central High School. My experience there has been all right. The school is your typical large high school. You know, about two thousand kids. It used to be one of the best in the city, but now it is getting a reputation for not doing so good. . . . A lot of students are failing the standardized exams, so there are questions about the school and the academics. Back in the eighties the school was on top, a lot of people went to Central and went on to good colleges, but not really now. My mom told me that folks were fighting to get in back then. That's why she wanted me to go. But then things started to change and the school started to go down. The school became less selective, you know. It was like folks from all over were getting in. People ain't doin' as well as back in the day.

Shawn described his urban high school as a school in decline. Central High School was indeed struggling and had recently been classified as one of the city's worst for academic test scores and graduation rates. The school was also over capacity, with more students crammed into classrooms than should be required. Shawn viewed the low passing rates of students on standardized tests as an indicator of school failure. In the high-stakes testing environment in most urban school systems, test scores have become the marker of whether a school is "good" or "not good," the primary evidence of academic achievement. Interestingly, the physical conditions of schools are never factored in or even considered in the measuring of a school's overall performance. Unfortunately, Shawn was one of the thousands of students in New York City public schools who feel the unnecessary burden of high-stakes tests.

Because of his school's low performance, Shawn viewed himself as a "good student, trapped":

> I classify myself as a good student trapped in an all right school. I am a good student 'cause academically I am strong and I get mad support from home. But I do well 'cause I have other things going for me. The thing is, a lot of kids go to bad schools and are doing bad too. Plus they are not getting real learning. So that's what's messed up. But I am a good student. I just focus on getting through the classes and passing the exams. I do what I got to do, you know. Go to class, take my notes, and bust the exams out. I just do what I have to do and pass the tests.

To endure being "trapped" in a declining school, Shawn resorted to a somewhat pragmatic approach of focusing his energy on passing the needed exams. At almost every grade level in high school, New York City students are required to take Regents exams, a series of state-mandated tests required for graduation. Shawn had been conditioned to believe that tests are the only important measures of academic success. Further, he asserted that listening to the teacher, taking notes, doing homework, and passing tests are characteristics of being a "good student." He did not reference any challenging curricula or inspiring lessons in his high school experience. He did not speak of any potential value he was gaining from his schoolwork. He simply referred to narrow measures of academic achievement—tests—as evidence of learning. Often in high-stakes school environments curricula and pedagogical practices are altered to meet test objectives, leading educators to argue that these practices are resulting in "too much schooling and too little education."[24]

"MATH CLASS IS LIKE A FACTORY": TEACHING TO THE TEST

Shawn's attempt to do what was required to pass tests in school, however, did not help him feel less "trapped." The low performance of his high school had led Shawn's teachers to readjust their teaching methods and curriculum approaches to ensure that students passed the mandated Regents exams. This was evident in Shawn's math class. As he described it:

> In math all we do is sample exams, problems from the Math Citywide Exam. Its like we just come to class, sit down, the teacher takes attendance,

and we like do the problems on the board for like fifteen minutes and then go over them. Then the teacher brings in a new topic that we take notes on and then do problems on. It's like the same thing over and over again. In eighth grade, see, math was fun, you know. We did all kinds of fun things looking at math in the real world. Took trips and looked at shapes and did the geometry on them. It was fun. You did worksheets and stuff, but that was like part of a bigger goal of math. We learned life math. Math was fun.

Whereas in middle school math instruction had been "fun" and linked to real-world problems, in high school Shawn found that math was disconnected from everyday life. He explained his frustration with this new approach: "My high school math class feels like a factory or something. Like a sweatshop or something [laughing]. 'Go to work, do this, sit down and focus. Y'all gonna fail the citywide test if you don't get this.' Stuff like that. . . . I can see how folks get bored, you know, and start doing other things. All you do is work." Shawn's assessment of his math class as a "factory" reinforced his feelings of being "trapped." His lack of interest in high school math was a direct consequence of the major shift in New York City public schools over the last twenty years away from using diverse, creative approaches to curriculum and pedagogy to doing more direct drill and skill activities so that students can pass tests. In many urban schools, to reach testing mandates, teachers employ unimaginative curricula and less creative pedagogical approaches. Shawn's use of the term *sweatshop* highlights not only the rudimentary or rote nature of his learning in high school math class but also the ways tests drive curricula, classroom learning, and, in too many cases, classroom discipline. Shawn's nostalgia for the teaching and curriculum he had in middle school math reflects his desire for more intellectual engagement in high school.

Shawn was simply coping with the conditions in his school and not experiencing a rich high school learning environment. As Patterson and others contemplate why so many young men of color take an "oppositional" stance toward school, Shawn's view of his high school education reveals his vulnerability as an intellectually curious young man in a deteriorating school environment. He was not receiving an education that allowed him to explore and to apply knowledge to the outside world as he had in middle school. So he "just takes notes and passes tests." His observations show that school conditions can drive even talented students out of school.

"I GET FOLLOWED IN BLOCKBUSTER"

Shawn's ability to attend a program like CAI while coping with a declining urban high school shows his strong resolve. His challenges, however, were not confined to his inner-city school. Shawn had also felt the sting of job and consumer discrimination. Patterson observes that young men's "cool pose," or performance of hypermasculinity, tends to limit their educational advancement and their employment options, ultimately leading them into dire circumstances such as prison. But Shawn's preppy appearance and seriousness of purpose to become the next "Johnny Cochran" ran counter to such assessments. In Shawn's case, his race and his youth, not his motivation or his attire, were key factors in his inability to secure part-time work. He described his experience trying to secure a job in neighborhoods outside Central Harlem: "I put in many applications for jobs over the summer at spots near big department stores in midtown and lower Manhattan. You know that big sports store downtown? I went there, and they ain't thinking about hiring young Black kids, especially if you don't live nearby or something. They ain't hiring kids from Harlem. Other friends of mine went there before, and they filled out an application and don't never get called. It's like a waste of time, almost." Shawn viewed his inability to get jobs in certain stores in the city as a by-product of being profiled as a thief because of his race. He knew that young Black and Latino men have been historically characterized as thieves and thugs, a perception amplified by the popular media, and believed that this stereotype played a role in limiting his work options. Consequently, Shawn adjusted to this discrimination in employment: "You just know what stores don't like to hire you," he explained, "and you just don't go there."

To Shawn, being denied a job and being followed in stores both occurred because of his race: race and employment were inextricably connected. His avoidance of certain stores to shop in or apply for jobs in because of likely discrimination meant that his personal freedoms and opportunities were greatly restricted. Indeed, nationwide the unemployment rate for African American men is double that of white males.[25] This chronic unemployment or underemployment is most prevalent in inner-city communities throughout the nation. Moreover, as Stuart Tannock explains, poverty, unemployment, and racial discrimination in the labor market "influence students' sense of whether schools provide access to greater opportunity and consequently whether serious effort" will be rewarded.[26]

Shawn's experiences with racism and job discrimination were not just perpetuated by whites in other communities. He also endured consumer discrimination in his own neighborhood. Shawn vividly recalled being followed in a Blockbuster video store in Harbor Hill, the only major video store in his neighborhood. He recounted:

> Yeah, I get followed in stores all the time. A security guard was following me in Blockbuster over the weekend. You know how they rent Play Station games and stuff. Sometimes kids come in and try to steal the CDs out, since they put them inside the cases. But I was there just checking out what they had in. The security guard just stood at the end of the aisle and looked at me the whole time. . . . I just kept looking, and when I got bored I left. But I am used to that, you know what I'm saying. Folks following you around, looking at you to see if you gonna do something. Sometimes folks look at you so hard you think you stole something even though you didn't. You be all nervous like you stole something even though you didn't. That's like some psychological control, you know what I'm saying. Like being watched and that makes you feel guilty.

Shawn's assertion that being watched in stores made him "feel guilty" shows that the intense surveillance had shaped his behavior and self-perceptions. Cornel West, in *Race Matters,* argues that the constant barrage of negative images of Black people often becomes internalized and exacerbates the feelings of hopelessness that pervade many Black communities.[27] Shawn's experience with job discrimination coupled with racial profiling in stores influenced his motivation at times. His attempt to find work ran counter to the prevailing notion that young men like him are not actively seeking work or are uninterested in legal forms of employment. He was quite willing to work. However, his experience with job and consumer discrimination was not uncommon. Stoll's research, mentioned above, highlights the pervasiveness of discrimination against young men of color in youth labor markets. Thus the argument that young men like Shawn are unemployed because of an oppositional stance or lack of a work ethic runs counter to facts.

"Spanish Is My Language": Miguel

Like Shawn, Miguel was a young man with ambitions to be the first in his family to attend college. He wanted to ultimately become a computer engineer. He came from a large Dominican family and lived in the Washington Heights section of Manhattan. An outgoing fifteen-year-old at the time this study was conducted, Miguel had an engaging smile and bright personality. He was in tenth grade at Mainline High School, a comprehensive high school in lower Manhattan that has been known for gang activity. He joined CAI after hearing a pitch from staff members at his high school about how the program supported students in college access and preparation. Miguel had the longest commute of the young men in this study, traveling over an hour to get to and from his high school and then an additional thirty minutes to get to the CAI program. He saw the benefits of the program to his larger goals. "I think CAI is going to help me a lot in getting into a good college," he explained. "That's why I come." Miguel also struggled each day to ignore the negative influences in school, juggle family responsibilities, and stay committed to his academic and career goals.

"SCHOOL IS OKAY"

Miguel asserted that he had little to no difficulty fitting in at Mainline. His focus was on his academic classes and doing well in the tenth grade. He maintained an overall B average and enjoyed several subjects. He stated, "School is okay. . . . I like history, Spanish, and gym. I like gym for obvious reasons. I am into sports . . . baseball and football mostly. History is good because it helps you understand things. It is fun. I like watching the History Channel [on cable] 'cause it's interesting. I knock history out. I get nothing but Bs and B pluses on my exams."

As Miguel presented it, he did well in history class, for instance, not because of stellar teaching but because of his profound interest in the subject matter:

> History class is not all that [great], it's just that I like history. My teacher tells stories and stuff like that. I just have an interest in it, so whatever he talks about I just listen 'cause I like all history. . . . I learned about how the Dominican Republic was formed. I am Dominican so that was

interesting. I learned about the negativity of Columbus's journey on Indian people. Most Dominicans have Indian blood. I learned about slavery.
I learned about how sad it was that when Columbus came a lot of Indians
were wiped out in like a decade or so. Like all these diseases came and
like wiped people out. . . . I was like, man, that's messed up. No wonder
people talking about Columbus is a murderer but like Italians saying he
is a hero.

Here Miguel illustrates how his passion for history opened the door to
learning more about his Dominican heritage. Through a lesson on Columbus's contact with the Americas, Miguel learned about the origins of
Hispaniola and was able to see the relevance to his life. He also became
more able to appreciate his Dominican culture. He explained: "On the
one hand I felt bad that folks were wiped out [by Columbus]. It opened
my eyes. I knew where Hispanics comes from and stuff. But on the other
hand I was proud 'cause I knew that we were able to survive as a people,
and look at us now, you know . . . I knew that we are strong people to survive that. We [Dominicans] are doing well with our own government and
here in this country. So I fault Columbus, but then I am proud."

Miguel also linked his identity to the Spanish language. He spoke Spanish at home and stated that it was one of his favorite subjects. "[Spanish]
is like my language," he explained. "I mean it's not like what we originally
spoke, 'cause we probably spoke some Indian language but we didn't get
Spanish until the Spanish came. But anyway most of us speak Spanish,
and so it is important to know the language." Miguel believed that mas-
tering Spanish was integral to affirming his Dominican heritage. Though
acknowledging that the language was a result of conquest, he saw it as
part of the legacy of Dominican people and believed that being bilingual
in Spanish and English was crucial to succeeding in life.[28] He elaborated:

I like speaking both English and Spanish. Like, being able to read different stuff. To be able to speak to different people. It's cool 'cause you are
able to talk to anyone. . . . I can help people out in my family, you know.
My grandfather is from the DR and does not speak English. I mean, he
can say a few things here and there. But it's not strong. When we are out I
need to speak for him in stores, or like on the phone when someone calls
he will have me speak for him. I feel good that he relies on me a lot. I
look up to him 'cause he still took care of his family even though he don't
speak English.

Miguel's respect for his grandfather for supporting a family with limited English ability drove him to strengthen his own bilingual skills. It is quite common for bilingual Latino children to help non-English-speaking family members navigate everyday responsibilities.[29] Often these children serve as interpreters for parents or younger siblings in educational settings.[30] Miguel embraced this role as translator for his grandfather. To strengthen his dual language ability, Miguel made an effort to translate his report cards for his grandfather and kept him abreast of his performance in high school and progress toward college. Thus Miguel saw the Spanish language and Dominican history as useful and relevant to his everyday life.

Miguel fortunately had found value in some of the subjects he was taking in school. But when the conversation shifted to his safety in school, he became less positive: "Gangs are a big deal in my school. . . . Fights be happening all the time . . . to the point where you don't know when things are gonna happen. We got security and stuff like that . . . metal detectors and cops. But that don't stop shit. It still gets crazy sometimes. . . . You get worried sometimes if things are gonna, like, get stupid when you walking out of class. It's real in my school." Miguel's worries about gang violence speak to his concern with safety and bodily integrity. Gang violence in and around schools in some urban communities is a major concern for young people. Although Miguel attempted to be academically focused, he attended a school that was (and is) riddled with gang activity that distracted him from his learning. He worried that violence would erupt as he walked out of a classroom, and the presence of cops and metal detectors did not seem to give him a greater sense of security. His comments raise the question of whether in general urban schools' adoption of more stringent security measures such as metal detectors, zero-tolerance policies, and armed police presence makes students feel any safer. The emphasis that Cosby and others place on "bad choices" as the reason young men of color drop out of or fail in urban schools does not consider students' concern about safety in these environments. Even the threat of bodily harm in school can influence a young person's ability to stay focused on learning. It shook Miguel at times to think that at any time he might become a victim of violence at his school. Transferring schools was an option for him, but he observed, "There's like not a lot of choices [in my neighborhood] and the schools downtown, if you get in, would take me more than an hour to get to." Working hard and staying focused on becoming a computer engineer did not shield him from the challenges and threats he faced in school.

"FINDING WORK IS HARD"

In addition to his full-time attendance at school, Miguel had been trying to secure part-time work after school to make extra cash and to "help his family out." However, his efforts had not yielded a job. "I tried to work and get extra cash but couldn't find a job," Miguel stated. "A lot of places want to hire kids who are like older, like junior or seniors in high school or like in college. . . . I left applications, spoke with managers and everything. . . . So I don't even try [now]." Many employers will hire older students, citing the need for more mature workers. Yet what is more surprising about Miguel's experience is that in his quest to find work he discovered that many of the part-time jobs in his community were being taken by adult men. He explained:

> I want to work at a sneaker store, but sometimes those jobs are taken up by like grown men and stuff. Like men in their twenties and thirties even. Like people ain't working and times are hard, so men are working in places and doing stuff that teenagers could do. You be competing with men for jobs. . . . But what are you going to do? If you got a family to feed and you ain't got a job, you gotta work doing something. So you gonna work in stores where you go all the time. They [store management] may know you, so they give you a job. [In my neighborhood] men are loading boxes, watching the front of the store for people stealing [unofficial security guards]. I mean, these stores make a lot of money, but you don't make any money there. I knew this dude who was working at a ninety-nine-cent discount store. He was straight from the DR and was making like $2 an hour or something like that. He gets no money. He is working all the time, standing outside in front of the store in the snow or rain. That is a bad condition to work under too. He works a lot of hours so you can make up for like little bit of money a day.

Miguel's experience of competing for jobs with adult men is not unlike what is occurring in many cities across the country. The staggering increase of immigrants from Latin America into urban centers is filling a demand for unskilled labor. A significant number of recent immigrants are working illegally or for far below the minimum wage and under sometimes harsh conditions.[31] Hence Miguel's story of the Dominican immigrant who is making $2 per hour under tough working conditions is, unfortunately, quite common. Low-skilled, low-wage work is being done by some of the most vulnerable workers.

Miguel also stated that he saw a great many unemployed men in his neighborhood: "There are a lot of guys in my neighborhood that I never I see work. Like I go to school, they on the corner. I come back home, they on the corner. I go to the store, they on the corner. Like they never work. It gets on my nerves when they hang out in front of my building. They look like they can work. I think they just don't get work." Miguel realized that motivation alone or ability did not necessarily translate into employment for the Dominican men in his neighborhood. Miguel's observation flies in the face of the assumption that "motivation can overcome poverty." Miguel was not only competing for unskilled work with men with families to support but also witnessing individuals who had the desire to work but were not able to pull themselves out of poverty. This was a reality he faced daily as he negotiated school and work options in his neighborhood.

"The NBA Is Unrealistic": Raymond

At slightly over six feet in height, Raymond, a sixteen-year-old African American, literally stood out among his peers. At the time this study was conducted he was living in Central Harlem with his mother, grandmother, and two younger sisters. He attended East Manhattan High School, a large comprehensive high school in midtown Manhattan. A self-described jock, Raymond was an avid basketball and football player. He dreamt of becoming a businessman who would own several restaurants in Harlem and real estate in different cities around the country. He stressed that despite his sports acumen he had no plans of going to the NBA or NFL. He believed that idea was "unrealistic." He did, however, want to go to college and study business to build his "empire." Raymond joined CAI after hearing a pitch from a representative during a visit to the school. Part of CAI's outreach involves conducting information sessions and workshops within schools, targeting classes where students are "classified" (i.e., tracked) as college bound. Raymond recalled being struck by the appeal of the program. He stated: "I knew a few people who went to CAI already, so when they came to my school it was what I was thinking about so I signed up. That's it. I know I want to get help to get into a good college. The other kids who went liked it, so it made it easier. But at some points I wanted to just not go [to CAI] and just go home, relax or play ball after school.

Sometimes all this [juggling the commitments of school, athletics, and CAI] can make you tired."

Despite the challenges, Raymond persisted at CAI because of a desire to "get into a good college." However, when assessing his educational experience at school, he was more critical.

"TEACHERS JUST PILE STUFF ON YOU"

At the time of the study, Raymond was a tenth grader at East Manhattan High School. He stated, unenthusiastically, that the school was your typical "public school . . . big and old." East Manhattan is not plagued with the high rates of gang violence, but it is struggling with low graduation rates. Roughly 20 percent of original ninth graders graduate in four years. Moreover, the school is overcrowded, with many students transferring from other city high schools. Students tend to transfer to East Manhattan because it tends to be somewhat safer than other neighboring school, not because of the academic program.

Raymond was critical of the curriculum and teaching in his school. He was impatient with the unchallenging lessons and uninspired teaching approaches. He often found that the school year was driven by testing, with the spring quarter being the most test-intensive: "It seems like when the spring comes teachers want to pile more on, like stuff just appears out of nowhere. You be having extra reading, assignments, and projects. Like as soon as the Regents (mandatory state exams) is coming, teachers start throwing more stuff at you than in the beginning of the year, the fall. Its like they had all this stuff somewhere and they want to catch up. . . . It makes me pissed off 'cause I'm like, 'Did you forget to teach this stuff in the fall?'"

When teachers are mandated to improve scores of standardized exams, "cramming" tends to occur as test time approaches. Raymond was frustrated with this practice. He explained:

> Teachers complain about students not taking time to study, but then they cram stuff on you 'cause they know the Regents is coming. . . . It's messed up. In history . . . he [the teacher] is putting all this extra reading, saying we need to know all this for the exam. . . . We were studying like one day the Great Depression and like moved on to like World War II by like the end of the week. Then we had to remember all the dates and stuff. I forgot what the time periods were . . . like what century it was.

Raymond argued that although teachers told students to "take time to study," they failed to give students time to study, instead "piling on" the work as tests near. He viewed this as hypocritical and counterproductive.

"I'm just bored with school now," he told me. "I just don't see what's fun about it. It's like you just need to go . . . that's it. Like it's not even about learning . . . it's about just getting the information. . . . You don't even need to be smart . . . just like pay attention and memorize." Raymond's assertion points up the rote nature of education in his school. School was for him a place to simply memorize facts for exams, not a place to develop ideas or learn anything meaningful. His idea that one did not "need to be smart, . . . just pay attention" echoes the sentiments of Shawn and Miguel. Raymond was quite aware that he needed to go to school, but he did not find much value in what he was being taught. His pragmatic stance on school ("I just need to go") did not shield him from the disappointment about his schooling.

"THEY DON'T FOLLOW WHITE KIDS"

Raymond had also experienced some setbacks in finding work. He had been turned down for many of the retail jobs he had applied for after school. "I go get an application, fill it out, then the person says, 'The manager will call you back' and never does," he stated. About a year earlier, Raymond had worked at an athletic store in Harlem, which he enjoyed. "I was selling authentic and replica [athletic] jerseys . . . plus I got a discount, so that was cool," he stated. However, he left after a year because the manager of the store reduced his work hours in favor of another employee:

> I had to leave the job 'cause [the manager] was cutting my hours. . . . I was like at fifteen hours a week, then down to like five or six hours a week. . . . I was making like six [dollars] an hour . . . so like that turned out to be no money. I was still working. . . . Then I found out that another guy on the job was asking for more hours and getting mine. . . . That didn't make sense to me. . . . I was making mad sales, like every Saturday I was selling. . . . He was always telling me how much I sold and that I am good and all. . . . I didn't understand why. . . . I did ask him [the manager], and he was like, "Oh, you asked too late" . . . but still didn't change anything. . . . Then I found out that the guy who got my hours was a relative or something. After a while, I was almost close to no hours,

then he [the manager] was like asking me to do things this other kid was supposed to do. . . . It was messed up.

Raymond's experience with the unjustified and arbitrary decisions of employers in youth labor markets is not uncommon. Most often youth are seen as "stopgap" workers, temporary and often disposable labor for the workplace, filling a void for employers.[32] The assumption is that since they are young and school age, they get a job simply for some extra spending money and as a stepping-stone to a bigger career after they graduate. This may be true for young people from middle- and upper-class families, where family networks tend to support young people's forays into the work world and where family resources usually supplement their meager wages. However, for young people like Raymond, from poor and working-class households, part-time jobs of any type are harder to come by, and most often the wages these young people earn supplement family wages. Raymond saw a disconnect between what he believed was good sales work based on the accolades of his manager and the manager's decision to reduce his work hours, hours that Raymond relied on to help pay for clothes and school-related items.

Raymond was also troubled by the manager's requirement that he conduct surveillance on Black and Latino youth who entered the athletic store. He stated:

> Every time like when a group of kids [especially Black and Latino males] came in, we had to move to the front of the store . . . near the door so if they try to cut out or something, we would stop them. We were told [by our manager], "Keep an eye on son" [slang reference to a Black or Latino male youth]. . . . I sometimes knew some the kids 'cause they from around my way. . . . They not lifting [shoplifting] . . . but we had to watch. . . . Sometimes he [the manager] would ask if they buying stuff and rush them out if they don't. . . . But when a group of white kids come in . . . like tourists off the buses and stuff . . . they don't follow the white kids, and there be a lot of them and a lot of times they don't be buying nothing.

Raymond stated that his maltreatment by the manager regarding his hours coupled by the constant harassment of Black and Latino youth and the blatant preferential treatment of white customers had driven him to leave his part-time job at the athletic store. His observation (and participation in) Black and Latino males being harassed and racially profiled resonates with Shawn's experience in Blockbuster. As Stoll has shown, discrimination against Black and Latino male youth in the labor market (in the inner cities and in the suburbs) is even more prevalent than we are led to believe.[33] Raymond endured this experience over a year, but the psychic toll was too much. He stated, "I needed to leave. . . . I felt played [disrespected], and I was straight with him [the manager] all the time, never late, never stole . . . and a lot of people [employees] stole." When he was asked if he was looking elsewhere for a new job, given his inability to land work in his neighborhood, he replied, "Where? Midtown [central business district of Manhattan]? That's worse. They never hire you in those stores. They act like they don't even want you to shop there."

"I Need to Make My Mom Proud": Angelo

A self-defined "Puerto Rican–Dominican," Angelo was a tall and athletic sixteen-year-old at the time of the study. He was the youngest of three children, the product of a Puerto Rican father and Dominican mother. Hector, Angelo's father, had left the family when Angelo was just a toddler, and Angelo had not heard from him since. Frances, Angelo's mother, had taken care of her family on a modest teacher's aide salary. Angelo stated: "My mom works at a good job, so we are doing better and have money for things. . . . My mom pushed me to go to a good high school so I can graduate and go to a good college. She did like three years at this college downtown. But she had to stop going to college because I was young and she had to stay with me. But she said after I graduate from high school she is going back and finish."

The pact Angelo and his mom made to attend college indicates how important they believed education was to change their circumstances. Although Angelo had not yet decided on a career, he was passionate about attending college. Since he had watched his mother struggle to support her family, Angelo felt compelled to do well in school as a way to help his mom. His desire to be academically successful was compounded with the responsibility to bring pride to his family. "I need to make my mom proud, you know. She works mad hard, works a lot of hours," he stated. Angelo was driven to reciprocate his mother's hard work. A solid "B" student, Angelo learned about the CAI program through a presentation by a CAI staff member at his public high school and left the meeting believing that CAI would help him get into the college he hoped to attend. Angelo went to CAI regularly, commuting over two hours by train and bus two days a week and every Saturday to participate in the program. This was a tremendous daily task for Angelo, not simply because of the time commitment and physical exhaustion that came with the commute but because of the mental energy needed to navigate different communities and the courage it took to face life in a troubled school each day. "I'm tired," he said, with his head on his desk at CAI. Angelo enjoyed CAI, but he too felt the strain of juggling so many responsibilities.

"TO ME I AM A GOOD STUDENT"

Angelo worked incredibly hard to do well in high school. He left his home every day by 6:30 and commuted over an hour on crowded subways to attend Washington High School, a comprehensive high school in the northern part of New York City. Washington has gone through changes over the years. Initially it was classified as one of the most dangerous in the city. Gang violence was prevalent, and students were typically harassed on a daily basis. As in Miguel's school, at Washington, metal detectors have been installed and armed police officers roam the hallways. Interestingly, Angelo viewed the increased security at school as positive development. "The school used to be bad before with gangs and stuff. Now it is nice," Angelo stated.

Angelo saw the enhanced security at his school as one less distraction from his academic pursuits. He viewed himself as a "good student" and explained, "My grades are like 70s and up. . . . I am cool in all my classes, really. I take notes and stuff. Do my homework. I do my work and try to pay attention. I knock my tests out and do my homework." To Angelo, as to Shawn, being a "good student" meant paying attention, doing your homework, and passing tests. This self-definition greatly supports prevailing notions about academic achievement, particularly in public education. The movement toward standards and accountability since the early 1980s has resulted in narrow definitions of academic success. Testing has become the sine qua non of public schooling, to the disappointment of a great many young people.

Despite his school's rote approach to academic work, Angelo found a creative outlet through poetry. He wrote poetry in a journal to express his dreams, fears, and aspirations. He stated, "It [poetry] is an outlet for me . . . it allows me to clear my head from all the stuff in my life." Angelo was under a great deal of stress to succeed academically, particularly because he was the first in his family to potentially go to college.

"I CAN EITHER GO TO COLLEGE OR TO PRISON"

Angelo shared a small bedroom with his twenty-five-year-old brother, Roy, who had dropped out of high school at the age of sixteen and had struggled to find steady work ever since. Roy represents the "disconnected." Because of being unemployed, Roy spent most days lying in bed, doing very little. Angelo stated, "Roy just likes sleeping. He sleeps a lot. He is probably sleeping right now. He just doesn't do anything. He lays around the house."

Angelo was perturbed by his brother's inactivity. He viewed it as an affront to his mother's sacrifice and hard work for the family. "It bothers me that he don't do anything. My mom works, so he should work," Angelo stated. Roy's situation very much exemplifies that of a number of Latino men in inner-city communities. By dropping out of school at sixteen, Roy had not made his life easier. However, Angelo viewed Roy's idle lifestyle as simply the cause of his unemployment rather than a consequence. He had largely bought into the notion that motivation alone is what leads one out of poverty. Further, when he stated, "My mom works, so he should work," Angelo suggested that Roy was refusing to work and that he was solely responsible for his unemployment.

Angelo disapproved of Roy's lifestyle but was equally critical of his thirty-one-year old brother, Jose, whose recent incarceration had turned the family upside down. Jose was serving a three- to seven-year term for burglary and assault in a maximum-security prison upstate. Angelo described the events leading to his brother's arrest:

> My brother was caught breaking into an apartment. When a security guard came up to them, apparently he hit him with a pipe or something like that and knocked the man out. The security guard had to get mad stitches. My brother and his boys thought the apartment was empty but it wasn't. The people were just away for a while, but they got caught like a few hours later. The police came by looking for him. But he was at one of his boys' house. It was like three of them who tried to get in and they got caught.

According to Angelo, Jose's crime had a great impact on his mother: "My mom was messed up about it. She was crying and stuff. I felt bad for her 'cause she tried to look out for him like she did all her kids. My brother always got caught doing stupid stuff, like trying to rob people and stuff like that. He was doing stuff when he was a teenager. My mom had a hard time with him. He usually got caught, do like probation and like only a few months in jail. This is the first time he had to go for a long time."

To Angelo, Jose's incarceration was simply a consequence of years of doing "stupid stuff," engaging in criminal acts as a troubled youth. Angelo viewed his brother's fate simply as a culmination of bad choices rather than an outcome shaped by adverse circumstances growing up in East Harlem. Having completed only the ninth grade, Jose, like the majority of Latino men in American prisons, came from a poor family, had less than a high school diploma, and grew up in a tough community. However, Angelo dismissed any mitigating factors that might have influenced Jose's unlawful choices. "I did not even want to go to court [when Jose was arrested]," he explains, "because I felt it was my brother's fault he got himself into stuff. . . . He chose to do his thing even though my mother looked out for all of us." As with Roy, Angelo maintained that Jose's present circumstances were solely his "fault." In the "cool pose" thesis advocated by Patterson, as in previous "culture of poverty" arguments, poor people's actions are a result of simply "poor choices," not the result of "poor conditions."[34] Moreover, some argue that the conditions faced by a disproportionate number of Black males are a consequence of angry, immature, and sometimes overtly hostile attitudes toward those in authority.[35] Therefore, criminal behavior among the poor males of color is viewed as a pathology rather than a result of systemic deprivations. Angelo seemed to have internalized this perspective. On the surface, he did acknowledge the influence of poverty or conditions in his neighborhood on his or his brother's circumstances. But he saw his brother's behavior not as part of a broader problem but as an entirely individual act of will.

"I CAUGHT MYSELF"

Interestingly, as Angelo asserted that his brother "chose" to be a criminal, he also admitted that Jose's incarceration had been the impetus for him to reevaluate his own life:

> Jose going to jail made me wake up and realize that I don't want to be like that. I want to go to college and do something. I realized that I could either go to college or end up like him or sitting around the house. That's not me. I want to do something. . . . I mean, I never got in trouble, but I could have gotten into stuff like that. I used to do stuff, not serious stuff.

Like me and my friends back in the day use to steal stuff, candy and stuff from stores. One time my friend got caught trying to steal from a Korean store. Nothing serious, but it was scary. But I caught myself. When my brother got caught, I was like, man, I don't want to be in prison like fighting for a bunk or something. Like calling my mother and asking for stuff. People visiting me in there with prison clothes. That's not the life I want. So him getting into trouble woke me up to like how I need to stay on track and get through school. . . . Too many people are depending on me to stay serious.

Angelo "catching himself" indicates how he avoided engaging in potentially destructive behavior. He stated that his fear of prison and his concern with not disappointing his mother played into his actions. However, his unlawful behavior in the past and his assertion that "I could have gotten into stuff" revealed how vulnerable Angelo was to the conditions that had befallen his brothers, such as chronic unemployment and poor educational institutions. Even though he was focused on college, Angelo continued to be in close proximity to hardship and danger.

Furthermore, by viewing his options as either college or prison, Angelo revealed the limited choices and freedoms in his life. To Angelo, college was not just a more advantageous route or choice than the ones his brothers had taken; it was an alternative to chronic unemployment or imprisonment. One cannot argue with that. However, what is more telling is that Angelo perceived the possibilities for his life solely in terms of these two choices. He did not see a full spectrum of options for himself—just a college education or prison. Moreover, his comment that "too many people are depending on me to stay serious" illustrates the tremendous pressure he was under to succeed. Beset by fears of disappointing his mother by ending up like his brothers, he had to overcome real obstacles to stay safe, complete high school, and continue on a path to a career and material success.

In this chapter, we have observed how four young men of color, Shawn, Miguel, Raymond, and Angelo, made sense of their schooling and engagement with the youth labor market. All the young men attended segregated and resource-starved high schools where increasingly high-stakes testing was driving the curriculum and instruction and safety was a major concern. They were critical of their schools and the quality of their education. Both Shawn and Miguel found some space to engage in what they were learning, however. While Shawn longed for the creativity that had been fostered in his public middle school math class, Miguel was able to connect what he learned in his history class to his heritage. Raymond and Angelo, however, experienced in school only the mounting pressure to pass the Regents exams and the cramming by teachers to achieve educational mandates.

All four young men had had personal experiences with job and consumer discrimination in and around their neighborhoods. Shawn, Miguel, and Raymond had sought part-time work during the out-of-school time not only to gain marketable job skills but to alleviate some of the financial burden on their parents. Subsequently, their challenges in securing work had a great impact on them and caused them to ponder their own personal worth and desirability in the labor market. Being monitored in stores (or in Raymond's case being ordered by his boss to closely watch other Black and Latino shoppers) or being denied work in certain neighborhoods because of race, age, or gender created a level of frustration and disappointment that surpasses what white males experience seeking work.[36] As we see, these experiences ultimately influenced these young men's outlook and perceptions of work.

The unemployment of one of Angelo's brothers and the incarceration of the other contributed to giving Angelo an unhealthy, zero-sum outlook on life. That he saw college as his only viable alternative to chronic joblessness or a life of crime speaks to the quality and quantity of choices Angelo perceived in his life. Whether there were truly more options available to him after high school (such as civil service jobs or the military) is not the main point. Crime and unemployment were widespread in his community and present even in his own home, and his acute awareness of them, coupled with the inadequate preparation in his school, made for deep-seated problems that affect a great many young men like him. The view of his options as "college or prison" is not widely shared by Angelo's better-situated peers in wealthier communities.

In all, the narratives of these young men showed how they grapple with serious life pressures that directly influence their motivation to continue in school, their outlook on finding part-time work, and their future aspirations. The young men struggled to believe in the prevailing message that dedication to school and an undeterred focus on college and career would ultimately enable them to overcome their present conditions. However, on a daily basis, they confronted family, community, and employment challenges that made the academic demands of a school and expectations to find work especially burdensome. As a result, the chances that they would fulfill their educational goals were precarious. We see that motivation to go to school and to seek work is not enough. Some factors can make even the most motivated student waver. Segregated and failing schools and unreceptive youth labor markets can deter even the most ambitious, disciplined individual. And for all four young men, the schools they attended, whether from a lack of resources or a lack of will, were not engaging their intellect or recognizing and inspiring them toward their chosen career goals.

For Shawn, Miguel, Raymond, and Angelo, their fears of failure in school, the unemployment or underemployment of family members, and job and consumer discrimination often undermined their abilities to stay focused, find pleasure in learning, and maintain optimism about their future. Yet individuals such as Orlando Patterson argue that these young men are the exception, that they represent the "promise" of Black and Latino males because they "rise above" the dysfunction of their schools and/ or are "never giving up" in trying to secure work in a discriminatory job market. The underlying assumption guiding that narrative is that these young men will make it because America consistently rewards perseverance and hard work above all else. History is replete with stories of groups that have garnered some level of success. Indeed, success is achievable for all, the myth holds, through a steadfast belief in a consumption-centered American dream combined with a Protestant ethic of temperance. This chapter, however, illustrates that these young men are not exceptions: the American dream both consumes and eludes them. They, like other young men either incarcerated or "disconnected," are in a precarious state, vulnerable to the adverse circumstances under which they live, whether they choose to engage in certain behaviors or not. Patterson and others fail to acknowledge the myriad obstacles that jeopardize the futures of Shawn, Miguel, Angelo, and Raymond and to examine the fragility of the goal of "making it" for young men of color. Unfortunately, daily issues concerning the bodily and emotional integrity of young men of color tend to be ignored and the focus shifted to the instrumental role of schooling and individual initiative in gaining an education and/or finding and maintaining work.

The life experiences of Shawn, Miguel, Raymond, and Angelo call for a new approach to equity in institutional practices and public policies that takes into consideration the heterogeneity of young men of color and their needs as human beings. These narratives call for a deeper understanding of the complex lives of young men of color as well as a reinvigorated, critical stance against institutions and institutional practices that limit the life chances and potential of young men of color in urban communities throughout the United States.

4

"Where Youth
Have an Actual Voice"

*Teenagers as Empowered Stakeholders
in School Reform*

CELINA SU

When Hector was a freshman in high school, he did not always study as hard as he could. At the urging of a friend, though, he joined Sistas and Brothas United (SBU) and began to work with them regularly after school. SBU is a youth organizing group that works to improve conditions at schools around the South and Northwest Bronx.

The school Hector attended at the time, John F. Kennedy High, reported high rates of violence, a severe shortage of guidance counselors, broken escalators, and unusable fire-safety mechanisms. Hector struggled just to get through each school day. Still, when he had a chance to talk to administrators about his experiences, he could not help but get excited. It had taken a whole lot of persistence—a barrage of faxes and phone calls—to even garner a meeting. Maybe they could get some facilities repaired, or even hire some guidance counselors? He practiced his short testimony, again and again, with other SBU members.

When Hector showed up, he found out that the school officials had, secretly and without authorization, pulled his school records. His grades were not exactly great, they said. In fact, they were straight-up bad. To these policy makers, Hector's critiques reflected his low valuing of education rather than a set of legitimate concerns. They therefore rebuffed any suggestions Hector might offer. He did not exactly have the right to make any criticisms about school, now, did he?

Did he?

By the time he was a senior, Hector had transferred to Satellite, a smaller, alternative high school. Satellite was much safer, and he got to know teachers there. Still, he had not given up on education reform campaigns. In 2004, Hector was one of the founding members of SBU's STARS, the Student-Teacher Alliance to Reform Schools.[1] He helped to collect survey data on the issues that concerned Bronx teachers most, like overcrowding and professional development, and chaired meetings on how teachers and students could join efforts to work toward reforms that were both ambitious and doable. He helped to strategize on whether press conferences, protests, petitions, or some other action would be needed to get the higher-ups to pay attention.

This time, the reception of the teachers was strikingly different. They praised his good work, talked about how they were in it together, commended him on his administrative skills and his passion, and invited him to join them in fairly exclusive meetings with the city's top Department of Education (DOE) officials.

At one of the first STARS meetings, Hector's friend Jeremy recited a poem he had written:

> There's many problems with our education
> . . . .
> Is it the students' fault? Just try and *think* about their status:
> Got books from when the colony's first established
> . . . .
> Constantly treating them like a statistic, treating them like lab mice.
> Scantrons mess up and lower scores, and *students* pay the price.
> Well, if we say it is not the students' fault, let's look at a new vision.
> Are the teachers to blame? Now let's just look at *their* position.
> . . . .
> Forced to teach 30–35 students, and feeling like they have no weight.
> Stressed while teaching, and the check ain't even that great.
> . . . .
> They are raising standards for us, and it sure ain't fun,
> And who's responsible for raising standards for all of them?

In a way, Hector's story began with how inner-city youth are portrayed in popular media—as wayward kids who struggle in school because they do not make sufficient efforts to do well, or as thugs who accuse their academically successful peers as traitors for "acting white"—but it did not end that way. What changed? How did Hector transform from being seen as an easily dismissed troublemaker to a teachers' darling? Part of the answer is that perhaps Hector was not a troublemaker in the first place. Rather, he did not have the means or support he needed to articulate well-constructed critiques of the school system in a manner palatable to administrators, and these policy makers never gave Hector the benefit of the doubt afforded to most teenagers.

Hector's story, and the stories of the dozen or so other youth leaders I present in this chapter, are much more than novelties or tales of human interest. They point to the real-life aspirations of inner-city youth and to what these teenagers are truly capable of *once they acquire the skills, encouragement, and power to do so.*

The voices of such teenagers are conspicuously absent from the public discourse about them. According to popular pundits like Bill Cosby or Orlando Patterson, students struggle in inner-city schools not because these schools are underfunded and economically and racially segregated but because they subscribe to a "culture of failure"—"almost like a drug, hanging out on the street after school, shopping and dressing sharply, sexual conquests, party drugs, hip-hop music and culture."[2]

Cosby et al.'s messages sell well because they fit preconceived notions of what poor African American and Latino teenagers are like, but they fall apart upon further investigation. Yes, some inner-city youth are disengaged from some mainstream social institutions, and many are not doing well in school. Yet their stories suggest that when they screw up or act up, their disaffection is hardly inherent or born out of a "culture of failure." Instead, these young people are responding to the concentrated poverty in which they live and the under-resourced schools that they attend. These schools have failed to provide them with a decent education—with some individualized attention, working bathrooms, some range of school activities, chairs, tables, books, and teachers who have been trained in the subjects they teach—conditions that are taken for granted in most of our nation's schools, and rightfully so.

This chapter draws from data I collected during eighteen months of hanging out with SBU, a group of teenagers organizing around school reform campaigns in the South Bronx. Not *once* during the eighteen months, not just with SBU members but with young people across the Bronx as well, did I hear anyone complaining about students who "act white." They knew they were missing something in their schools even if they did not always know what, exactly, and they were resentful about it. *This* was their preoccupation, not fear of success.

The youth were used to the near-complete disconnect between their values and their academic performance. They knew that the latter did not reflect the former. Many of them, like Hector, were struggling in school when they joined SBU. By and large, they were not "the chosen," the anointed "good students" like those (who nevertheless held deep, well-considered reservations about the school system) presented in chapter 3. Even so, SBU leaders craved for any sort of collective, meaningful action they could find, and sadly, school was not where most of them found it.

SBU's case study demonstrates that inner-city youth have been actively disempowered by school conditions that treat them like criminals to restrain rather than active learners to teach and mentor. They have been dehumanized by public discourse that justifies the severe segregation, underfunding, and punitive surveillance that characterize their schools. As a consequence, the success of SBU members lay not in spiritual conversions that gave them better morals—the "attitude adjustment" recommended by Herman Badillo in *One Nation, One Standard*[3]—but in empowerment and engagement with something akin to a real education.

In this chapter, I roughly follow the trajectory of Bronx youth discovering and becoming active in a collective movement for education reform. I examine their reasons for joining SBU, how they came to trust peers in the organization, and how they make sense of Bronx schools. Via SBU, these students got the chance to tackle challenging, substantive work and to both take and eventually teach skills-building workshops—on statistics, governmental administration, federal and philanthropic funding, critical analysis, persuasive writing, research, and collaboration.

The myth of inner-city youth as screw-ups is so powerful that adults often dismiss these students before even listening to them. How are these student activists supposed to force institutional change without antagonizing policy makers? That they are able to do so is a testament to their strength and collective will and to the validity of their critiques.

Finally, I present stories from a couple of the school reform campaigns pursued by SBU regarding teacher quality and public safety. As these students became active at SBU, they also became more adept at taking responsibility for their own education and working toward meaningful school reform, but not without the support of policy makers.

Right now, inner-city youth like those at SBU are suffering from the consequences of our indifference: these youth, the ultimate stakeholders of public education, are bombarded with media messages that high-stakes tests show they are stupid and that increased school funding is a waste of time. After all, as Cosby said, inner-city youth do not care about school anyway.[4] As education specialist John Ogbu told the *New York Times* in 2002, "No matter how you reform schools, it's not going to solve the problems."[5] Without the means to refute these messages, it is no wonder that some youth eventually begin to believe them or feel confused. If only they did not care so much . . .

Who Would Have Known?
A Youth Social Movement, Right under Our Noses

Before plunging into the case study, we must keep in mind that stories like Hector's are much more representative than they might first appear, since SBU is hardly the only youth education organizing group around. Between 1995 and 2000, over twenty youth organizing groups were formed in New York City alone. These groups have focused on working together to demand substantive and sustainable school reform. In 2004, Make the Road by Walking and Youth on the Move joined SBU to form the Urban Youth Collaborative (UYC) and raise the scale of their collective efforts. By 2007, twelve other groups (and counting) had joined UYC in their attempts to secure a decent college preparatory education for all New York City students.[6] This coalition is racially diverse and includes groups from all over the city, with participants like Desis Rising Up and Moving (DRUM), Ezperanza del Barrio, and YouthCAHN (of the City AIDS Housing Network).[7]

In 2002, a comprehensive survey of education organizing groups at eight research sites (Baltimore, Los Angeles, the San Francisco Bay Area, Chicago, New York City, Philadelphia, Mississippi, and Washington, D.C.) showed that thirty-eight of the sixty-five active organizations surveys had already pursued campaigns led by youth.[8] The Funders' Collaborative for Youth Organizing, currently the main financial force behind youth organizing groups around the nation, only began to award grants in 2001. Since then, both the number and intensity of youth-led campaigns have risen dramatically.[9]

What are these students, almost all from inner cities, asking for? For one, they demand the basic right to get to school and learn. In the "teeming maze of homeless shelters and transitional housing centers of Ohio's urban centers," youth members of the Coalition for Homelessness and

Housing in Ohio lobbied for the state's first law guaranteeing homeless students the right to a public education.[10] In Oakland, California, Kids First! staged a walkout of hundreds of students (with parental permission slips ready and signed) and successfully lobbied the city to subsidize $27 monthly bus passes for low-income families so that they would not have to choose between groceries or school toward the end of each month.[11] In Washington, D.C., the Youth Action Research Group conducted a "read-in" when their schools were shut down for two weeks because the public school system never made essential repairs. In Philadelphia, Youth United for Change insisted that the city council require college preparatory, not generic, versions of math and science.[12]

Students also ask for room to learn and the support they need to do so. In Denver's Westside High School, Students 4 Justice resisted the over-crowded school's policy that forced all 1,700 students to eat lunch at the same time, scrambling for the cafeteria's 350 seats, and prohibited them from leaving campus.[13] As Philadelphia Student Union's founder Eric Braxton put it, "We questioned why shootings in suburban schools, like at Columbine, triggered the addition of support services, while our schools respond by putting in metal detectors and more cops" and taking away basic education and counseling funding.[14] These students led a march of over two thousand people to demand that a $15 million reallocation be put *back* into education. In Chicago, Generation Y's Breakin' the Chains campaign protested a set of cruel and unusual policies that prompted *thousands* of expulsions, many accompanied by police arrests, for infractions such as snowball fights.[15]

Back in New York, Make the Road by Walking rallied every student at the Bushwick Community High School to pledge to refrain from name-calling and homophobic language. They also convinced Bushwick High School to open a second entrance so that students would not have to wait more than half an hour each morning just to go through metal detectors and enter the school.[16] In the Bronx, 1,500 students walked out of Dewitt Clinton High School and marched two miles to the district headquarters to protest the use of metal detectors and excessive force by armed police at their school, often for infractions such as coming to school late.[17] Just two weeks later, hundreds of seniors orchestrated a silent sit-in outside the administrative offices at John F. Kennedy High School, which serves approximately four thousand students. They were protesting the elimination of four of the ten guidance counselor positions there.[18]

In his 2004 *Brown* speech, Cosby claimed that "these people" are spending their money on "$500 sneakers—for what? They won't buy or spend $250 on Hooked on Phonics."[19] Yet in each of hundreds of youth organizing campaigns around the country, inner-city students have gone out of their way to demand access to a meaningful, challenging, college preparatory education.

There is often an assumption that middle-class families drive school reform. When mothers in affluent Scarsdale, New York, or professors in Cambridge, Massachusetts, boycott standardized exams, their campaigns are seen as legitimate and the protestors as even praiseworthy in their social conscience.[20] However, when low-income, inner-city students ask for similar policy changes, they are labeled as insolent rather than insightful. For instance, when UYC members complained that their administrators were pressuring overage students to move into untested alternative programs, or presented a Bill of Rights and Responsibilities with provisions like "educators who are certified in their licensed subjects,"[21] the DOE's responses "vacillated between defensive and dismissive."[22] Amy Cohen, a former UYC coordinator, has worked with parents and taught in public schools in the past. Yet she asserted that "the threshold [for involvement, before policy makers are willing to listen,] is so much higher for youth, particularly young people of color. As the policy makers insist on fewer resources for those who are most affected, the students see their experiences being invalidated."

During one meeting with schools chancellor Joel Klein, UYC students asked to see the data proving that the Memorandum of Understanding (MOU) between the New York Police Department and the DOE, which focused on punitive measures and use of force in the schools, was effective. Originally, the DOE was supposed to revisit the MOU and see if its policies were working, but this was never done. The UYC requested data that examined not only incidence rates but also graduation rates. The youth wanted to know what happened to the students who got pushed out of schools, and they requested that infractions such as being late to school be punished via school-based measures, such as detention, rather than via the Police Department. They also called for mediation programs to get to the root of disciplinary problems. In response to every question or request, Chancellor Klein repeated his mantra about the MOU being effective, but he also promised the youth that they would receive the relevant data. As soon as the meeting ended, however, then-head of Safety, Rose DePinto, stated that the data would not be sent to them. Instead, the

DOE would set up another meeting, where they would themselves present the data. UYC representatives called again and again to arrange such a meeting. It was never scheduled. In response to a series of similar incidents, the youth could not help but make statements such as "If we were adults, they wouldn't treat us like that."

In an unscientific experiment, I entered the words "Black Latino education New York" into the *New York Times* Web archives and took a close look at the top twenty articles I got in return. Mostly I learned about how poorly these students were doing and about how they consequently needed not more resources (since these were being cut) but instead mental strategies and motivation for success. The following story lines were representative:

- One Queens student was stabbed on the way home from school and ran back to the school lobby, bleeding. It took almost half an hour for an ambulance to arrive.[23]
- In schools without arts or music programs, almost all of the classes focus on the *five* high-stakes standardized tests students are expected to take each year. Funds for highly successful after-school programs are being cut.[24]
- A Harvard economist will be paid around $195,000 for "incentivizing" schooling to inner-city students, primarily by giving them payments for perfect scores on exams and applying marketplace principles to education.[25]

A focus on the supposed values and preoccupations of inner-city students blames them for their failures while denying them the basic services all youth need to succeed.

I then entered "Westchester education" into the *New York Times* database. Among the top twenty articles in this search, the intense competition and high anxiety of high school students in elite schools was *by far* the most common theme.[26] Desperate times call for desperate measures, so now parents do more than pay for $560-an-hour SAT tutors.[27] They have taken to purposefully holding their children back in school or enrolling them in kindergarten as many as three years later than they should in order to give their children a developmental advantage over others. Even though this practice makes teaching much more difficult, white children are more than twice as likely to enter kindergarten late as Black children.[28] Some parents at elite private schools have encouraged their children to "refresh" themselves by purposefully repeating their freshman year in high school, to improve their grades, and to prevent the grades of their first ninth-grade iteration from getting on their transcripts when they apply to colleges. Although some schools report that 10 percent of their incoming freshman classes consist of repeaters, this is "a strategy available only to . . . those who can pay $25,000 to $35,000 a year."[29]

From these articles, I also learned that

- Students traumatized by the online insults of classmates have prompted Scarsdale, Horace Mann, and other elite high schools to hire special counselors and the Westchester County district attorney to open an investigation.[30]
- In wealthier school districts, private donations on top of district spending help schools to finance new "must-have" items in schools, like weather stations and smart boards, computerized blackboards that embed video lectures and connect with students' laptops and iPods. "Smart boards are the new air-conditioning."[31]
- In Westchester, refreshments at PTA meetings are catered rather than homemade, and lawyers and marketing executives lobby policy makers for more resources and do not take "no" for an answer.[32]

For the most part, I learned quite a bit about the dismal statistics measuring the performance of Black and Latino students *as a whole*. When I read articles about white students, they were labeled not as white but as *individual students*. (I was able to guess at their racial backgrounds, however, because all nonwhite students were labeled so and because articles on white students were more likely to have accompanying photographs and multimedia presentations in which we heard the students themselves speak about their attempts to do well in school.) In other words, the white students were humanized in the eyes of the reader.

While my experiment was highly unscientific, I believe that a more comprehensive survey of the most pervasive narrative tropes about white, Black, and Latino students would have yielded similar results. Indeed, when members of Youth Force, an organization dedicated to reducing the incarceration of young people, systematically analyzed all ninety-three *New York Times* articles about youth crime in a three-month period, they found that identifiable white youth defendants were quoted in roughly half of the articles, while identifiable Black or Latino youth defendants were quoted zero times.[33]

There is virtually no media attention on the hundreds of youth organizing efforts being pursued across the nation's cities, even though *each* of their school reform campaigns involves hundreds, and sometimes thousands, of students. It is easy for concerned citizens in the public at large to swallow hackneyed, misleading media portrayals of hypercompetitive suburbanites and troublemaking urban youth when most live in one segregated world or another and do not traverse both.

The rampant and patent misrepresentation of inner-city students in the popular media strategically obscures more nuanced views of what they are really like, what they want, and what they aspire to. In the meantime, to even suggest that these students struggle with schools serves as an excuse to give up on them, as if they were disposable lives. It also follows that, since these students are spending their time stealing sneakers or popping out babies anyway, the government and our society as a whole can abdicate all responsibility for decent schools in America's cities.

Complaining about the faults of youth will not improve their academic performance, but addressing their circumstances and schooling will. This chapter looks at some of the concrete ways in which inner-city youth, the very ones who struggled in school and are regularly maligned by Cosby et al., have taken matters into their own hands. Together, they declare: "GET A GRIP ON MY REALITY. DON'T PUT ME DOWN AND THEN SMILE AT ME."[34]

Where We're At: Introducing the State of South Bronx Schools and SBU

The four or five main high schools attended by SBU members each report occupation rates at 175 percent to 300 percent of capacity. Some schools meant for 1,200 students instead enroll 3,000. There are bathrooms missing stall doors or toilet paper, gyms that have been taken over as teachers' parking lots, and upper-floor windows missing glass panes and safety bars. The metal detector is often the only thing working properly. Even when students avoid or cope with such hazards, there is the daily grind of teachers not having assigned rooms because there is not enough space and making do with very little. Between classes, students and teachers have to make their way through the crush of awkwardly carried adolescent bodies packing the hallways like huge, squirming, pushy sardines. It often takes such exertion to get to the next class on time that it is a wonder more fights do not occur.

SBU's story is not just one of an inadequate education, but one of persistent, pervasive, all-encompassing segregation and severe economic inequalities. It is inconceivable that South Bronx schools would be in such physical and financial distress if *Brown v. Board of Education* had been more forcefully implemented. After white families fled to the suburbs, partly to escape integration with students of color, *Milliken v. Bradley* (1974) weakened the *Brown* decision by stating that neighboring suburban districts did not have to participate in regional integration programs, even if racial integration was impossible otherwise.[35] Since then, as the next chapter examines, other attempts to uphold *Brown* have also been struck down by the courts.[36]

Thus these teenagers continue to attend separate and inherently, astoundingly unequal schools. Among school districts with five hundred or more students, sixty-seven of the top hundred spenders in the nation are located in Westchester County. Some spend more than $25,000 a year per student.[37] The majority of school districts on Long Island and in Westchester County spent more than the state average per pupil but boasted of tax rates below the state average.[38] In contrast, schools with high rates of low-income students average around $7,000 a year per student.[39] Although 70 percent of the state's poor students and 80 percent of its limited-English-proficient students attend New York City schools, the city receives far less funding than wealthier, suburban districts.[40]

Unfortunately, patterns of racial and economic inequality are not limited to the schools. There is severe, concentrated poverty in the neighborhoods of SBU members. In 1999, the Bronx had the lowest per capita income in New York City, $13,959, around one-third of that in neighboring Manhattan, $42,922. Looking at numbers for the Bronx as a whole obscures patterns of segregation within the borough, as North Bronx neighborhoods are much wealthier than South Bronx ones. Once we separate out South Bronx neighborhoods, we see that their per capita income is $10,148, only one-quarter of Manhattan's.

As compared to New York City overall, the South Bronx also reports much lower percentages of white and Asian persons. Whereas Blacks and/or Latinos constitute 53 percent of New York City overall, 84 percent of Bronx residents and 96 percent of South Bronx residents are Black and/or Latino.[41]

Thus, if we examine the demographic makeup of the specific neighborhoods from which SBU draws constituents, we see that SBU members are the poor, primarily Latino and Black, inner-city youth referenced in public debates about the "culture of failure" (table 4.1). The numbers clearly show that poverty is indeed a major force in these students' lives. Exactly what their "culture" looks like, however, is a different question altogether, and one that we will look into in the remainder of this chapter.

TABLE 4.1
Basic characteristics and constituency of SBU

Organizational Characteristics	SBU
Number of education organizers	2 to 4
CONSTITUENCY BY RACE*	
% Black	35%
% Hispanic/Latino	59%
% Non-Hispanic white	5%
CONSTITUENCY BY INCOME	
% at or below poverty level	39%
LEADERSHIP AND MEMBERSHIP	
Core leaders	20
Estimate of base membership	300
Estimate of education campaign membership	100

Note: Demographic data were tabulated by the author according to the neighborhoods served by SBU and drawn from the 1999–2000 U.S. Census and state and city surveys, using Community Studies of New York's database Infoshare Online at www.infoshare.org (accessed 2004). The information on constituency by race is from the Education Trust, "The Funding Gap 2005: Low-Income and Minority Students Shortchanged by Most States," Winter 2005, www2.edtrust.org/NR/rdonlyres/31D276EF-v72E1-458A-8C71-E3D262A4C91E/0/FundingGap2005.pdf.

SBU's Background

SBU is a youth-led community organizing group affiliated with the Northwest Bronx Community and Clergy Coalition (NWBCCC). It operates in neighborhoods that became "South Bronxed" in the 1970s and 1980s. That is, as white flight and concentrated poverty took their toll in southern neighborhoods in the Bronx, some landlords decided that it was more lucrative to commit arson and collect fire insurance payments than to collect rent from their apartment buildings.[42] Eventually, the "South Bronx" label came "to signify a syndrome of social ills, an era even, but not exactly a place."[43] When adjacent neighborhoods in the Bronx began to report deteriorating housing stock and rising crime rates, they became "South Bronxed."[44] When NWBCCC first formed in 1974, it helped neighborhood residents to address these tenant issues. Over time, it came to address education and environmental justice concerns as well.

SBU was born around 1997. Encouraged by their parents, high school students in the Mosholu-Woodlawn South and Kingsbridge Heights neighborhood associations of NWBCCC began to actively participate in education organizing campaigns. These students quickly became ex-cited at the prospect of policy makers listening to their concerns and saw that sometimes school repairs were made in response. They decided to stick around, forming the Kingsbridge Heights Youth contingent of NWBCCC.

Soon their membership grew exponentially and expanded beyond the Kingsbridge Heights neighborhood. In 1998, the youth won not one but two seats on the NWBCCC board as the association called Sistas and Brothas United. Although SBU is officially part of NWBCCC, the youth have made it their own organization in important ways. First, it has its own by-laws, leadership, and more youth-friendly dues system. Its staff members are NWBCCC employees, but the majority of its funding comes from SBU-specific foundation grants. More substantively, its continued expansion has been accompanied by development of its own political campaigns and strategies and a very different vibe from NWBCCC as a whole.

At SBU, unpaid active members, those who do more than just occasionally show up to meetings and pay dues, are called "leaders." Organizers are paid staff at the organization. One of its organizers, Elena, and several leaders have been with the organization since its inception. SBU staff also include a second full-time organizer, a full-time tutor coordinator and in-house education expert, and at various times additional part-time organizers and workshop coordinators.

Every day from 2:00 to 8:00 p.m., dozens of high school students show up to volunteer on outreach and political campaigns. These days, SBU works on large campaigns on new school facilities, school safety, and overcrowding. It has helped South Bronx students win thousands of dollars' worth of repairs, staged large protests for more New York State school funding, garnered new school safety protocols in the schools, and created a small school from scratch, complete with its own administration and pedagogical mission. These campaign wins are no small feat and prove that inner-city youth can work on long-term, large-scale projects that require planning, strategy, critical analysis, and immense amounts of discipline and hard work. The rest of this chapter focuses on how SBU got to this point.

More of a Love Thing: Coming to Sistas and Brothas United

Rosalinda is the sort of young woman one might expect to be active at SBU. She got good grades and so earnestly gushed about her favorite books that teachers, at meetings with her, sometimes looked as if they were ready to swoon. I once observed several teachers, within the span of a few minutes, lament that if only there were more students like her, then . . . well . . .

The popular assumption is that if more students were like Rosalinda and loved books, then students and schools would succeed. A complementary assumption would be that Rosalinda and her friends joined SBU specifically because they valued education and wanted to do something about it. If these assumptions were true, then SBU members would not be representative of inner-city youth. However, even an obviously successful student like Rosalinda first came to SBU not for its education organizing per se but because she wanted to do something both "good" and social after school. As she described it, "Lisa knew me from our classes, and she approached me in our biology class. 'You know, you're too smart! I want you to come to our program! We need tutors. I see that you have a lot of potential.' I was not doing anything after school, so I came, and I started to tutor, and I started to get involved, also, in the different campaigns."

Assumptions that SBU members are somehow self-selecting or exceptions to the "culture of failure" rule simply do not hold up, especially when we consider not just why members join but why they become committed as activist leaders. Rosalinda said that she stayed because the other youth and organizers taught her to think "outside the box" and because she developed critical thinking skills, lasting friendships, and a new level of ownership, responsibility, and pride:

> At the beginning, I did not speak at all. I felt so overwhelmed, so intimidated with all of these . . . *youth* who spoke like they did not care about anything else. It was different from what I saw in school. The way they talked about different things, and the way they cared about all these issues . . . they spoke about it with a passion. Sometimes it was like, "Oh, we've been at this meeting for hours," but they were actually excited . . . about the kind of work they did. And the enthusiasm is kind of contagious.

Though she was an "A" student, Rosalinda was not used to students who loved working on school reform. This alone suggests that we should not assume that good students are the ones who value education most, and more pointedly, that those who struggle in school do not care.

Between helping out others on their homework and completing her own, Rosalinda spent many of her afternoons tackling vision statements for new policy proposals. She explained that the constant feedback and affection at SBU kept her going. In other words, what ultimately wed Rosalinda to SBU was a sense of empowerment and work toward her visions of social justice. While the prevailing culture talk about the "cool pose" argues that hard-working youth care about school reform and succeed and lazy teenagers do not, the reality at SBU is more complex. Even good students need to be empowered.

Sometimes the so-called "good" students themselves wanted to believe that they deserved a good education more than the other youth at school. Indeed, Rosalinda herself had previously bought into popular stereotypes about inner-city youth. The fact that she herself had made the distinction between "good" and "bad" students hints at just how pervasive Cosby's culture talk is. Then Rosalinda found out that her distinctions were not just artificially imposed or slightly off but plain wrong. She stated that SBU had made her a less "judgmental person" because she had gotten

> to know them ["bad" students] and know what they've gone through, and why they made the choices they made. . . . I was young; I was kind of naive. . . . I was so ignorant about things and the world outside me. I used to look at young people and see them cursing, talking about things in the street. I used to look at them with contempt, to be honest. Now, I kind of understand. . . . I've met a lot of people here who are those kids who have changed or seen things happen. To be honest, to use a term I've been using a lot lately, I was "in the box."

If the process of getting to talk about the schools, learning more about the state of the school system as a whole, and working on campaigns for school reform was so transformative for someone like Rosalinda, it is life-changing for the supposedly "bad students" she used to fear. After all, these less-than-stellar students had not necessarily experienced the same sort of pride and accomplishment Rosalinda had felt in studying. Nor had they consistently reaped the rewards of good grades. Yet less-than-stellar students constitute the overwhelming majority of SBU. Why did *these* folks join SBU?

Discovering the Possibility of Accomplishment

Nathaniel spent ninth grade in western Pennsylvania, living in a trailer. He had moved there to get to know his father a bit better. He came back to the Bronx at the end of the school year, though, because his mother's apartment had burned down in a fire. He gave her all the money he had earned at his after-school job during the year before and moved into a shelter with her. He had a brother in prison, plus a couple of younger siblings to help care for. He was not doing that well in school, but frankly, that was not Nathaniel's priority. Nathaniel joined SBU in his tenth grade because Michael, another leader there, asked him to. "Since we were friends already, it was a connection we already had. It was partly because it was *him* asking me. . . . I thought I could relate, so let me go in there, and we can do it together. . . . If it had been a regular Coalition organizer, it would have been, 'Oh, another routine thing, you got to listen to older people do this, and say that.'"

Nathaniel became inspired because he had seen another Bronx teenager *just like him* in a powerful position. Whereas more privileged youth often look to accomplishment as an entitlement, Nathaniel had to see it happen before his eyes to even realize that it was possible for him. He felt that the stories of other SBU youth resonated with his own. "When I first came here," he recounted, "I heard a whole bunch of youth speak, and actually, Michael was in charge of my orientation, so I really felt like, 'Whoa, my homey's really doing it!' It challenged me! 'Wow, they know so much! I want to get to that level!' And I worked until I got to know that much stuff, too. . . . Maybe, I can be just like them. I want to be a leader, to be called a leader." The fact that Michael is the son of a gang leader, became involved in gangs himself at an early age, and was briefly placed in a mental institution at the age of twelve made his story even more poignant to other potential leaders. These comments suggest that Nathaniel wanted to engage in meaningful, challenging work but that he was not necessarily exposed to similar opportunities or encouragement in school.

Again and again, SBU leaders spoke of how they became more involved in both official and unofficial school affairs *after* they learned to trust people and learned about positive collective activity and a sense of agency via political participation in SBU. This does not mean that they did not value education until SBU showed them how important schools were. Rather, SBU gave them the confidence they needed to realize that other people were on their side, that their opinions mattered, and that, collectively, their hard work would pay off.

Igniting a Long-Standing Passion for Schooling with Love and Support

Another SBU leader, Lisa, enjoyed going on outdoor walks, so she joined a primarily social group called NYC, or New York Conservationists. There she met SBU organizer Ernest. Even though she was recruited by an organizer, Lisa clearly viewed her relationship with Ernest as one of friendship. "We got really close, and talked about our lives. . . . I loved him, and he told me to check . . . out [SBU] . . . I could relate to all the people here." Eventually, Lisa switched to spending all her time at SBU, partly because she felt that SBU was more active and was doing more constructive things than NYC and partly because she felt that the SBU youth understood her better. Her participation in SBU, in turn, led to substantive changes in her relationship with schools. She had never been apathetic about the state of Bronx schools, but it was participation in youth organizing that helped her to vocalize her outrage: "Before, I never knew where to start, or where to go from here. . . . I thought, 'What could I do, here, by myself?' And the truth is, you can't really do anything by yourself; you have to have a crowd of people with you to make sure you'll be heard. And when I came here to SBU, people said, 'Hey, you think school sucks? So do I! That's great; let's work on it!'"

SBU has been able to bring out the young people's passions because it integrates campaign work with social work. SBU is about much more than the campaigns per se, so members like Nathaniel also emphasized factors that appear irrelevant at first glance: "We have fun things. We do trips. And, on a personal level, we chill with each other." At the SBU offices, the youth were constantly saying "hello" and yelling greetings of affection across the room. Jeremy noted that the amount of time they spent together had substantive effects: "We get to take trips far away and sleep in the same house, like in [MTV's reality show] *The Real World*. We argue and have mad fun. In the end, we're good, true friends, develop a sense of trust and depend on each other, even through the vicious arguments." Nathaniel elaborated, "We definitely relate differently, because we spend a whole lot more time together. . . . It is just more of a sense of community. More of a love thing in our SBU thing." Further, even when individual leaders disagreed with one another, they expressed gratitude for the attention and support they received: "Sometimes, people can get a little too involved, but it is all good."

That a "love thing" appears to make such a big difference is hardly a novel notion. Yet the extent to which the students emphasized its importance in their empowerment, and their subsequent investment and involvement in school affairs, might still strike policy makers as surprising. At the very least, it is discordant with the assumptions held by so many pundits today: that only tougher standards will get students to motivate and suddenly do better in school, that anything else is coddling, and that these youth do not value education. This does not mean that these students want lower standards—nothing of the sort. When they are challenged, work hard, and find the way to communicate with their teachers, for example, they become incredibly excited. Yet they need some sort of structured means of empowerment before explicitly tackling their own roles in school.

Articulating Long-Standing Concerns over Schooling

SBU provided these students with the means to express frustrations with their schooling that they could not convey before. Many of these students had become resigned to the notion that their opinions would never be taken seriously, that their pitiful attempts to change things would not make a difference, and that they did not have the power or recourse to gain the attention of people who mattered anyway.

Once they got to SBU, a recurrent theme among the students was how their SBU experiences had "opened their eyes." According to Nathaniel,

> SBU made me . . . more of a person that is open to things and realizes that everybody is not the enemy. At SBU, when people first come here, you have to introduce yourself to them. Me, I was always closed, "I do not know you," so I kept my mouth closed, "I do not need to meet you." But after a while, you got to go up and introduce yourself, you gotta be a leader, and say, "Hi, my name is Nathaniel, and I do this, may I help you." . . . And when I see people on the street, I go and help them, and say, "Hello," and "You have a good day.". . . No one's against you, do not worry, nobody's trying to kill you.

Nathaniel had never been safe or comfortable in his school or neighborhood before; he felt powerless, and SBU helped him to better comprehend and navigate the difficult conditions in which he lived. Only with these changes did Nathaniel become ready to accept more responsibility as an activist leader at SBU and as a good student.

Several years after the organization's inception, SBU began a peer tutoring program that greatly affected Lisa: "My grades were horrible when I first came to SBU. I had a 60-something average." Then, as she became more involved in SBU, she received the support and encouragement needed to raise her school grades considerably. Ironically, after she had worked to improve her grades and her teachers *then* gave her more fulfilling work, Lisa became more enthusiastic about school. Until SBU helped her to prove to her teachers that she deserved more fulfilling work, however, the teachers were either so overtaxed or unresponsive that they assumed Lisa would not be up to the task.

Until Lisa joined SBU and learned how to articulate her concerns, and just how compelling and fun projects that mattered to her could be, the education she received in school did not connect with the rest of her life. It had just felt frustrating, and it did not seem to be worth the trouble. Still, once SBU leaders are exposed to well-constructed opportunities for good work, they quickly become committed to, and even absorbed in, consequential campaigns for school reform in the Bronx.

Getting Policy Makers' Attention

SBU leaders had to prove to policy makers, again and again, that they should have a say in their own education. With determination, they presented themselves as serious stakeholders and decision makers.

Students at SBU knew that their schools were appalling and inferior. They were told this in the media every day. *These schools are full of violence*, announced the evening newscasts, and even if they were not, the students nonetheless experienced overcrowded school buildings full of police officers, metal detectors, and harried teachers.

When the students met teenagers from elsewhere, they were often asked, as Nathaniel was, "Oh, you're from there, have you gotten shot before?" Even though Nathaniel dismissed these folks as "closed-minded and ignorant," there was no denying that his school was certainly full of people, even strangers, who constantly gave students like him a watchful eye. He knew that he was good and that these people were wrong to assume that he is a troublemaker, but the burden was on him to prove them wrong. This forced him to constantly walk on eggshells in school, to sometimes lose focus on his schoolwork, and to dampen simmering resentment by channeling his energy toward SBU campaigns.

So if their schools were not inferior, perhaps the students themselves were? At SBU, students frequently debated the extent to which they needed to put their best foot forward in order to gain respect from higher-ups in the administration. If so, then what should this self-presentation look like? Should they have to change the way they dress, for instance? While some of these higher-ups were themselves African American or Latino, the students could not help wondering whether they would speak the right language and whether they would be taken seriously. Some wondered if they should wear different outfits that they did not necessarily own, though baggy T-shirts and jeans are the most common uniform for teenage boys across the nation— even white, suburban youth. Common perceptions and misperceptions influenced by culture talk about what "good" students look like made it that much more difficult for SBU members to prove to higher-ups that they were worthy of attention and made the process of school reform even more bewildering. This was especially so when misperceptions about "good" students were racialized. Black and Latino youth were being told that they, as a group, lacked values, even if white youth would probably perform similarly in similar circumstances and perhaps with less dire consequences.

Several of the leaders noted how difficult it was for them to get policy makers to take them seriously. Rosalinda, for instance, observed that some adults, like Joel Rivera, their city council representative, "listen to us, when we're youth. But not everybody is that way. Some people say, 'You're students, you have no place in the system, what are you doing here?' 'Yes, we do, and that's what we're demanding.' Sometimes it is hard because people do not listen to us. But that's another motivation to keep us going. We'll go to the next person." While it is encouraging that repeated rejections made SBU leaders more motivated rather than less, it is striking that the main message they got was, *You're students, you have no place in the system.* This was not always intentional; often what policy makers actually meant was, *You're students, please, go to school and learn, and let us take care of the rest.* If SBU leaders were not succeeding academically along the way, well, perhaps they were not trying. By not listening to what the ultimate stakeholders in the system really thought, the policy makers were not doing their job or examining the conditions in which these students were attempting to learn.

The obstacles facing SBU youth were (and are) high. Sometimes it took guts for these students to show policy makers that they meant business. As Michael described one incident:

> Once, at a huge meeting we were having with Dennis Wolcott, the Deputy Mayor of Education, in a huge auditorium at Martin Luther King High School, I see that he's not paying attention. He's sitting there, playing with his Palm Pilot like this, when I am talking about the concerns we have. So I stop talking, lift up my chair, and walk across the room, around the table to where he's sitting, and plop my chair down next to him so that I am in his face and he can listen to me. I saw [the then-director of NWB-CCC] looking at me like, "What are you doing!!?" But after I did that, he listened. And at the end of the meeting, we were all going, and he comes up to me and says, "Do not leave me without shaking my hand."

Ironically, Michael had to risk *furthering* his (false) image as a trouble-maker—breaking rules of meeting decorum—in order to get administrators to listen to him and eventually realize that perhaps they should have in the first place. Even with its happy ending, this anecdote suggests that the administrators originally presumed that the students at the meeting did not value their education enough or have anything worthwhile to share. These students did not receive the sort of childhood—with decent schools, "boys will be boys" excuses, second chances, and a sense of dignity—accorded to almost all other children. Even elementary school students knew that outsiders had a poor opinion of their neighborhoods and perhaps of the people who lived there. Outside the offices of another Bronx education organizing group, a local youth, maybe eight years old, marveled that all his teachers were milling around there. He asked what they were up to, and since none answered, I told him that we were taking a neighborhood tour. "Not a pretty sight, huh!" he retorted. The teachers laughed.

Learning to Making Sense of Schools

To be taken seriously by policy makers, SBU members needed to make sense of their schools and present high-quality policy proposals. They also needed the resources to realize their ideas. In this section, I outline the different ways SBU members attempted to learn about and contextualize the state of their schooling.

Acquiring the Means and Skills to Express Concerns about Schooling

Would leaders like Lisa have gotten to know what meaningful schoolwork looked like if she had not become so involved with SBU? Would she have been able to articulate what good schooling looks like?

We cannot be sure, of course, but Lisa did not think she would have known what vision statements to write, or what policy proposals to submit to the DOE, if she had not joined SBU. She, Nathaniel, Rosalinda, Hector, and Michael were interested in school reform, but they did not think the department was likely to help them, and they had no confidence or political skills. Finally, they had limited knowledge of how schools are supposed to work. To make further progress, these students trained themselves to grapple with, understand, and glean lessons from the kind of schooling their wealthier counterparts received.

While their participation at SBU clearly gave them a sense of empowerment, social support, and responsibility to work toward school reform, the students also had to articulate visions of better schools in order to forward proposals to fulfill their mission. In short, SBU students could always name some of the problems with their education, but it was difficult to gain a warm reception if they did not have school credibility and an array of positive policy proposals to boot. Where did these positive policy proposals, which outlined what *could* and *should* be done, come from?

To a certain extent, these proposals came from the training at SBU, especially in statistical analysis and political structures. The students were trained by organizers and each other to read government documents, access and process public data, and work with research institutes of local universities to collect good evidence of inequalities in the school system. The youth could then contextualize their schools and present concrete data to corroborate their sense that something was amiss in their education. Indeed, many of the SBU students became whizzes at basic statistical analysis and rattled off numbers on how disadvantaged their schools were at public meetings.

Often these statistical analyses also gave the leaders a better sense of how government, especially city and state agencies, operated. Jeremy, for instance, noted how "the [physical plant] funding works so that you're reimbursed nine cents for a building and seventeen cents for repairs. So you have built-in disincentives against getting new school buildings. And then we look at how different things are in the suburbs."

Almost all hard numbers—regarding discipline rates, overcrowding and building occupation rates, percentages of certified teachers, and so on—demonstrate that profound inequalities exist, but the students were also quick to note that numbers did not give a full sense of what their experiences were like and that city agencies tended to understate their problems. For example, statistics show that the Bronx has fewer experienced teachers than other boroughs, but they do not quite capture the experience of sitting through classes without enough books and with young, well-meaning teachers who do not quite know which pedagogical techniques work best in these schools. The students were thus careful to corroborate quantitative evidence with qualitative evidence and vice versa. Nathaniel, for instance, stated that despite the numbers he had not believed that funding disparities really ran along racial lines until he visited schools in other districts and witnessed it firsthand: "It also really does come down to race, in some ways. From my observations. A person might say, 'White people get this and that.' I am like, 'Well, maybe this person is pretty ignorant, and is just saying that because they do not like white people.' It was put in my mind that white people usually get this, and others that, [but] until I really saw the comparisons, and I really saw it myself, I [had not] thought that it was kind of true."

All SBU leaders could name the heads and deputies of all relevant agencies in local, city, and state education agencies and were not afraid to speak to them. Nathaniel observed, "SBU has definitely changed me. It is just that it made me more aware of politics and the government, the system. You have to see things and read between the lines, really. For example, if I wanted to talk to my principal, I'd learn to go see the boss in charge; if I can't see that boss, I'd go to an even higher boss. You know, I learned to not just settle until I get an answer, or get something out of somebody, that would help me towards my goal." The comment demonstrates how inner-city youth have to learn and acquire a sense of entitlement to good schools, or at least accountable school administrators, that many students and parents at more elite public schools may take for granted.

Finding Positive Visions of Schooling

In trying to come up with school reform proposals, the students often sifted through their own experiences, trying to glean lessons to use as a basis for policy arguments. Rosalinda noted how she became equipped to pinpoint frustrations with less successful teachers because of her experiences at SBU and also because she had some classes with truly inspiring teachers:

To be honest, I've noticed a lot of flaws in the structure of the school system itself. Like in standards in English classes, I am really passionate about [that]. . . . I would be open to organizing for other issues, but not in the same way as education. . . . I can pay attention every day to connect what I am learning to what works in the school system. It encourages me to learn about the issues more. Like, if I see any bias in the classroom, I would know what I can do about it; I would investigate.

Sadly, these young people mostly came up with stories of how *not* to run a school. Michael recounted:

With my little cousin—he went to summer school, and that's punishment alone. Then, I am helping him with his homework and picking up his book, I see that I can't help him with his homework because there's a hundred pages missing. Before, I would just feel like it is all right, that's the way it usually goes, and just leave it alone. This time, I thought of the history of resources going into the different schools, and about school budgets, how they are determined. Me, myself, and I need to learn about the larger picture. I got mad.

In contrast, when Rosalinda spoke about the teachers she adored, she was practically overflowing with enthusiasm:

Because I've had the opportunity to have really great English teachers, who are open-minded themselves, who I can relate to, who teach me a lot about society. . . . Mr. Correa, he calls himself a radical and a dissident. I love that guy! You do not understand, I just love him so much, what he believes, and what he stands for. We've read Plato, Noam Chomsky, Orwell, I love Orwell as well, *Fast Food Nation*, it is just aspects of society that we get to go deep into. With *1984*, we read three related things that opened my mind extremely about society. I connect it a lot to this place. I feel so good about it.

For all the talk about how inner-city youth need to spend virtually all their time preparing for high-stakes tests, Nathaniel expressed gratitude for opportunities to engage in critical analysis, think independently, and take responsibility for his own education. He wistfully thought back to the few chances he had to learn creatively or to showcase outstanding work:

[The principal in junior high] talked to me like I was a young man, even at that early age in my life. And it was more the shows that she had. . . . And you know, it was great to be performing, chilling, become famous in our school! I am real proud of that; I felt like a star! . . . There was none of this in high school. It was crazy, because high school's when you're really supposed to do that. . . . My high school, we do not have our own building—They took out the third floor and put another school in there. We also have a preschool in there. . . . The place is cool . . . [but we have] nothing to get our pride up.

Almost all of the students expressed some moment of pure joy in their schooling. These students held onto these moments in trying to envision what schooling could be like, the encouragement and motivation for learning and schooling it would provide. Unfortunately, many of the students discovered for the first time what *consistent* good schooling looks like by visiting *other* people's schools. Nathaniel, for instance, felt that life in Pennsylvania was luxurious, perhaps because he held overcrowded conditions in the Bronx as his basis for comparison.

My father was already living out there, so I decided to go out there and live with him. . . . In the trailer park, it was beautiful; all that space! Whoa! They had a good sense of community in the school, too. They had Homecoming, they had a football field, they had basketball games, they had concession stands, they had Pajama Day, when you wore your best pajamas there, they had Halloween parties, Christmas parties, parties all the time. . . . These things made a *big* difference because schools are kind of like a home; you're there most of the time. . . . I never knew what field hockey was until I got there. I was like, "What is that?" I thought it was a new sport they just made up when I got there!

Living in a working-class district in western Pennsylvania, then, gave Nathaniel a notion of what school could be like. Often there were dramatic differences in classes. Nathaniel continued, "I felt like there was better education out there. They had resources. . . . I do not think they had money problems. Like when it comes to science class, you actually get to do science experiments. Now, we just take notes. . . . We do not have science labs; we do not have any of that stuff."

When Nathaniel came back to the Bronx, he felt that his life had become that much tougher because he had become used to schooling and life in Pennsylvania. Students thus measured the quality of their education by comparative as well as absolute criteria. The SBU leaders explicitly linked all school quality issues again and again to their campaigns against inequities, and not just inadequacies, in schooling.

It was also through experiences in other school districts that the students realized suburban residents were not necessarily more deserving of a good education than they were. Nathaniel, who is African American and was greeted with the Confederate flag and quite a bit of overt, racist hostility in Pennsylvania, also observed:

> There just isn't enough diversity in both parts—not enough whites in our schools, and not enough Blacks in their schools. And most of the kids there, they had all this money! And people say, oh, that they want it based on academics? No, they can't. A lot of the kids out here, that are the same as out there. It is not based on academics at all. Many people out there, they are poor and on welfare just like here, but they get to go to great schools?! I was like, "Wow." A lot of people out there were poor, but they had better schools, resources . . . better gyms, with the equipment there were no problems, no problems.

Because Nathaniel never had the chance to attend a racially integrated or majority-white school before, he had not examined what other academic experiences might look like. Would the quality of one's school be mainly attributable to class? He was used to hearing about the rich kids in neighboring Manhattan or Westchester County. And would levels of student achievement be mainly attributable to students' efforts? On the basis of his experiences in Pennsylvania, Nathaniel came to suspect that race was a key factor in these differences.

While not all of the other students had lived in other school districts, especially in majority-white ones, they had visited other school districts and met with education organizers from other cities via SBU. Such experiences were integral to the students' ability to articulate positive visions of schooling.

SBU members' descriptions of their own personal transformation invoked themes of collective action and empowerment, not the acquiring of a previously absent concern for education. It therefore seems disingenuous to interpret urban students' passivity on educational reform issues as apathy when they are not exactly equipped to express and tackle such concerns. Youth like Nathaniel and Lisa were not actively involved in education reform either until SBU showed how they could make a difference. If all students from the South Bronx and other urban areas were so equipped, we might find more stories of the kind told here—those of poorly performing students, as well as superstar ones, driving policy reform campaigns.

SBU Campaigns for Better Schools

SBU's campaign on school safety, which presents nuanced views on how to best abate violence in schools, goes against the popular stereotype of inner-city young people as primarily initiators of violence. School safety officers, many of them actual New York police officers, patrolled the hallways of the schools that the campaign addressed. While SBU youth disagreed on whether the police *primarily* intimidated or protected students, none of them denied that in actual practice police officers did both.

The campaign therefore created a forum in which safety officers and SBU youth would make up respective teams and perform skits about how they perceived each other. Later, the youth and safety officers came up with a new, official protocol for respectful, "open-minded" interaction in schools. This set SBU's proposals apart from more common demands for more school safety officers. In this way, the campaign addressed issues of racial profiling in the schools, an aspect of school security often overlooked or avoided in community organizing campaigns. The students also drew maps of violence and drug dealing from students' perspectives, pointing out trouble spots that had not been effectively patrolled by the police.

As in meetings with higher-ups in the DOE, SBU leaders were conversing with many officers who were themselves African American or Latino but who had nevertheless succumbed to negative, racialized stereotypes of what "good" students looked like. These upper-level administrators were familiar with the culture talk story lines about urban youth that opened this chapter. Like Cosby, some of them differentiated themselves from today's inner-city students by claiming that today's young people of color do not want a decent education—despite overwhelming evidence to the contrary.

Further, because American schools remain so racially segregated, most SBU leaders did not know about and could not immediately point to white student populations and show that they too behaved sometimes well and sometimes poorly. The larger context of segregation makes it easy for policy makers and media pundits to sell racial stereotypes, since most individual students do not have the personal experiences to definitively refute these messages. Only by banding together and by engaging in nuanced conversations with one another and with police could SBU leaders present their critiques of poor school conditions productively.

The other major campaigns pursued by SBU, namely the STARS teacher quality campaign and the (ultimately successful) attempt to open a new Leadership Institute small school, based on SBU's leadership development model, underlined two key difficulties faced by the youth—how they were not taken seriously as stakeholders, at least at first, and how their pedagogical imagination was limited by their experience.

Regarding the STARS program, Rosalinda noted: "When I first joined, we were starting to do interviews of teachers, we worked on making a survey. We came up with survey questions, formatted them, put them in order, and then we started to talk to teachers and students about how they felt about each other. . . . I was discouraged a little by it because it was not as active as it should've been. . . . We had asking questions face to face in mind, but then teachers never had time to meet with us; there was always something going on." At each step along the way, SBU members went through a slow, painful process of proving themselves to each new authority figure they wished to impress and disproving the stereotypes about lazy teenagers who cared for nothing but "bling" and sex. Like Hector, whose story was recounted at the beginning of this chapter, most SBU leaders were told at some point or another that they have no right to speak about their schools. But they persisted, and ultimately they won over most of the public officials, teachers, and administrators that they involved in their campaigns. As Laura, one of the youth organizers, explained in a report written by her and several of the youth leaders,

> The teachers who came to these meetings were blown away. They saw students who they had pegged as troublemakers leading discussions about teaching and learning. Our point was to show teachers that youth do care about their learning. If teachers took the time to talk with the students, they would know what is going on in that student's life and why they missed school or acted the way they did. We said, "Your job is to find out—What leadership qualities does this student have? How can you draw out those qualities at school?" If students had a chance to shine in schools, they would do better. But that means someone inside the school has to take the time to get to know the student.[45]

Eventually, SBU members were invited by New Visions for Public Schools (often referred to as "New Visions") to submit a proposal for a new school under the New Century High School Initiative, a program that began in 2002 and focused on opening dozens of small public high schools in New York City.[46] New Visions was used to receiving proposals from either veteran educators or young, innovative, entrepreneurial ones, but not proposals put together largely by young people, the students themselves.

Fernando Carlo, one of the teenagers who worked on the proposal throughout his high school years, commented, "We are trying to design a school where youth have an actual voice—besides sitting on a student council and figuring out what parties to throw—in figuring out what funds go to what programs and how teachers are hired, and in designing the curriculum. . . . A lot of educators are not used to hearing that type of thing from youth, and it scared them."

The resulting proposal from SBU, called the Leadership Institute, was ultimately approved by New Visions, but only after several annual rejections. The school opened in September 2005. The Leadership Institute focuses on leadership, social justice, and community action, the themes that made such a difference in the lives of SBU members.

According to Shoshana Daniels, a teacher who became an education coordinator at SBU before returning to teaching as a Leadership Institute faculty member, SBU struggled not only with the receptiveness of adults to their ideas but also with their own difficulty, given their limited experiences in poor schools, in envisioning what a good school would look like. Here the comparative analyses made possible with the help of SBU and its connections proved helpful. In the end,

> We developed an interdisciplinary curriculum that links academic learning with . . . the skills they need to develop campaigns for social change: how to conduct research on land-use policies, for example; how to analyze and present data about available tracts of land in our neighborhood that could be used for new school facilities; how to interview experts; how to develop well-supported position papers on key reform strategies; how to write compelling letters to elected officials; and how to speak persuasively at press conferences. We believe that true learning happens when students, not teachers, are at the center of the learning experience. The role of the teacher is to create an environment in which students can ask critical questions and develop projects that help them find answers.[47]

SBU campaigns reveal members' sensitivity toward all constituency groups, their emphasis on peer support, and the importance of empowerment in creating meaningful schooling.[48] For example, one campaign began when SBU compared their school experiences with those of the Young Intellects, a group of young Muslim women also from the Bronx, and realized that, as under-resourced as their districts' schools were, other students within them were nonetheless getting preferential treatment. Specifically, members of the Young Intellects were being contacted by guidance counselors for precollege advisement several times a year, though SBU members had been unsuccessfully attempting to reach their guidance counselors for many months. The Young Intellects themselves voiced the suspicion that because many of them were Asian or African immigrants they were perceived as different from typical African American and Latino inner-city youth and consequently as "good" students who should receive more counseling services.

SBU youth decided to collaborate with the Young Intellects to carefully collect and document all homework assignments they received, their attempts to arrange appointments with guidance counselors, and any actual meetings with counselors in order to gauge and authenticate disparities in the quality of schoolwork and counseling received. Only by teaming up with another group of Bronx youth, then, was SBU able to prove that there were severe counseling inequities even within Bronx schools. Youth know that their experiences are not just reflections of their merit or worth, but outsiders do not necessarily know this, and popular media usually promote the opposite message.

In their campaigns, SBU youth learned that their experiences do count for something and can be put to good use in campaigns. They also learned to trust one another, and ultimately teachers and other stakeholders of the school system, enough to assume that good relationships would naturally bring about positive change.

SBU Forever

SBU leaders were (and remain) close, and so passionate about school reform that they have stayed committed to their campaigns, even when the rewards are not immediate. It is a good thing, too, because education reform does not come about quickly—not in a few months, or even a few years. Students like Lisa, Nathaniel, Hector, Rosalinda, Michael, and Jeremy worked toward rewards that many of them did not reap themselves.

Many of the youth expressed anger at the systemic inequalities in New York education. These activists knew that helplessness can sometimes manifest itself in poor academic records and that this is not the same thing as apathy, indifference, or poor values. Still, they also understood that good education was so precious that their efforts were worth it, even other young people would be the ones to benefit. Before the Leadership Institute opened in fall of 2005, one of its main creators commented, "The Leadership Institute, or every campaign we've been working on, some of the changes will happen later on, after we leave high school. That's the funny thing. . . . I guess it is because we've been through the issues, we have experienced them, we do not want it to be that way any more. We do not want our kids to be fighting for the same things. We want things to be better for the future."

After so many heartening anecdotes, it would be easy to imagine that these were special teenagers, those who stood out amid their peers in disadvantaged neighborhoods, who were destined to make a small difference. According to public discourse and popular media, most inner-city young people are abandoning their chance to accomplish something and do well in school. But a careful look at a youth movement disrupts this popular culture talk. It shows just how badly these teenagers craved a feeling of achievement.

Teenagers like Hector, Lisa, Michael, and Nathaniel had no such destiny circumscribed from the beginning. They were struggling in school. Their stories do not suggest that that inner-city young people are actually angels rather than troublemakers; in fact, no sweeping stereotype applies. At the same time, these students were missing, not values, but schools that nurtured and challenged them. They lacked a sense of empowerment, of agency, of feeling and knowing that their actions could make a difference and that hard work could pay off. They wanted teachers, school safety officers, and policy makers to judge them by how they acted instead of how they looked—poor or working-class, African American or Latino.

To a certain extent, the ways these youth are talked about in the media, in popular discourse, and sometimes by teachers, administrators, police officers, and even parents frustrated by them—as troublemakers, as lazy, as stupid—are so pervasive, and yet so disconnected from the everyday, nitty gritty preoccupations of SBU leaders, that it has been difficult for them to battle such misconceptions head on. How can they suddenly prove everyone wrong and succeed if they do not have the resources to do so? Despite what Orlando Patterson and others have suggested, young people's values cannot be guessed from their appearance or from other superficial signifiers like the music they listen to. There is a difference between being told that hard work makes a difference and being shown how, with the guidance necessary to actually make it happen.

Using their firsthand knowledge of schooling in the Bronx, SBU members were able to pursue campaigns to obtain more adequate funding, more appropriate pedagogy, and more equitable education policies. Along the way, these teenagers had to earn one another's trust; compare notes and glean patterns from their collective experiences; earn the respect of teachers, police officers, and administrators; and learn New York City's convoluted, bureaucratic regulations from the inside out. Only through such collaborative efforts could these students make sense of their public schooling. Often conversations with residents of other school districts or experiences with living in other districts themselves were also necessary before SBU leaders could begin to envision what school could be—a safe place, full of pride, decent science labs, and good teachers.

The discrepancy between the myth of "disconnected" inner-city young people and the reality of disempowered urban teenage students has dire consequences. Implicit in the myth is the idea that the schools these students attend are just fine. This myth naturalizes and reifies the egregious economic segregation of our nation's schools and the racial hierarchy in our society as a whole. On the basis of this false assumption, a whole slew of corresponding policies, all taking power further away from these students, have been proposed. Taxpayers are told that their well-earned money is going to young people who would use bathroom doors not for a modicum of privacy but for plenty of criminal mischief, to those who do not give a damn about education and are in fact fearful of academic success lest they lose their street credibility and look like wimpy whites. Questions about the public school system's money management skills notwithstanding, funding should not be withheld because of the myth that the students would not take advantage of science labs, or better facilities, or well-trained teachers. The assumption is simply untrue.

These stories suggest how dangerous it is to base public policy on fuzzy conceptions of "good" or "bad" cultures. Our society generally asserts that each and every young person deserves a decent education, and the more privileged ones get it. Do students in Westchester County really deserve science labs more than Lisa or Michael? Michael flirted with gangs, but this is no reason to withhold educational opportunities; on the contrary, it suggests that a decent education would make that much more difference in his life. Instead of dismissing the academic struggles of inner-city young people as predictable given their supposed lack of motivation, the story of SBU suggests that these students have legitimate criticisms of the school system and should have a real say in education policy.

Ultimately, SBU's story is not an argument about good or bad values. It is a chronicle of empowerment and disempowerment. To a certain extent, teenagers will be teenagers, and SBU members should not be denied the opportunity to make mistakes and learn from them. Social control and cultural training programs will not yield a better future for children in the nation's inner cities, but listening to and acting upon their critiques will.

Until the sort of ownership, leadership, and empowerment present at SBU becomes more consistent and widespread throughout the New York City public school system, students like those described here will continue to strive to make sense of their schooling and to take matters into their own hands. As Nathaniel said, "In the meantime, you fight together. You learn. You get education. The best thing is to educate yourself. . . . There's a lot of things in books that they would never ever put into movies or anything like that." The movies are filled with stories of the one great teacher, the one great student who overcame all the odds. The rest of the youth, the ones left behind, may not all have the chance to participate in school reform movement organizations like SBU, but they are no less worthy of great teachers or of public education that makes a difference.

Substantive school reform is certainly a slow process; as an SBU organizer observed, "Our approach does not fit the model of 'Let's restructure these big failing schools quick, now, in a big way, before the next election.'"[49] But to calmly tolerate the status quo, or worse, to operate under the impression that the status quo is what these young people deserve or want, is to actively disempower them. It is to ignore their collective cries of anger and smother their dreams of hope.

Conclusion

Jeanne Theoharis

The separation provision rests neither upon prejudice, nor caprice. . . . Separation of white and colored "children" in the public schools of Virginia has for generations been a part of the mores of her people. To have separate schools has been their use and wont. We have found no hurt or harm to either race.

—*Davis v. County School Board of Prince Edward County,*
Federal District Court (1952)

In these days it is doubtful that any child may reasonably be expected to succeed in life if he is denied the opportunity of an education. Such an opportunity, where the state has undertaken to provide it, is a right which must be made available to all on equal terms.

—*Brown v. Board of Education* (U.S. Supreme Court, 1954)
347 U.S. 483 (1954)

It was not the inequality of the facilities but the fact of legally separating children based on race on which the Court relied to find a constitutional violation in that case *[Brown]*.

—*Community Schools v. Seattle* (U.S. Supreme Court, 2007)

Barbara, an African American junior, attended a school that enrolled no white students and contained twice as many children as it was built to hold. Classes sometimes took place in the school auditorium and other makeshift spaces. The district's only concession was to erect tarpaper shacks to hold the extra students that often were very cold. The school lacked a cafeteria and a gym. It had limited science labs, and the school did not offer physics, world history, or Latin. Teachers were underpaid and had to do jobs reserved for janitors in other schools.[1]

Tanisha, an African American junior, also attended a school that enrolled no white students and held nearly twice as many as students it was built to hold. Sometimes there were not enough desks, and students had to work at the teacher's desk or on top of the bookshelves. It was often too hot or too cold. The district's only concessions were to add trailers as extra classroom space and then move the school to a year-round schedule. The cafeteria was much too small and lunch period was only a half hour, so many of the students did not eat lunch. The school had limited science labs and few AP classes. Teachers were underpaid, and many were temporary.

The separate and unequal conditions of these young women's schooling bear a striking similarity. But a significant difference lies between them. Tanisha Smith attended Fremont High School in 2004. Barbara Johns, on the other hand, was one of the student leaders at Moton High School in 1951. The student strike she led against the poor and inequitable conditions at her school compared with the white school across town helped spur the lawsuit *Davis v. County School Board of Prince Edward County* (1952). This case, along with four others, formed the basis of the NAACP's suit in *Brown v. Board of Education* more than fifty years ago.

Much of our public conversation about *Brown* has sidestepped the similarities between the schools that educated Black and Latino students in the pre-*Brown* era and many of those that educate Black and Latino students today. Indeed, much of the public debate in the aftermath of the fiftieth anniversary of *Brown* has misrepresented the nature of the cases and the realities of present-day segregation. One of the key strands of the NAACP's case—embodied in the Moton High School student protest—was that these differences in resources, facilities, and teacher pay fundamentally compromised the kind of education Black children were receiving and, accordingly, Black advancement in American society.

Barbara Johns organized a student strike in 1951 after some of the Black male students who worked at the white high school after school came back and told her and her friends how nice the white high school was. She recalled, "I remember thinking how unfair it was." This difference between the schooling they were receiving and what white students were getting at the more well-equipped high school across town had become an inequality too great to bear. Students assembled in the school auditorium to hear Johns speak. She told her classmates that "it was time that Negroes were treated equally with whites, time that they had a decent high school, time for the students themselves to do something about it."² Segregation was a means of ensuring that school resources and high caliber education were financed collectively but not distributed equally. The NAACP's decades-long legal fight for desegregation thus arose as a challenge to these inequities and to the psychic cost exacted by living under an unequal system.

The narratives of the students gathered in the previous pages echo Johns's stirring speech. While Johns's schooling is all too similar to the experiences of the students in this book, the kind of education Tanisha Smith receives is now being justified by many people as the fault of her own values and the mores of her community rather than a disgrace to the spirit and substance of *Brown*. This book recenters the issue of segregation in the public discourse around education, in the process exposing the methods used to mask and maintain inequality in post–civil rights America. Like Barbara Johns, all of the young people in this book attend segregated schools—schools where the overwhelming majority of students are African American and Latino and where classes are dramatically overcrowded, bathrooms often in disrepair and unusable, AP classes and science labs few and far between, college counselors extremely scarce, and security guards often plentiful.³ These students, for the most part, tell us that they do not want to go to schools like these. They are, as CAI student Shawn explained in chapter 3, "trapped in an all right school." They do not like classes where they are not challenged, where they have more worksheets and less substantive work, where a number of teachers and administrators do not deem them to be capable of excellence. And some of these very students have organized strikes and rallies, attended town halls, and written petitions—all, like Johns, to protest the kind of education they are receiving. It is "time that they had a decent high school."

These students' perspectives give us an important window onto public schooling today. These young people insist on the right to tell their own stories and to criticize aspects of their schooling without that being distorted into a measure of their attitudes or motivation. As they talk back to those commentators making broad generalizations about their character, they reveal the deficiencies of many inner-city schools and the insufficiency of current reform efforts to address these problems. This final chapter pulls together the findings from these three case studies to show the kind of damage that the culture talk examined in the first chapter inflicts on young people's sense of self and the ways it helps justify the insufficient and inferior education they are provided. Beginning by situating the voices of students within the legal legacy of *Brown* and contemporary culture talk, the chapter then looks at how these students' experiences in school point to two central areas of concern: the bodily experience in school, which flows from the resources available in their schools, and the punitive, anti-intellectual way their schools are organized. Following that, an analysis of many of the popular reform efforts—No Child Left Behind (NCLB), mayoral control, and pedagogies for the poor—demonstrates that much of what currently passes for school reform is misguided and insulting. These reforms provide little accountability to students and do not actually address the concerns young people have with their schools. Thus we conclude with a proposed reformulation of NCLB to achieve more substantive public accountability to students and a call for a constitutional right to a quality education that would help establish the kind of equality that the *Brown* decision initially promised.

Moving Away from Equality

Contemporary American society has largely obfuscated the fundamental issue of educational equality that drove the NAACP's case in *Brown*. The five cases that were aggregated in *Brown* all showed significant disparities in the kind of education Black children were receiving in comparison to white children in the same district.[4] These inequalities took a toll on the material education Black children were receiving and on their sense of self and possibility. In its decision, a unanimous Supreme Court recognized that "the opportunity of an education . . . is a right which must be made available to all on equal terms."[5] The Court put off for another year the implementation order of the *Brown* decision, often referred to as *Brown II* (1955). After hearing testimony about how and on what time line desegregation should proceed (with the NAACP pressing for a strict timeline while the states urged gradualism), the Court returned oversight to the states, set no timetable for desegregation, and called for a "prompt and reasonable start towards full compliance . . . with all deliberate speed."[6] This put the onus back on Black parents and civil rights allies to push for desegregation, equity, and compliance with the law and meant that the principles of *Brown* would not become the reality of it.

As a result, ten years later, the overwhelming majority of school districts in the North and South—including New York and Los Angeles—remained segregated. Nevertheless, by the mid-1960s, both cities were engulfed in movements that highlighted the tremendous disparities between the education that white and nonwhite children were receiving.

Local activists, such as Kenneth Clark (whose research formed part of the basis for the NAACP's case in *Brown*), Ella Baker, Rev. Milton Galamison, and Annie Pearl, called on New York public officials to create a comprehensive desegregation plan that would address and remedy the educational inequities rife within city schools. In 1958, parents in Harlem and Bedford Stuyvesant refused to send their children to segregated schools.[7] The Parents' Workshop started by Galamison and Pearl joined with the NAACP and CORE to press the city to create a plan for desegregation. On February 3, 1964, 464,361 students boycotted New York's public schools to demand a plan and timetable for comprehensive desegregation of the city's schools—the largest civil rights demonstration to date in the history of the United States, eclipsing the numbers of the legendary 1963 March on Washington. Yet no substantive plan resulted; the Board of Education, like the *New York Times,* claimed that "there is, of course, no official segregation in the city."[8] Caving to the pressure of white parents, the New York Board of Education refused to implement any comprehensive desegregation of New York schools and substantially address the inequities in education that white and nonwhite children in New York experienced.

School segregation also worsened in Los Angeles after the *Brown* decision. As the *California Eagle* subsequently reported, "More Negro children attend all-Negro schools in Los Angeles than attend such schools in Little Rock."[9] The overwhelming majority of Black students were not tracked for college, and the curriculum reflected racial biases and "happy slave tales." Contrary to prevalent belief about northern segregation, school segregation did not simply derive from racialized housing patterns. Local and state officials systematically and methodically worked to solidify residential segregation and to distribute educational resources inequitably through the creation of racially homogenous districts, restrictive hiring, and other bureaucratic measures. During the early 1960s the NAACP, CORE, and ACLU pressed the Board of Education and organized local protests at schools. The summer of 1963 brought regular downtown marches to protest at the Board of Education, which *still* had not responded to civil rights groups. Movement leaders grew increasingly frustrated with the board's inaction, and national civil rights leaders—like Martin Luther King, James Farmer, and James Forman—joined local activists to protest L.A.'s school inequities. They held silent protests in the boardroom, conducted sit-ins, held protests at individual schools, and filed suit in court. Yet, like New York's administrators, LAUSD officials refused to carry out any substantive desegregation and blamed the problems of schools largely on the values and motivation of students of color and their parents.[10]

These movements met not only local resistance but also a Supreme Court that by the 1970s limited the implementation of *Brown*'s promise of equality. In 1973, in *San Antonio Independent School District v. Rodriguez*, the U.S. Supreme Court reversed a Texas District Court's decision that education was a fundamental right which thus rendered inequities of school financing constitutionally pressing. While the Supreme Court acknowledged that *Brown* had affirmed that "education is perhaps the most important function of state and local governments," it found that "education, of course, is not among the rights afforded explicit protection under our Federal Constitution. Nor do we find any basis for saying it is implicitly so protected."[11] Having ruled that education was not a "fundamental" right or interest, the Court maintained that reliance on local property taxes to fund public schools, even while causing significant disparities, was constitutional because local control over schools represented a legitimate state interest.[12] This decision, in effect, ensured that poorer districts would never receive equal funding to build equal schools—and that having a right to equal protection did not extend to attending an equally funded school.

In *Milliken v. Bradley* the next year, the Court reversed a district and court of appeals remedy that had created metropolitan superdistricts (linking the city of Detroit with its suburbs) to remedy the de jure segregation found in Detroit's schools. Despite extensive evidence of the intentional nature of Detroit's school segregation, the decision exempted suburban districts from any role in or responsibility for remedying segregated urban school systems and subsequently reinforced the existing trend of white flight from cities to suburban school districts. Calling the decision "a giant step backwards" from *Brown* and an "emasculation of our constitutional guarantee of equal protection of the laws," Thurgood Marshall in his dissent observed, "Notwithstanding a record showing widespread and pervasive racial segregation . . . this Court holds that the District Court was powerless to require the State to remedy its constitutional violation in any meaningful fashion . . . , thereby guaranteeing that Negro children in Detroit will receive the same separate and inherently unequal education in the future as they have been unconstitutionally afforded in the past."[13]

Rodriguez and *Milliken* had far-reaching consequences for schoolchildren in urban areas like New York and Los Angeles, as they sheltered inequality through a legal claim of local preference and control (much as the lower courts had done in the Moton High School case back in 1952). The well-to-do suburbs that ringed both New York and L.A. spent far more per pupil than the city could and sent more of their students to college and beyond, even as many of these suburban residents continued to use the city for work and leisure. Thus school inequities continued to widen in the 1980s and 1990s. Tellingly, while the percentage of adults with college degrees in L.A. County has climbed to over 25 percent (from 4 percent in 1940), the percentage of college graduates among adults who have attended Fremont has remained largely the same *over the past sixty years* (hovering just under 5 percent in 2000).

On the fiftieth anniversary of the *Brown* decision, many public figures and institutions—including the Supreme Court in its 2007 decision in *Community Schools v. Seattle*—obscured these widening inequalities and their consequences for American democracy. Claiming that the task of *Brown* was to end legalized racial classification and separation (rather than promote equity), the Court maintained that *Brown's* goal was long since realized. Writing for the 5-4 majority in *Seattle,* Chief Justice John Roberts asserted that voluntary school desegregation programs in Seattle and Louisville were an "extreme approach" and that striking these programs down was "more faithful to the heritage of *Brown*."[14] In a rhetorical sleight of hand, Justice Roberts explained the Court's decision: "When it comes to using race to assign children to schools, history will be heard. . . . *It was not the inequality of the facilities but the fact of legally separating children based on race on which the Court relied to find a constitutional violation in that case [Brown]*" [emphasis added].[15] The Court now stated that *Brown* had sought to address the use of race in school assignment rather than the ways race was used a mechanism to promote inequality.[16] It was as if Barbara Johns had staged protests because she was excluded from the company of white students, not because she observed a pattern of superior resources and facilities in the white high school. The use of racial categories, rather than the existence of two very different kinds of education being offered fifty years ago and tragically still here today, had become the social evil.

While many commentators (including the *New York Times* editorial page and four members of the Supreme Court) deplored the *Seattle* decision, there has nevertheless been a dangerous capitulation to these terms of the debate. Much of the public conversation has been trapped in a false debate around whether the remedy in *Brown* implied that color-blindness was the goal. On the cover page of the *New York Times Week in Review*, Jeffrey Rosen summed up the question before the Court in *Seattle* as "Was the purpose of *Brown* to achieve a colorblind society or an integrated one?"[17]—a question that serious scholars of the period (not to mention Johns herself) would argue misses the central challenge to educational inequality at the heart of the NAACP's case in *Brown*.

The response to the *Seattle* decision has been a further shrinking of what is imagined to be possible and a hardening fatalism about the kind of education that will be provided for many of our nation's young people. In his *New York Times* editorial on the decision, *Enough* author Juan Williams called on the nation to "bury" the *Brown* decision, claiming that its time and utility were over. Ignoring the Court's own record of retrenchment in the 1970s and 1980s and the hypersegregated, unequal schools many young people attend in a country that boasts some of the best public schools in the world, Williams still claimed that "the last 20 years . . . *Brown* [was] in full force."[18] A certain naturalizing of inequality has come to characterize public discourse. *New York Times* columnist David Brooks in his response to the *Seattle* decision observed, "But it could be the dream of integration itself is the problem. It could be that it was like the dream of early communism—a nice dream, but not fit for the way people really are. . . . People say they want to live in diverse integrated communities, but what they really want to do is live in homogenous ones, filled with people like themselves."[19] Equitable primary and secondary education has now been reduced to a fanciful dream of integration rather than a substantive constitutional guarantee. Williams similarly concludes in his aforementioned editorial, "And today the argument that school reform should provide equal opportunities for children, or prepare them to live in a pluralistic society, is spent."[20]

The fatalism embodied in giving up the fight for equal opportunities for children seems contradictory to the nation's professed beliefs. Americans hold fast to the idea of democratic meritocracy embodied in our educational system, a system that is supposed to give every child a chance to succeed, no matter the circumstances into which she or he is born. We distance ourselves from countries with elitist screening processes that reserve access to good education to a chosen few. In post–civil rights America, many people maintain that while the country might have been flawed by racism in the past this is no longer the case. On the heels of the Supreme Court's *Seattle* decision, Gallup asked Americans, "In general, do you think that Black children have as good a chance as white children in your community to get a good education, or don't you think they have as good a chance?" Overall, three-quarters of Americans polled said "yes," they believed Black children had the same chance as white children in their communities to get a good education.[21]

Pick on Someone Your Own Size

> I wonder, too, what is invisible in today's world that allows so many in our polity, few of whom are declared segregationists, to think that an all-white classroom is exactly the same as an all-Black classroom is exactly the same as an all-Asian or all-Hispanic classroom. . . . What narratives are we inventing to justify the gross racial divisions, the callous disproportions, the cruel imbalances . . . in the equality of citizenship that begins with the image of that eager, lonely child on her first day of school, for whom all things might be possible, if we only willed it so?
>
> —Columbia University law professor Patricia Williams,
> "Invisible America" (2007)

The disjuncture between the culture talk surveyed in chapter 1 and the perspectives of young people highlighted in the subsequent three chapters reveals "the narratives we [are] inventing to justify the gross racial divisions, the callous disproportions."[22] This post–civil rights discourse of segregation—lambasting African American and Latino youth for their "cool poses," fears of "acting white," and lack of work ethic and regard for education—creates a false and frightening image of these young people. In doing so, it helps hide the existence of two very different kinds of education available in this country.

While presenting the problem as unprecedented and urgent, scholars and public figures who locate the problem in the values and motivations of African American and Latino communities are actually repeating a timeworn explanation for the racial achievement gap. In the postwar period, and particularly post-*Brown*, local and state officials in many northern cities, seeking to distinguish themselves from their southern counterparts, deployed very similar culture talk to deflect burgeoning movements for school desegregation in their own backyards.[23] While school officials in many northern cities did not feel comfortable publicly proclaiming "segregation now and forever," they did not mind calling Black, Chicano, and Puerto Rican students inferior, unmotivated, and culturally deprived and framing parents as "uncommitted to their children's education."[24] In both New York and L.A., teachers and administrators in the 1950s and 1960s often took up a sociological language of "cultural deprivation" and devoted increasing amounts of money to programs to address "delinquency" but refused to systematically deal with resource differentials and segregated schools. Simultaneously, they built a security apparatus in many city schools and introduced new forms of school discipline, including expulsion, which by the mid-1960s was used on increasing numbers of Black and Latino students. Revealingly, facing a growing desegregation movement in Los Angeles, the Board of Education issued a report in September 1963 that placed responsibility for problems in the schools outside the district's purview, notably "the lack of hope and motivation among some of these [Black and Mexican American] families which leads them into negative attitudes toward education and the demands the school makes on their children."[25] Since overt support of segregation was seen as the distasteful purview of southern racists, this culture talk gained force in postwar political discourse because it provided a socially acceptable rhetoric to forestall desegregation and equity for African American and Latino young people.

Thus when contemporary public figures like Orlando Patterson, Elijah Anderson, John Ogbu, Bill Cosby, Herman Badillo, and Alejandro Portes background issues of overcrowding, decrepit physical plants, insufficient resources, and lack of access to college preparatory curricula in favor of highlighting a newly urgent crisis of declining values in the African American and Latino communities, they are actually deploying a language public officials have been using for more than fifty years to maintain the segregation of children of color. Talking about the culture of Black and Latino students has long been a successful way to deflect issues of segregation precisely because it provides a socially palatable rationale for differential educational outcomes.

The voices of the young people in this book return our attention to the structure of their schools, the content of their classes, and, more broadly, the ways their beliefs and their very personhood have been distorted. They demonstrate the profound ways in which most students value education and wish to succeed academically and make their families proud, as well as the degree to which the nature and character of the education they are receiving compromises this. Looking at schools from South Central L.A. to the South Bronx demonstrates what a feat it is that students work hard and stay focused despite the deplorable condition of their schools. With "so many in the class," young people often have trouble getting noticed, let alone receiving the individual attention they deserve. The students in each case study eloquently critiqued the boring, punitive nature of much of their schooling and the ways high-stakes testing and heavy school security compromised the educational climate of their schools. They yearned for, and spoke lovingly of, classes where they "really learned" and teachers who "really pushed them," and they repeatedly acknowledged parents who believed in them—"My mama is the reason I have a future."

These three ethnographies spanned a diversity of urban students, of young people on both coasts, of native-born students and immigrants, of Africans Americans, Latinos, and immigrants from Mexico, Central America, and the Caribbean. They were politicized students and athletes, hip-hop youth, church choir singers, and punk rockers, students who had seen little success in their high school context as well as those who had been identified by teachers as academically talented. All three ethnographies reveal the vulnerability of these young people and the ways their sense of self was influenced by the damaging public discourse about them. They measured their souls, as W. E. B. Du Bois observed a century earlier, "by the tape of a world that looks on in amused contempt and pity"[26] and in so doing sometimes lost confidence in themselves and in their capacities as writers and creators, innovators and thinkers.

As young person after young person in each of these studies outlines his or her aspirations for college, describes favorite classes, expresses a desire for more challenging coursework, and explains the ways in which he or she is treated with suspicion by many teachers, storeowners, and employers, the disingenuousness of claims that African American and Latino youth no longer value education becomes clear. But there is a great distinction between believing that education is important and necessary for future success and believing—and being treated as if—you are capable of succeeding academically. While a number of these students were not succeeding academically and some have subsequently dropped out, this occurred not primarily because they devalued education but because they had lost confidence in themselves and the school to do right by them. Aspirations do not equal opportunity: wanting to go to college and working hard to achieve that goal is a far cry from getting to go. Most of the young people in this book hoped to attend college, yet only a minority are now attending four-year institutions.

Through their insistence that cultural values rather than structural conditions are the culprit, public figures like Bill Cosby, Juan Williams,

Barack Obama, and John McWhorter have grown prominent and prosperous. But there is something unseemly about the way powerful men are attacking much less powerful young people who have little opportunity to fight back and make their own case. When young people grow demoralized, taking these insults and the kind of education they receive as a sign of the society's disrespect toward them, they are chastised for their bad attitude. And when they dare complain, when they say that their school "sucks," or self-protectively assert to a well-meaning sociologist that they "didn't care anyway," they are treated as *the* problem.

While public figures like Barack Obama harp on the problem that "if you conjugate your verbs and if you read a book that somehow means you are acting white,"[27] the young people in the previous pages did not frame this as a central concern for them. The students who were succeeding in school did not talk about being reviled for that success, nor did students who were struggling in school justify their position by denigrating academic success as a form of "acting white." Indeed, not a single student across our three studies ever mentioned the fear of "acting white." Instead, these young people talked back to adults who treated them as "fxxx-ups," "aliens," and "criminals." These young people were acutely aware of how others looked at them. As CAI student Shawn poignantly explained, the ways in which he was viewed with suspicion affected his own sense of himself: "Sometimes folks look at you so hard you think you stole something even though you didn't. . . . That's like some psychological control. . . . Like being watched and that makes you feel guilty." These young people chafed under the weight, as Du Bois had a century earlier, of being seen as a "problem" and could not simply separate themselves from the ways they were viewed. Many, like Fremont student Johanna, praised teachers who asked "for a lot more than the usual person," adding, "but that's a good thing." Others were sidetracked by adults who lacked confidence in their abilities: Jacobo, for instance, wrote of wanting to study architecture or computer science in college but explained that his counselor "said that she wants me to get a job for next year and drop three classes so that I can get out by lunch."

Like Barbara Johns fifty years before them, the teenagers we studied knew that other kids' schools were cleaner, less crowded, and more well appointed—and understood the social value conferred with these differences. Indeed, their experiences point to the ways such young people see the substantial inequities still found in our nation's schools as a reflection on themselves. These young people were quick to blame themselves when things went wrong. Over and over, most expressed a deep sense of personal responsibility, explaining how "it depends on me" and "it's all about not giving up." Kinyel, a Fremont student, explained that he didn't "want to be the guy in a couple of years in a trash can." CAI student Angelo worried about landing "in prison." The fear that making one mistake or losing focus would end in catastrophe pervaded many of these young people's narratives.

These young people are judged by a different standard than their peers. In most suburban high schools, many young people show little enthusiasm for school—but this is not used as a rationale to justify phasing out science and history from their high schools' curricula, nor does it prevent most of these young people from going on and often excelling in college. Anti-intellectualism pulses throughout American society from the White House to White Plains, from inner-city high schools in Chicago to suburban ones in Wisconsin. President George W. Bush often boasts about the merits of being a C student, in the process denigrating academic success: "When I'm with Condi I say she's the Ph.D. and I'm the C student, and just look at who's the president and who's the advisor."[28] And at Yale's 2001 commencement, he proclaimed, "To the C students, I say, 'You too can be president of the United States.'"[29] Despite the president's repeated jokes about being a C student, no one suggests that a more focused curriculum with more reading and less science, social studies, and electives at Phillips Academy, on top of stricter disciplinary procedures, would have made the difference in the president's academic performance. One also wonders if President Bush would make the same comment at Fremont or Clinton high schools or if this kind of anti-intellectual camaraderie is reserved for the Ivy League. In a society that celebrates equal treatment, there seems to be no need to grant young people of color treatment equal to that of their more affluent, white counterparts—the room to make mistakes, adopt various poses, and come into their own in an excellent school environment.

Prominent African American and Latino men like Cosby, Williams, and Badillo have been granted a tremendous public platform and praise for "telling hard truths" in calling out and criticizing the anti-intellectualism of young people of color.[30] Garnering immense publicity, including a one-hour special of NBC'S *Meet the Press* with limited commercials, Bill Cosby and Dr. Alvin Pouissant teamed up to create a self-help book for parents and committed adults entitled *Come On, People: On the Path from Victims to Victors.* They have been celebrated for their courage and leadership when in fact what they say corresponds to views already held by the public. Cautioning against "packaging the center right wisdom of the moment as a well-considered, yet bold and personally risky challenge to convention," political scientist Adolph Reed has explained the allure of Black middle-class men speaking out about the problems within the Black community. "It flatters their success by comparison and, through the insipid role model rhetoric, allows fawning over the allegedly special role of the Black middle class."[31]

Advancing cultural theories may be a way to gain prominence and prosperity in American society today, but it also helps sustain a system of educational inequality. Indeed, when placed alongside the perspectives of the young people gathered in this volume, these cultural theories appear more complacent than courageous, more nihilistic than truth-telling. If these kids are believed to be the problem because of their self-inflicted actions and unrestrained behaviors, there is no need to expend precious resources on them—no need for Patterson or McWhorter to roll up their sleeves and teach ninth grade, no need for Cosby and Badillo to expend their political capital to press school districts like LAUSD to make college preparation the default high school curriculum, no need for Williams to rally his journalist friends to mentor students in schools strapped for counselors. Rather, these young people have to demonstrate their worthiness for efforts to be spent on them, which sets up a dangerous Catch-22: once you have to prove your worth, you affirm the possibility that you are not worthy.

While these public figures seem nostalgic for the pride and determination of the pre-*Brown* Black community, there is little recognition that pre-*Brown* calls for uplift and self-help explicitly recognized that educational conditions were unjust and unfair. Now, Cosby and Poussaint declare, "The doors of opportunity are no longer locked, and we have to walk through."[32] This is part of the setup that leads young people to try hard and then lose confidence in themselves, when real opportunities—or even decent treatment by adults—are not forthcoming. However, the focus on poor values, baggy clothes, broken English, and fears of "acting white" offers a tremendous amount of psychic comfort to a society that does not want to provide these young people with a quality equal education but still wants to maintain that all people are treated equal. In post–civil rights America, where people want to believe that everyone has an equal opportunity for a good education, the existence of schools like Fremont and Clinton would produce too much cognitive dissonance without it.

There is a revealing difference between the students at Fremont and CAI and the young people who make up SBU—not in terms of character or life experience but in terms of empowerment and self-confidence. Many of the SBU students gained a language and a larger frame with which to view and analyze the structure of their schooling and, through this, a sense of personal and collective empowerment. "I did not want to sit in all of those long meetings," SBU student Lisa explained. "I'm hungry, I just finished a day of school, and I want to go home and sleep. But I have to sit there, because if not, there won't be enough representation there." SBU students came to see the troubles with their schooling not only as a result of their personal decisions but also of the disparate structures of education that exist in American society. Rosalinda explained the sense of empowerment that came from having adults take seriously her analysis of New York's schools: "It has helped me a lot to understand how New York City itself works, not only the education system, but the government itself. . . . And sometimes we say, 'Hey, you have to go back and do this,' and they [city officials] actually listen." By rejecting the ways they were seen as "a problem," the SBU students were able to critique the structure of the schooling they were receiving and imagine a different educational future for themselves and their peers.

When Young People Talk Back: Findings from the Schools

The young people's perspectives explored in the three studies reveal a great deal about the problems with urban public schooling today and provide a roadmap for educational change. They demonstrate two central areas of concern: the bodily experience students have in school, which derives largely from the resources available to their schools, and the governance and organizational structure of their schools and the anti-intellectual nature of many of their classes.

In terms of the bodily experience young people have of inner-city schools, these schools are variously too hot, too dirty, too crowded, with too much security but not actually safe, and often without reliable access to the bathrooms. They often smell of urine, disinfectant, and too many bodies. The halls, bathrooms, and guidance offices are crowded. Students are often forced to wait for long periods of time to see a guidance counselor, let alone a college counselor. And in some schools, it can take an hour to even enter school through the metal detectors. Classrooms often lack windows (or have windows that cannot open or close). Bathrooms are not always open, there are often fewer available than even what is required by law, and access is severely restricted. As SBU student Lisa explained, there was only one bathroom at her school, and only one of the stalls had a lock; the other four stalls had no doors. The lack of dignity conveyed through these conditions is palpable. "And it's crazy overcrowded: one teacher for thirty-seven students," which meant that Lisa had to sit on a radiator in her classroom. "It was turned on, and it was hot. You shouldn't have to go through that."

Yet students felt like they had to make the best of it. Trying to be nonchalant, they attempted to take it all in stride. Lisa continued, "Clinton's a good school. Facilities aren't that good, and the bathrooms are the most disgusting things in the world, but . . . I try to make the best out of everything." In sum, there is not only a great deal of bodily disrespect that students are forced to endure simply in attending urban schools but also an expectation that they should endure these indignities without being discouraged.

Is it possible to learn under these conditions? Absolutely—and many of these young people attested to that, over and over, in their attempts to make the best of difficult situations. But would they have learned more and better if their classrooms had been clean and spacious and the right temperature, if they had had reliable access to bathrooms and an adequate lunch break in the middle of the day, if they had not had to wait in long lines to come into school or see a counselor? No doubt—and this is the opportunity question that many of these commentators have avoided asking.

Resources are in short supply in such schools. There are not enough books, chairs, or working computers and often no science equipment, music rooms, or art classes. Students have to find makeshift workspaces in crowded classrooms, working at the teacher's desk, perching on bookshelves, or sitting atop radiators or ledges. Indeed, many schools rely on truancy to make the classrooms livable—and there are few resources to call students who are absent from school. The libraries are small and often not open or are being used for other school functions (such as testing and meetings) and not available to students. Science labs are rare or nonexistent. Up-to-date computers and working printers are hard to find—and few classrooms exist where every student could use the computer. Art, music, photography, graphic design, architecture, world religions, law and society, multiple foreign languages—the high-powered electives offered by elite public high schools like New York City's Stuyvesant High School or Beverly Hills High School—are nowhere to be found in these inner-city schools. Such rigorous electives are not extra luxuries, as parents who send their children to elite schools attest. These kinds of classes open up intellectual terrain for young people to imagine trajectories for themselves and then gain knowledge and experience in those fields even before they go to college. At schools like Lisa's, worksheets and other skill-and-drill exercises are plentiful, and the right classes are hard to get. So students are shoved into classes that are much too easy and often inappropriate to their college aspirations.

Finally, these schools resemble warehouses or juvenile detention centers in their organizational design and governance. Often there is ample police presence on campus. The trappings of security rather than educational excellence are the operational fetish in the kinds of schools these young people attend. In some schools, there is the daily humiliation (not to mention the tremendous amount of time) of waiting in line to pass through metal detectors. In all of them, security officers form a regular, aggressive presence. This security apparatus, accompanied by the regime of high-stakes testing, contributes to a largely punitive, rather than challenging or interesting, school experience. Classes are built around the testing standards, and increasingly electives and even science and history are short-shrifted for the "basics." Raymond, a CAI student, explained, "Like, it's not even about learning. . . . It's about just getting the information. . . . You don't even need to be smart . . . just, like, pay attention and memorize." Shawn, also from CAI, likened his math class to a "sweatshop." But this had not always been how Shawn felt about math. He recalled fondly, "In eighth grade, see math was fun, you know. We did all kinds of fun things looking at math in the real world. Took trips and looked at shapes and did the geometry on them. It was fun. You did worksheets and stuff, but that was like part of a bigger goal of math."

Like Shawn, numerous students looked back nostalgically at history or math classes they "used to love" and extolled the classes that had "bigger goals" in which they "really learned." The climate of high-stakes testing has influenced the curriculum and simultaneously produced a deeply individualizing effect: students learn to see themselves as responsible for what they have learned. As Fremont student Amy explained, "About math and science . . . there is some problems that I really don't know, don't understand, but I think that if I try and try I could understand it." Exacerbating this punitive environment is tremendous overcrowding and a lack of individualized attention. Year-round schooling, extending the school

day, and other kinds of jerry-rigged scheduling may fulfill district prag-
matics, but they also create overly long and tiring schedules that make it
difficult for students to learn to their potential.

What's Wrong with Current Approaches

> The purpose of education, finally, is to create in a person the ability to
> look at the world for himself, to make his own decisions, to say to him-
> self this is black or this is white, to decide for himself whether there is a
> God in heaven or not. To ask questions of the universe, and then learn
> to live with those questions, is the way he achieves his own identity. But
> no society is really anxious to have that kind of person around.
> —James Baldwin, "A Talk to Teachers" (1963)

These young people's discussions of their schooling and its problems differ
greatly from those initiated by pundits, policy makers, and many school
officials. On March 19, 2005, the Education Committee of the New York
City Council devoted a Saturday to hear testimony from young people
and noted a similar gap. Fifty-four students testified, with more than a
hundred attending. They described harassment by security guards, little
physical education and art in their schools, limited science classes and
few labs, and closed and dirty bathrooms. In its report, the committee
was "especially troubled by the disconnect between student testimony and
previous statements made by high-level Department of Education representatives. What is happening on the ground in classrooms differs sharply
from the 'reality' described by the officials at Tweed [the location of the
New York City Department of Education]."[33]

What the committee pointedly observed—and what is clear from the
students in these pages—is that student perspectives diverge profoundly
from the picture being painted of the schools by education officials. Urban
schools are approached as a political abstraction, not as a lived experience
of millions of young people each year, and thus the bodily experience of
going to an overcrowded, undermaintained school is often glossed over.

Many recent reform efforts, from the federal No Child Left Behind
(NCLB) to more local initiatives (such as charter schools, mayoral control, and vouchers) to targeted pedagogies for poor students and their
parents, have concentrated on accountability measures and governance
structures. These reform efforts operate from the twin principles of ratio-
nal technocracy (that the problem with schools is ineffective governance,

so with better standards and more effective control they can be fixed) and a fundamental trust in institutions (that racism has been corrected and that institutions now operate fairly and openly). As a result, they keep segregation and inequality in place and offer little accountability of the school system *to* students and their families.

NCLB's Counterfeit Accountability

With its promise "to close the achievement gap," NCLB was advocated by President George W. Bush and passed in Congress in 2001 with over-whelming bipartisan support.[34] NCLB marked the national culmination of what Jonathan Kozol has deemed as the application of "the 'scientific' model of accountability and measurement that conspicuously applies to the practices of business management to guarantee efficiency in operation of a classroom, school, or district."[35] At the federal level, NCLB promised accountability but has instead pushed schools to give sixty-five million more mandated tests on top of those already being given.[36] At the same time, it has provided little in actual school resources, increased teacher salaries, or the additional counselors needed to change academic perfor-mance at these schools.[37] Indeed, NCLB's form of accountability has not included much accountability in the reverse direction: the federal govern-ment is not making itself responsible for failing schools and committing itself to transforming them.

Under the act's provisions, schools that for the first two consecutive years of its implementation fail to meet specified Annual Yearly Progress (AYP) goals are deemed to be "in need of improvement." These schools have to notify parents of their failure to meet NCLB goals and of parents' ability to transfer their children to better-performing schools within the same district at the school's expense. Schools that fail to meet AYP goals for a third year have to continue to offer parents the ability to transfer their children. They also have to put in place "supplemental services" to help improve students' test scores. Schools that fail to meet goals for a fourth year are then required to take "corrective actions," such as increas-ing district control of the school and firing staff members. Schools that fail to meet the goals for a fifth year must be "reconstituted" by being closed down, placed under state control, or placed under the control of a charter school or private education firm.

Half a decade after the passage of NCLB, there is mounting evidence that a majority of public schools, perhaps as high as 70 percent, will not meet the 2013–14 AYP goals. Schools that serve large minority and/or immigrant populations have been particularly hard hit. A study of California schools found that those with a large number of racial or ethnic subgroups were "penalized" during the first two years of NCLB implementation. Specifically, the study found that "schools serving lower income families and their children, *on average*, are less likely to have achieved their AYP growth targets." Schools in which students' scores do not improve face sanctions that require them to shift funds toward financing the transfers of students to other schools as well as the contracting of "supplemental services" mandated by NCLB. When they most need their operating budgets, they are forced to slash them for the sake of private contractors. However well intentioned, NCLB in effect tells the nation's poor schools to do more with even less. At the end of the fifth year of the act's implementation, close to two thousand schools have failed to meet AYP goals and will need to be "reconstituted."[38] Thus, as Kozol has noted, "All these schools, under the stipulations of No Child Left Behind, will soon be ripe for picking by private corporations."[39]

Preliminary studies also suggest that the NCLB-fueled drive to improve scores on standardized tests has led schools to increasingly "teach to the test," focusing on the content and baseline skills necessary to pass tests to the exclusion of other content and skills. A study by the U.S. Department of Education found that about 52 percent of school districts have reformed their curricula to concentrate more on content areas covered by state tests.[40] In 2007, the Center for Education Policy surveyed 349 school districts across the country and found that since NCLB had been implemented, "about 62% of districts reported that they have increased time for English language arts (ELA) and/or math in elementary schools." The survey revealed that "to accommodate this increased time in ELA and math, 44% of districts reported cutting time from one or more other subjects or activities (social sciences, science, art, and music, physical education, lunch, and/or recess)." On average, these districts reported a 31 percent reduction of instructional time for these subjects.[41] As more and more school time is taken up by test preparation or by testing itself, students are being given a very impoverished vision of the purpose and breadth of education.[42]

NCLB thus provides a "counterfeit accountability," as educator Stan Karp has noted, "that sorts and labels kids on the basis of multiple-choice questions as a substitute for the much more difficult and more costly process of real school improvement."[43] The promise that children attending low-performing schools will be able to transfer to better-performing schools in the same district has largely turned out to be a mirage. There are not enough good schools to which such students can transfer, especially in many urban districts where African American and Latino students are concentrated. Unable to transfer, poor and working-class students of color remain trapped in racially segregated and unequal—and increasingly stigmatized—schools where teachers face mounting pressure to "teach to the test."

Mayoral Control and Local "Reforms"

In local school reform efforts, the emphasis on accountability over equality has also reigned supreme. Both New York and Los Angeles have engaged in far-reaching educational reform efforts, with Mayors Bloomberg and Villaraigosa leading the charge for more local accountability. The subject of a *60 Minutes* special, Mayor Bloomberg has emerged as a major voice in urban school politics, and in April 2007 Villaraigosa invited Bloomberg to Los Angeles to discuss his strategies. Both Bloomberg and Villaraigosa have spoken candidly about the problems facing their school systems (the two largest in the nation) and have pushed for widespread reform. In both New York and Los Angeles, the move to mayoral control, the breaking up of large high schools into small schools, and the use of so-called "learning communities" constitute the battery of reforms recently on display.

With an increasingly technocratic approach to education, school reform in both cities has been ushered in through the centralization of authority and power. Shortly after coming into office in 2002, Bloomberg convinced the New York State Legislature to turn control of city schools over to him rather than the Board of Education. Doing away with the last vestiges of community control, the state also allowed the mayor to appoint eight of the thirteen members of the board—now called the Panel for Education Policy—and abolished the thirty-two community school boards. Bloomberg hired former Bertelsmann counsel and Department of Justice antitrust lawyer Joel Klein, who had little experience in education policy or pedagogy, to be chancellor. In 2003, Bloomberg unveiled his "Children First" plan. The plan included a mix of increased principal authority, centralization, subcontracting of school services, and an overriding emphasis on a narrow definition of accountability. Bloomberg has approached this with an authoritarian streak—when members of the Panel for Education Policy communicated their intent to vote against his policy proposal on third-grade retention, he simply dismissed them from the panel.

A key part of Bloomberg's governance strategy has been an expansion of school discipline and policing. School security had changed dramatically in New York City under Bloomberg's predecessor Rudolph Giuliani, who succeeded in getting the board to transfer control of school safety to the New York Police Department. Bloomberg continued this policy—and the lack of public accountability that has attended it, since the police do not answer to teachers or principals in schools. Mayor Bloomberg placed more security agents in the city's most dangerous schools and then announced the opening of a series of "New Beginnings" suspension centers for disruptive students who were being removed from their schools.[44] In 2004, Bloomberg announced a new school safety initiative known as "Impact Schools," which targeted twenty-six schools with high levels of reported crime. This initiative expanded three zero-tolerance strategies in the public schools: doubling the number of police officers in these schools, cracking down on even minor incidents of disorderly behavior, and expediting the punishment and often the removal of students who broke the rules. But a report by the Drum Major Institute found that the Impact Schools "were more overcrowded than the average city high school, were far larger than most city high schools, received less funding per student for direct services, had more students overage for their grade, and served a student body that was disproportionately comprised of poor and Black students as compared to the average New York City public high school."[45]

The city has refused to disclose the number of schools with permanent metal detectors, but an investigation by the New York Civil Liberties Union estimates that at eighty-eight schools students must pass through metal detectors every day (with most having long lines with students waiting for long periods just to get into school)—not to mention the roving metal detectors that Mayor Bloomberg announced in 2006. Notably, within New York public schools, the schools with permanent metal detectors receive less funding than others—a $9,601 per-pupil expenditure against a citywide average of $11,282.[46] They are also significantly overcrowded: New York public schools overall enroll 6 percent higher than the city has the physical capacity to educate, but at metal detector schools there are 18 percent more children than seats. The number of school safety officers that now police New York schools is up to 4,625 from 3,200 in 1998.[47] This expansion in school policing has resulted in increased complaints of excessive violence. Police commissioner Ray Kelly reported to the city council that there had been almost 2,800 complaints about excessive violence by school safety agents in New York City schools since 2002. Of these, 27 percent have been substantiated thus far, a much higher percentage than by the Civilian Complaint Review Board for the NYPD in general.[48]

In the spring of 2007 the city announced a pilot program, to be run by Harvard economist Roland Fryer and paid for by private money, to pay students and their parents for doing well on standardized tests. They followed this move with another program to pay teachers that could boast good test scores in their classes, and then a third program to pay students for doing well on AP tests.[49] Money that could be used to improve the schools—for instance, to actually provide AP classes for all students interested—is now being directed toward a largely untested incentive system. While the Bloomberg administration has touted this compendium of authority-centralizing, market-based reforms as finally dealing with the quality of schooling being provided, the policies miss other crucial issues of school organization, such as overcrowding (and double-session scheduling), tracking, and the structure of the curriculum and available classes. Moreover, in a number of the small schools in New York City, the class size remains high, and teachers are not given additional time to plan together. The pedagogical advantages of these models as they have been implemented (rather than originally conceived) have been slight, but the ideological advantages of the repetition of "small schools" over and over in public discourse has been more significant (as if saying "small schools" could erase large class sizes). Additionally, some small schools in New York admit better students and shunt off English-language learners and students who struggle academically to other schools.[50] These selective small schools have posted higher test scores and graduation rates—and have subsequently been held up as proof of the soundness of the mayor's plan. Moreover, many schools have pushed out students after age eighteen, even though they are allowed to stay until age twenty-one. Thus the gains of the Bloomberg reforms to the *entire* student population have been minimal.

As part of the school reforms being implemented in both cities, students and families are encouraged to "choose" to move away from high schools of last resort like Fremont and DeWitt Clinton. These schools then become schools of last resort, and students who attend them are believed to be those who are unable or unwilling to gain admission to better schools. This "reform" reinforces the dominant view that effective parents and students have real options (even as the vast majority do not, since there are simply not enough spaces in these better schools, charter schools, or magnet programs) and thus that enrollment at schools like DeWitt or Fremont is a bad "choice" students and their parents have made. Ultimately, it encourages what UCLA professors Jeannie Oakes and John Rogers have described as a "triage" mentality: that the best that can be done by policy makers is to "save" a few rather than to build a system that would serve every student well.[51] The image of a free marketplace of schools, while trumpeted as providing more and better options to students who avail themselves of the opportunities, functions largely as an excuse for leaving low-performing schools as they are. There is no meaningful way for all students to succeed in these schools, and hard work alone is no match for the obstacles to education that the schools present. Certain young people are "rescued" to underscore the failures of the rest.

This approach also obscures the fundamental issues of resources. Our nation's most powerful citizens (politicians and lawyers, business executives, doctors and professors) all want a similarly structured education for their children: small classes where students receive individualized attention, ample facilities, well-appointed, up-to-date classrooms and libraries, highly trained and compassionate teachers—all of which cost money. But when the topic turns to the education of poor and working-class children, money suddenly becomes not the "real issue." Hoover Institute economist Eric Hanushek claims, "Funding is not related either to overall student performance or to the performance of specific groups—minorities, disadvantaged students, or urban students—it is not a good index of equity. . . . Thus, when legislatures search for adequacy in funding or when courts demand it, they do not realize that it is a search for the Holy Grail—a noble but ultimately futile effort."[52] The Manhattan Institute—home to Badillo and McWhorter—has repeated this line of reasoning in numerous publications.[53] Yet curiously, for all of their insistence that money is not the solution, they take this attitude only toward urban public education, rather than expounding on the limited utility of expensive private or suburban schools.

Mayor Bloomberg echoed this mantra in a prominent 2007 speech to the Urban League when he stated: "Politicians have pandered to us by selling us on the idea that all we need is more money and smaller classes—and we've bought it. . . . If we want to truly improve the education our children receive, and fulfill the promise of the Civil Rights movement, we have to stand up and tell them: 'No more!' No more pandering to special interests. No more fear of the tough issue."[54] If young people with the right motivation and upbringing can succeed, why have upper-middle-class parents in increasing numbers chosen to send their children to charter schools, magnet schools, exam schools, suburban districts, and private schools—any place to get them away from the urban comprehensive schools that they allow for *other* people's children?

Indeed, it is many of the same public figures mentioned above, not the urban youth they deplore, who act as if educational aspirations *are* white. While New York chancellor Joel Klein claims that the Bloomberg plan will "finish the job that *Brown v. Board of Education* began," their reform plan does not treat all students of color as requiring the excellence embodied in specialized New York exam schools like Stuyvesant or Bronx Science or even high-performing ones like Midwood, Benjamin Cardoso, or East Side Community High School. Mayor Bloomberg revealed these assumptions in his 2007 speech to the Urban League. Believing he was embodying a far stronger commitment to these young people's educations, he trumpeted, "To encourage more students to start preparing for college, we've begun paying the fee for all 10th and 11th graders to take the PSAT, which has allowed us to substantially increase the number of Black and Latino students who take the test." Yet in suburban public high schools, as well as the city's exam schools, this has been standard for decades. While certainly a step forward, Bloomberg's celebration of something that is routine in other schools as a major accomplishment is telling in its condescension.[55]

Pedagogy for the Poor

Another popular area of school innovation has been the recent focus on developing particular pedagogies for poor children. Following from the premise that poor children suffer from a cultural disadvantage that interferes with school success, these approaches center on remedying the supposed cultural deficiencies that prevent the educational achievement of poor children: teaching students how to look at the teacher, dress right, and act and speak accordingly. While framed as a new innovation, this approach has much deeper roots in the vocational training celebrated at the turn of the century by Booker T. Washington. Following from these cultural deficit assumptions, these methods treat educational underattainment as fixable through a strict program of cultural remediation. Recent media coverage of the KIPP (Knowledge Is Power Program) academies has largely portrayed them as successful in improving the educational attainment of poor children because of their emphasis on teaching mid-dle-class mores and aspirations. As *New York Times* reporter Paul Tough explains in a lengthy article on this subject, "Their work also suggests that the disadvantages that poverty imposes on children aren't primarily about material goods. True, every poor child would benefit from having more books in his home and more nutritious food to eat (and money certainly makes it easier to carry out a program of concerted cultivation). But the real advantages that middle-class children gain come from more elusive processes: the language that their parents use, the attitudes toward life that they convey."[56] In his explanation of the academies' success, Tough, like others, skims over the dedication, long hours, and quality of the KIPP teaching staff and the extra resources they have managed to garner.

In June 2007, Tough followed up this emphasis on a pedagogy for the poor with an extended profile of Ruby Payne, a fifty-six-year-old educator-turned-inspirational-speaker and author of "A Framework for Understanding Poverty."[57] Hired by dozens of school districts, Payne has become a prominent speaker on children in poverty and provides training for thousands of teachers each year in teaching poor students "explicitly about the hidden rules of the middle class . . . how to speak in 'formal register,' how to restrain themselves from physical retaliation, how to keep a schedule." Admiring in tone, the article focused on Payne's idea that middle-class teachers need to better understand the culture of their poor students if they are to help those students succeed in school. The article dismissed academics who have criticized Payne's preference for anecdotes over systematic evidence as "a few angry assistant professors whose collective audience is a tiny fraction of the size of hers."[58]

The *New York Times*'s proclivity toward these cultural solutions is telling. To argue that the "real advantages" middle-class children have are "attitudes toward life"—to insist that teaching poor children to look at the teacher or to speak in a "formal register" is the key to getting on track for educational success—functions as a smokescreen for being cheap about some young people's education without having to admit to that stinginess. Middle-class *New York Times* readers can be comforted in their knowledge that it is not money but their culture that sets their children apart.

But young people are not the only ones subjected to this pedagogy of moral uplift. Bill Cosby and Dr. Alvin Pouissant target parents and committed adults in *Come On, People*. Urging parents to speak standard English, teach their children self-love and the value of hard work, turn off the television, pass on the salt, and avoid junk food—and Black fathers to reconnect with their children—they argue that schools in many neighborhoods may be poor but young people can succeed there. "Even bad schools produce smart kids," they proclaim. "Make sure your child is one of them." A jeremiad for personal responsibility published by a Christian press, Cosby and Pouissant's book identifies the problem of institutional racism in its numerous guises. However, most of the book's 243 pages suggest personal remedies to turn victims into victors. "No one can stop you from getting educated other than yourself," they declare, framing problems in schools as simple "hurdles" to be overcome.[59]

There is an obvious appeal to these pedagogies of moral uplift. They come cheap. They ask little of society except a cathartic relinquishment of responsibility. At the same time, by extending the deliberations over why the achievement gap between white and nonwhite students exists, these pedagogies gain the reputation of being bold and innovative when they are actually attempts to avoid confronting the real structural causes of the gap. Offering nonwhite students a never-ending repertoire of self-help strategies to remedy the achievement gap contributes to a larger tendency to deem these young people less worthy and less capable of excellence than other students. Certain young people get admonitions to follow the speaker with their eyes, but they do not get enough teachers with the time to provide individualized instruction.

The point of schooling, as writer James Baldwin reminds us above, is "to create in a person the ability to look at the world for himself, to make his own decisions."[60] Yet only a few of the students in this book were granted such an education; the rest were denied the kind of schooling that systematically encouraged critical thinking and social analysis. Ultimately, these cultural pedagogies frame poor children of color as deficient and seek to tell these young people how to think, rather than enabling and encouraging them to think for themselves. This raises the uncomfortable question: As a society, whose children are we educating to look at the world for themselves and make their own decisions—and whose children are we more comfortable educating in such a way that we make the decisions for them?

A Return to Brown: *The School Financing Lawsuits*

> Public accommodations did not cost the nation anything; the right
> to vote did not cost the nation anything. Now we are grappling with
> basic class issues between the privileged and the underprivileged. In
> order to solve this problem, not only will it mean restructuring of the
> architecture of American society but it will cost the nation something.
> —Martin Luther King Jr., Gandhi Memorial Lecture,
> Howard University (1966)

While most contemporary reform efforts have sidestepped the issue of equality, parents and other urban school advocates have attempted to re-center the issue of school equity through a series of school financing law-suits. Because the Court found in *Rodriguez* no "fundamental" right to education in the U.S. Constitution, the struggle against financial dispari-ties in public education largely shifted to state courts after 1974.[61] In both California and New York, as in other states such as Texas and New Jersey, parents and civil rights groups have gone to the courts again to try to ad-dress the issue of educational equity.

In 1993, the Campaign for Fiscal Equity filed a constitutional challenge to New York State's school finance system, claiming that it underfunded New York City's public schools and denied its students (predominantly students of color) their constitutional right to a "sound basic education." In 2001, Judge Leland DeGrasse ruled that the state's system of financing public schools disproportionately hurt minority students and deprived city students of a "sound, basic education" as required in the state constitution and in violation of federal civil rights laws. DeGrasse cited insufficient textbooks, libraries, classroom supplies, and instructional technology as key pieces of evidence. "Contrary to the defendants' argument," DeGrasse concluded, "increased educational resources, if properly deployed, can have a significant and lasting effect on student performance. There is a causal link between funding and educational opportunity."[62] Despite this damning verdict, New York State remained unapologetic and appealed the case. In 2002, the appellate court reversed DeGrasse's decision, claim-ing that an eighth-grade education was adequate for opportunity and suf-ficient for citizenship and that "society needs workers in all levels of jobs, the majority of which may very well be low level." The court of appeals (the state's highest court) in 2003 ruled in favor of the Campaign for Fis-cal Equity and ordered the state to undertake sweeping reforms. After much stalling and political wrangling, the 2007–8 New York State budget included a $1.76 billion increase in school funding. Fourteen years after the suit was filed, New York City received a total of $710 million in new state school aid, of which $469 million was new foundation aid.[63] This was much less than the $4 to $6 billion that experts convened by Judge De-Grasse had deemed necessary.

Three thousand miles away, on the forty-sixth anniversary of the *Brown* decision in May 2000, students and parents with the aid of the American Civil Liberties Union and the Mexican American Legal Defense and Educational Fund filed suit against the state of California in *Williams v. State of California*. Their case rested on two premises: that the state of California has to provide all students the basic resources they need to learn (qualified teachers, adequate materials, and decent facilities) and that all students have a fundamental right to an equal education. The *Williams* plaintiffs argued that California's public education system failed to give students the necessary educational resources and allowed unequal opportunities across schools. Charging that the state of California is responsible for ensuring that classrooms have the qualified teachers and textbooks that students need, *Williams* called on the state to increase funding and create an accountability system so that schools have to live up to these standards.

The state spent $20 million over the next four years to defend itself against *Williams*, claiming that whatever problems did exist were the responsibility of the local school districts and threatening a reverse suit against local districts.[64] But in August 2004 the state agreed to an out-of-court settlement on the major points brought by the students in the case. The state formally acknowledged its responsibility to ensure quality and equal education for all California's students. It committed to providing enough textbooks and materials to use in class and to take home; clean, safe, classrooms; and well-trained teachers according to standards set by California and federal laws.

To ensure compliance, the settlement set standards for measuring whether schools have the basic resources for learning; these standards have to be posted in every classroom. Each year, officials from each county in California visit schools with the greatest need (as measured by the lowest test scores) and report these findings to the public. A new complaint system was also put into practice where parents and community members can raise concerns about school conditions that then have to be investigated. The settlement also provided almost $1 billion to fix decrepit school conditions that exist across the state and promised to phase out multi-track school calendars in some of the most overcrowded schools over the coming years.[65]

But despite the achievements of the *Campaign for Fiscal Equity* and *Williams* cases, there were notable limits to what these cases could accomplish. Since they were both based on clauses within the state constitutions, what they could attain was not equity but adequacy, not educational excellence but a sound and basic education.[66] Education clause cases thus tend only to attain enough funding to bring the quality of schooling in poor districts up to an "adequate" level rather than to equalize spending across districts.[67] Moreover, not all state constitutions contain education clauses, and even in states in which such clauses do exist there is wide variation in their language—"general and uniform," "thorough and efficient," "sound and basic," and "adequate." There is no constitutional way to ensure that what the most powerful parent, in the words of educational theorist John Dewey, "wants for his own child, that must the community want for all of its children."[68] Because New York and California were so far from providing even an adequate education to all their young people, these settlements required years of struggle to produce any significant change, even without attempting equal educational opportunity for all children. Both cases, then, highlight the degree of segregation in American schools today, as well as the resistance and legal stumbling blocks parents and students face in addressing it.

The limitations of *Campaign for Fiscal Equity* and *Williams* have not prevented young people and their allies from continuing to push for an equal and excellent education. Activists and community workers have made explicit connections between the civil rights movement of the 1950s and 1960s and the struggle for educational equality today. Former Student Nonviolent Coordinating Committee activist Bob Moses founded the Algebra Project in 1982 "to impact the struggle for citizenship and equality by assisting students in inner city and rural areas to achieve math literacy." On the basis of its twenty-five years of work in more than two hundred schools across the country, Moses and the Algebra Project are now calling for a federal constitutional amendment "that says every child in the country is a child *of* this country . . . and is entitled to a quality public school education."[69]

Through the Urban Youth Collaborative, students in New York have issued a Bill of Rights outlining a series of basic rights currently being denied to them in the city's schools. They have asserted the right to receive college preparatory courses; a challenging and diverse curriculum; small class settings; educators certified in their licensed subjects; respectful treatment by appropriately trained school principals, staff, safety agents, and police officers; excellent, up-to-date facilities; and safe, and respectful learning environments free from physical harassment. Maintaining their right to participate in decisions about their schooling, they have also demanded the right to obtain information and data about their schools and how they operate, to be informed of structural changes and other reforms before they occur, and to participate in school decision-making processes alongside parents, teachers, and administrators concerning the use of law enforcement tactics in their schools.

Students across California have used the *Williams* process to highlight conditions in their schools. With Californians for Justice, young people and their allies have demanded that college preparatory classes be the default curriculum for all public schools and have held rallies across the state.[70] Groups like Californians for Justice, Community Coalition, and UCLA's Institute for Democracy, Education, and Access have pushed for real educational transformation within California's public schools, organizing against the exit exam, pushing for real empowerment through the *Williams* complaint process, and demanding that the A-G curriculum required for admittance to a four-year college be the default for schools across the state.

Where We Go from Here

> That a child forced to attend an underfunded school with poorer physical facilities, less experienced teachers, larger classes, and a narrower range of courses than a school with substantially more funds—and thus with greater choice in educational planning—may nevertheless excel is to the credit of the child, not the State. Indeed, who can ever measure for such a child the opportunities lost and the talents wasted for want of a broader, more enriched education? Discrimination in the opportunity to learn that is afforded a child must be our standard.
>
> —Supreme Court Justice Thurgood Marshall,
> dissent in *Rodriguez* (1973)

Back in 1951, as the strike at Moton High School began, Barbara Johns explained to her fellow students the role young people needed to play in advancing the struggle. "Our parents ask us to follow them but in some

instances—and I remember her saying this very vividly," her classmate recalled, "a little child shall lead them."[71] Johns also called the NAACP to
ask for their assistance. They sent lawyers Oliver Hill and Spottswood
Robinson to meet with the students. Hill and Robinson initially aimed
to caution the students against their action and to convince them that
Prince Edward County harbored few whites who would be receptive to
the strike. But Johns and her group of 114 striking students won the lawyers over, and Hill and Robinson agreed to represent them as long as their
parents agreed to support a legal case that attacked segregation head on.
Hill recalled, "Their morale was so high that we didn't have the heart to
say no."[72] The initial case was lost in Federal District Court in 1952 when
three judges unanimously ruled that, while significant disparities existed
between white and Black schools in Prince Edward County, separate
schools and the differential education they provided did not result from
racism but stemmed from local practice and preference. Two years later,
the U.S. Supreme Court would decide otherwise, ruling in *Brown* that
"separate educational facilities are inherently unequal." And so a young
woman of sixteen years helped push the fight that led to one of the most
important legal decisions of the twentieth century.

Fifty years later, the young people in this book demand that we be outraged by the injustice embedded in our continuing system of separate and
unequal schools and, as the young people in SBU emphasize, that we join
them in the struggle to change it. Like Barbara Johns, these young people
are asking adults to step up—to refuse to be resigned in the face of persistent
inequality and to imagine something better for them and for the nation.

If we take these young people's perspectives seriously, popular reform
ideas such as paying students to do well on tests (or making testing itself
evidence of accountability) constitute an insulting brand of "reform." The
"reforms" discussed above do not actually address the bodily experience
that young people have in school or the punitive, anti-intellectual climate
in the schools that these young people attend; instead, they further the
notion that something mysterious and elusive is needed to turn these
schools around. Far from eliminating inequality, they merely mask it.

If we are going to make good on the idea that the door of opportunity is open and that hard work and determination will lead to success in
this society, then our first responsibility is to acknowledge that students
like those in this book not only would benefit from changed schools but
would be delighted by them. Most of these students, after all, craved—
and praised—classes where they "really learned" and that prepared them

to go to college. In many ways, as numerous students in all three case studies pointed out, the inadequacies of their schooling are exemplified by the widespread use of worksheets. The students hated worksheets, calling them "boring," "stupid," and "not really learning." But the problem demands a twofold solution. First, it requires resources: money to bring class sizes down and provide a wider range of learning materials in every classroom, so that worksheets do not become a staple of teacher survival. Second, it necessitates a changed vision: if we come to see that schools in inner cities such as the South Bronx or South Central L.A. are also educating the world's leaders, worksheets (and other forms of skill-and-drill exercises) become inappropriate for the task at hand. Creative problem solving, facility with advanced math, an ability to analyze and speak thoughtfully about art and literature, the skills to discern multiple causes of social phenomena and to fashion complex approaches to social problems, hands-on science experiments—this is the kind of education needed to educate such citizens.

These students' perspectives make clear that the task of school reform is extensive but not mysterious—while many current reform efforts are misguided and deeply pessimistic, there is a real path for change. First, these students' experiences in school demonstrate that added resources are needed to ensure young people's bodily integrity and dignity in their schools. The public conversation around resources has been mired in a debate around whether added resources produce better test scores—whether "money matters" in closing the racial achievement gap.[73] For the students in this book, the issue of resources is fundamentally about dignity, about creating educational spaces where real learning can take place, and about fulfilling the task of equality that *Brown* began. "Money matters" not because social science experiments tell us that more of it could raise the achievement level of many students but because we have a moral and civic responsibility to provide the funding that is necessary so that each child can receive an education to fulfill her or his human potential.

Creating an environment where students can learn to their potential requires attending to the bodily experience students have in school. All schools need to have ample working bathrooms that students are free to use; clean facilities without bugs, rodents, and other vermin and with adequate temperature regulation; windows and light; and enough chairs and desks for every student in school to learn comfortably in class. Moreover, these classrooms need to have working computers and printers and up-to-date books for every student to take home plus a set for classroom use. They need well-appointed libraries and science labs. These schools need enough fully credentialed, well-paid teachers so that class sizes are manageable and teachers can follow up with students and provide more individualized attention. Hiring more qualified teachers also means being able to offer more classes, more AP courses, and a full college preparation curriculum that includes foreign languages, art, music, and other electives. These schools need more guidance counselors who can help shepherd students through the college selection and application process.

Creating schools that respect the fundamental humanity of *every* child requires money, real accountability, and mechanisms of oversight, essentials that our society has thus far not been willing to commit to. As documented in the Introduction, we know that there are huge disparities in funding between and within school districts. We also know that because of these disparities the children of the rich and powerful are granted an education far more challenging, enriching, and dignified than the young people in this book. No one on the left or right, no commentator, politician, or scholar, disputes this, yet most maintain that the doors of opportunity are now open and that young people going to urban schools such as these still compete on a level playing field. As student after student in this book holds to the belief that hard work and motivation will translate into opportunity and success, adults either need to step up and make that actually true. Or they need to be honest with young people and acknowledge that race and class continue to play a far bigger role in determining success than any amount of motivation or hard work.

For all the fetishization of increased accountability in mayoral control and NCLB, these reform efforts have resulted in little actual accountability of schools and administrators, politicians, and citizens *to* students. The *New York Times* can run a front-page article in 2008 about teachers in New York City regularly using umbrellas in class and schools serving twice as many students as they were built to accommodate—and Mayor Bloomberg is not even made to answer for it. There is little outcry that under this "education mayor" in President Bush's "age of accountability" such conditions are allowed to exist.[74] The culture talk framing our public conversation around schools has been an effective way to obscure our poor values and lack of responsibility as a society.

NCLB changed the national conversation around education by promising new accountability and federal oversight over all public schools.

Indeed, NCLB gave the federal government new forms of jurisdiction over education, partly replacing the federalist model of education that has long prevailed in the United States.[75] But it then defined accountability solely through standards, annual testing, and penalties linked to performance on tests. While NCLB tied federal money for schools to student test scores (and schools risk being closed after five years if they do not meet these), it did not set benchmarks for public accountability. Indeed, the version of NCLB Bush signed into law did not even penalize states for low test scores, only schools.

Any reauthorization of NCLB, then, must address this gaping hole by including school proficiency as well as student proficiency.[76] If we are going to talk of "adequate yearly progress" and set twelve-year goals for test proficiency that all students must meet, then we must set goals for local, state, and federal officials as well. The idea of "no child" gave us the goal of 100 percent student proficiency—that the nation cared about the performance of each and every student. But what about the idea of "no school left behind"—the goal of 100 percent school proficiency? If we can imagine 100 percent student proficiency, then surely we can also imagine each and every school fulfilling a set of basic standards—a set of standards that we can see from these case studies is far from being met. A public guarantee that no child will be educated in a school that does not live up to basic standards is certainly part of our social responsibility to leave no child behind. Real accountability must therefore include benchmarks that every school has to satisfy, as well as penalties for local, state, and federal officials if these are not met.

Drawing on the experiences of the students who speak in this book, we suggest that such benchmarks for high schools should, at the very minimum, include the following:

- Each school must have clean, open bathrooms to which students have ample access.
- Each classroom must have a working window and adequately regulated temperatures.
- Each classroom must have enough seats and desks for every student.
- Each student must have his or her own textbook for each class. There should be a classroom set as well.
- Each school must not be allowed to enroll more than 10 percent over building capacity and must fulfill all health and safety codes.

- Each school must provide students access to science labs, libraries including online resources, and other facilities necessary to complete college preparatory coursework.
- The maximum class size must be set at twenty-five in secondary school and seventeen in primary school.
- Each school must have one counselor for every 250 students.
- Curricula must be updated, and a college preparatory curriculum must be the default curriculum in every school.

Most of what NCLB has accomplished thus far is to label schools rather than fix them. The young people whose stories guide this book ask us to demand much more of our leaders—to hold our mayors and governors, congressional representatives, and president accountable to provide quality schooling to each and every child.

Education as a Right

The Supreme Court's *Rodriguez* and *Milliken* decisions, in concert with citizens and state officials, undid the promise of *Brown* by undermining desegregation and equity plans through the rationale of local control. Thus, to address the problem of disparate and unequal schooling, we need a federal constitutional amendment establishing the constitutional right to a quality education.[77] Carrying out the real goal of *Brown*—equity and access of all children to an equal and excellent education—requires no less. Such an amendment would establish that, just like the right to vote, education is a "fundamental right." If the federal government can set standards for schools, it must be accountable to all students in those schools, and ultimately that accountability must rest in rights.[78] Affirming the right to a quality education need not take away from local school boards their control over curriculum, staffing, and other aspects of educational policy and can ensure that constitutional protections extend to equitable schooling.

Part of establishing such a right would mean rethinking whom urban public schools answer to. Given the punitive, hierarchical natures of the schools that the young people in this book attend, treating education as a right would necessarily alter the position of students and their parents within the school structure. It would require transforming every school into a challenging, intellectual one and creating a structure where students and their parents have a real voice in school governance (a practice already in place in many elite public and private schools). Fundamentally, then, treating all students as rights-bearing individuals necessitates structuring schools around their concerns—and ensuring that the local, state, and federal governments that maintain these schools are truly answerable to students and their families.

These young people make clear their desire for classes where they are free to explore and ask questions, and for schools that listen to them and take their perspectives seriously. They want schools where their voices—as well as their parents'—count. The sense of empowerment and critical analysis that SBU students have developed outside the classroom needs to be developed within schools as well.[79] Indeed, creating school governance structures that bring students to the table would facilitate the kind of empowerment that these students demand.

Bringing about these changes requires that we as a society commit to a new kind of culture talk: to social responsibility that enables personal responsibility; to a constitutional right to a quality education and guaranteed funds that permanently ensures for all schools the kind of adequate resources that the *Williams* and *Campaign for Fiscal Equity* cases sought to produce; to substantive community, parental, and student input into schools; and to a public commitment to the kind of quality schooling that educates all young people to be thinkers, creators, and innovators. More than fifty years after *Brown*, the nation needs to face up to all the ways in which we have never lived up to its mandate. *Brown* did not fail, nor has it lost its utility; it never was fully implemented. We must acknowledge that as a society we have not moved beyond race and racial inequality. We have not committed the same kind of resources to the education of nonwhite children that we have to white children—or forged a social vision that considers the future and potential of nonwhite and white students on similar terms. These young people deserve and desire equal and excellent schooling without constantly having to justify the ways they deserve it. And there is no such equality in twenty-first-century America.

Ultimately, we must forsake the cheap posturing of culture talk for a more substantive public responsibility for all children's schooling. The problems with schools fundamentally are not personal flaws but social failures; therefore, the remedy is not an individual challenge but a collective task. Young people need adults who are willing to work with them to transform their schools. We must set up mechanisms that provide real accountability to students—through improved school conditions and shared governance. Ultimately, this requires no less than a new civil rights movement where adults join with young people to ensure an equal education for each and every student.

Methodological Appendix
Listening to Young People

GASTON ALONSO

> The commitment to get close, to be factual, descriptive, and quotive, constitutes a significant commitment to represent the participants in their own terms. This does not mean that one becomes an apologist for them, but rather that one faithfully depicts what goes on in their lives and what life is like for them.
> —John Lofland, *Analyzing Social Settings* (1971)

In the introduction to this volume, Celina Su recounts how at a 2006 meeting of the New York City Department of Education a young woman affiliated with the Urban Youth Collaborative implored the gathered officials: "Please. You keep staring at your piece of paper and referring to questionable 'data.' Please look up and listen to us. We're sitting in front of you. We are the data." *Our Schools Suck* takes this young woman up on her plea. In the preceding pages, African American and Latino high school students testified to their experiences growing up in inner-city communities, attending the overcrowded and underfunded schools found in such communities, looking for employment in racialized labor markets, and working to change the conditions in which they study and live. They also told us about the school subjects they love and those that they hate, about their desire for "real learning" and their dislike of standardized tests, about their aspirations for the future and their fears about the present, and about their yearning for schools with good teachers, caring counselors, clean bathrooms, and safe hallways.

In taking the self-interpretations of students as our data, we insist that social scientists and policy makers treat young people as social agents in their own right rather than as the mere objects of their studies and policy discussions. The students who are the subject of this book are actors capable of placing themselves in history, interpreting the objective conditions of their lives, and contributing to the scholarship and public policies that shape those conditions. If we are willing to listen, they have much to tell us about "what life is like for them" in the hypersegregated and under-resourced schools in which we as a society have confined them and about the kind of schools and teaching that would engage them as students.

As described in the Introduction, during the spring of 2006 the authors of this book became concerned with the tone that public discussions about the education of students of color were taking. As one high-profile figure after another denounced these young people as "cool pose" troublemakers doomed to academic failure by their cultural norms and values, we came together to discuss how such simplistic representations did not match the complexity of the data that we had gathered in our previous research with young people of color. Rather than simply relying on how adults describe young people of color and their values, scholars and policy makers, we believe, need to do the hard work of documenting and grappling with how such young people understand themselves and express their values.

We began to imagine constructing a collaborative ethnography that brought together three distinct critical ethnographic projects, each guided by different scholarly interests and questions and each focusing on a different research site and deploying a variety of methods. Despite such differences, the case studies focused on the same population—inner-city African American and Latino high school students. By placing Jeanne Theoharis's study of the written self-expression of eleventh graders from Fremont High School in Los Angeles alongside Noel Anderson's interviews with young men of color attending a New York City Upward Bound program and Celina Su's ethnography of high school student activists from the South Bronx, we could examine how these young people—so hypervisible and talked about in our society but so seldom heard from—interpreted themselves and their schooling. "Humans are complex, and their lives are ever changing," Andrea Fontana and James Frey observe. "The more methods we use to study them, the better our chances will be to gain some understanding of how they construct their lives and the stories they tell us about them."[1] As we read the cases together, we noticed that despite the methodological differences among them, the data gathered consistently told us that African American and Latino youth construct their lives in far more complex and contradictory ways than those suggested by the heated public discussion about them. In the following pages, we reflect on what it means for researchers to take young people's voices as data; describe the methodological choices we made in order to, as John Lofland suggests, represent our research participants "in their own terms"; and discuss how this form of research can be used to reframe theoretical paradigms and reimagine public policies.

Young People as Social Agents

Our goal in this book has not been to replace the popular one-dimensional representation of young people of color with another one-dimensional representation—to say that all African American and Latino youth, instead of being "cool pose" troublemakers, are well-behaved model students. To do so would have entailed misrepresenting the complexity of the data and failed to represent our informants "in their own terms." As researchers concerned with the education of young people of color, we did not set out to discover and reveal their inner essence but rather to understand the complex and contradictory ways in which they interpret their world, interpret themselves in that world, and fashion themselves according to those interpretations. Thus our focus has not been to declare that young people of color *are* this or that particular way—as many of the journalists, pundits, and even scholars discussed in chapter 1 do— but rather to understand how they come to make sense of the world and how their understandings influence their aspirations and fears regarding schooling.

In insisting that researchers consider young people as "experts" of their lives, we challenge popular and scholarly representations of them as not emotionally mature enough or intellectually competent enough to properly understand and articulate their experiences. Too often, as a society, we dismiss the voices of young people by proclaiming, "What do fifteen-year-olds know, anyway?" "Aren't teenagers too young, too stupid, too emotionally unsettled, too moody to say anything significant about anything?" or "You are either crazy or foolish to listen to what kids have to say." This stance, as Rebecca Raby points out, is rooted in assumptions from the field of developmental psychology that have shaped our contemporary understandings of individuals in their teen years.[2] Drawing on the turn-of-the-twentieth-century work of G. Stanley Hall,[3] this field crafted a typology of discrete life stages through which all individuals were assumed to pass. As individuals move along an unidirectional path from infancy to childhood, adolescence, and adulthood, the model holds, they move closer to emotional maturity and intellectual competency. As a result, we tend to dismiss what individuals in their teen years have to tell us—waiting for them to reach adulthood before we seriously consider what they say as informed, insightful, and valuable.

Researchers have challenged this developmentalist model by pointing to the socially constructed and historically contingent nature of categories such as "childhood," "adolescence," and "adulthood." Rather than universal categories that apply to the life path of all individuals in all societies, they are constructs of twentieth-century American psychology researchers.[4] Nancy Lesko, for example, has explored the ways in which the dominant conceptions of "adolescence" are "twice naturalized" in that "they portray characteristics of youths between the ages of 12 and 17 years as naturally occurring and as having natures that essentially are distinct from those of adults and children."[5] Scholarly and popular representations of young people as "adolescents" portray their "nature" as determined by the psychological and hormonal changes associated with puberty. In these representations, "adolescents" simply *are* "hormonally driven, peer oriented, identity seeking,"[6] psychologically confused, "out of control," and in a constant state of "crisis." This is particularly the case with young people of color, who are also subject to racialized representations that, as discussed in chapter 1, portray them as dangerous, violent, and too fearful of being labeled "white" by their peers to attempt to do well in school.[7] These representations work not only to call into question the value of young people's voices but also, as Lesko points out, to grant authority and importance to the voices of the adult "experts" who produce knowledge about them. "When groups such as . . . the young are constructed as other and problematic," she notes, "social regulation of these others is supported and specified by the social science experts who represent them."[8]

Since the 1970s, scholars associated with the Centre for Contemporary Culture Studies at the University of Birmingham in the United Kingdom and the field of new childhood studies in the United States have moved away from the developmentalist view of young people as "adolescents" or subjects in the process of *becoming* adults—too young, too immature, too undeveloped, too dependent to be considered autonomous reflexive agents—and have instead embraced a view of young people as social agents or subjects in the process of *being*—autonomous and competent actors capable of reflecting on and articulating their own conditions.[9] These scholars have rejected the category "adolescence" as a socially constructed concept that blinds and prevents them from appreciating the meaning-making capacities of young people. This book embraces this approach by listening to the voices of young people in their own right and exploring their meaning-making practices. Such a stance, in Sari Knopp Bilken's words, "does not mean that adult researchers have to agree with youth. It does mean that we have to take their views seriously."[10]

To assume that high school students are too undeveloped to be able to competently articulate their own interpretations of the world around them is also to assume an ahistorical position. Young people have always been at the forefront of school reform efforts, as illustrated by Jeanne Theoharis's discussion in the previous chapter of Barbara Johns's activism against school segregation (which formed the basis of one of the cases in *Brown*). Young people have articulated what needed to be done and, whether by testifying in front of school boards, filing lawsuits, staging school walkouts, or marching in the streets, have pushed society to respond to their concerns. This point is borne out by Celina Su's study in chapter 4 of student activism and self-empowerment in the South Bronx. To recognize the importance of listening and learning from the voices and actions of high school students is to recognize their role as history-making actors.

Doing Qualitative Research

Practitioners of qualitative research methods, as Norman Denzin and Yvonna Lincoln point out, "stress the socially constructed nature of reality, the intimate relationship between the researcher and what is studied, and the situational constraints that shape inquiry."[11] Skepticism regarding researchers' ability to remove themselves from the social field they are investigating and thereby achieve the objectivity advocated by positivist social science has led many qualitative researchers to explore the ways their social positions—their race, gender, sexuality, and class and educational background as well as their research interests and political commitments—"filter knowledge," to borrow Denzin's phrase.[12] These researchers have rejected what Donna Haraway refers to as the "dazzling—and, therefore, blinding—illuminations" of the "god trick"[13] that allows researchers to remain invisible and thus supposedly neutral. Instead they have moved toward making their social positions known. "We need to avoid the 'objectivist' stance that attempts to make the researcher's cultural beliefs and practices invisible while simultaneously skewering the research objects' belief and practices to the display board," Sandra Harding has argued. "Only in this way can we hope to produce understandings and explanations which are free (or, at least, more free) of distortion from the unexamined beliefs and behaviors of social scientists themselves." For her, "Introducing this 'subjective' element into the analysis in fact increases the objectivity of the research and decreases the 'objectivism' which hides this kind of evidence from the public."[14]

While we agree with the call to "introduce the subjective element into our analyses," we are skeptical of facile analyses that read analytical consequences into particular social positions. Clearly, our analysis has been deepened and broadened because the four of us represent a wide range of social positions—men and women; queer and straight; Black, white, Latino, and Asian American; public school and private school educated; and so on and on. Our different genders and sexualities, racial and class backgrounds, academic training and intellectual curiosities have influenced our interactions with research participants and "filtered" our knowledge. However, it is too simple to assume that our analyses have been "filtered" in particular and obvious ways because, for example, some of us are men and some of us are women. Thus, while in the book's introduction and in the separate case studies we reveal our different social positions and examine how they might have influenced our interactions in the field as well as our analyses of the data, we refrain from making any definitive claims regarding their consequences and leave the job of making such judgments up to our readers.

But given that our research involved high school students, age is an aspect of our social positions that deserves some extended consideration. "Age," Lesko points out, "is a positional superiority in which adults always come out better."[15] Studies of young people entail what Amy Best refers to as a process of "studying down" on the part of adult researchers, a process structured by generational differences and the corresponding power inequalities. "The authority adults command and structures of power are deeply entangled," Best notes, "inasmuch as their authority flows from and is bolstered by a set of institutional and ideological arrangements."[16] These arrangements include the ideological mechanisms, discussed above, that render what young people have to say about their lives as less "insightful" and "valid" than what we as adults have to say about them. They also include the institutional resources, such as academic credentials and access to publishers, that provide social scientists with the authority and the ability to make our voices—including our representations of "adolescents"—heard in public in ways not available to young people.

The relations between adult researchers and young participants are further complicated by the fact that such researchers enter the field, in Raby's words, as "outsider[s] who may imagine insider status based on memories of adolescence."[17] Thus, during their fieldwork, Jeanne, Noel, and Celina all reflected back on their experiences as teens. Further, as we wrote up the case studies and discussed the book manuscript, we were all forced to engage with our own memories of high school. At times, these memories served as points of identification between the students and us, pointing to similarities in school experiences, while at other times they served as points of disidentification, pointing to differences in school experiences as well as to obvious generational differences. But we resisted the temptation to either overidentify with the students through our reading of their and our experiences as shared or to disidentify with them through our reading of their experiences as exotic and Other.[18]

"We are not, or at least I am not, seeking either to become natives (a compromised word in any case) or to mimic them," Clifford Geertz reminded fellow ethnographers. "Only romantics and spies would seem to find point in that. We are seeking, in the widened sense of the term in which it encompasses very much more than talk, to converse with them, a matter a great deal more difficult, and not only with strangers, than is commonly recognized."[19] Conversing with high school students, both in the field and in our analyses, made us conscious of the importance of acknowledging and addressing rather than dismissing the differences in social positions and power—including age—that exist between informants and researchers. Thus, for example, we recognized that our position as adults and educators who had been exposed to far better and substantive educational opportunities and possibilities meant that we could be critical of the schooling these young people were receiving and imagine better for them. Many of the young people in this book were making the best of their schooling (trying to act positive or unaffected by the problems and conditions around them). We, however, had the distance and the luxury of seeing it from afar and thus could be critical (and even indignant) about its shortcomings.

Case Studies

Despite the variety of methods Jeanne, Noel, and Celina deployed in their case studies, they all related to their research participants as "informants" rather than "respondents." Researchers who view and treat project participants as "respondents," James Spradley points out, are interested in gathering participants' responses to specific questions that are crafted prior to engagement with the participants. Through surveys—such as the survey used in Portes and Rumbaut's Children of Immigrants Longitudinal Study (CILS) discussed in chapter 1—and closed-ended structured interviews, researchers seek answers to the same questions from different participants. They thereby hope to examine patterns in the opinions of a bounded research population. On the other hand, researchers who approach participants as "informants" are interested in allowing participants to identify what issues are salient in their lives and to frame the questions themselves. To borrow Spradley's language, in the first case "the questions arise out of the social scientist's culture" and in the second case they arise "out of the informant's culture."[20] In each case study presented in the preceding pages, the researcher deployed methods that allowed the young people participating in the project to frame the discussion on the basis of their own "culture," experiences, and self-interpretations.

In the Field

Jeanne Theoharis's case study presented in chapter 2 is based on research she conducted while teaching at Fremont High School in Los Angeles. From September 2003 to June 2004, Jeanne assisted two eleventh-grade U.S. history teachers, Steve Lang and Sarah Knopp. Two days a week, she taught four classes of around thirty-five to forty students each with Steve and two classes with Sarah. Drawing on her expertise in the field of African American history, Jeanne augmented the history curriculum with African American and Latino history, crafted and explained essay assignments, and helped students with their writing. From March 2004 to June 2004, she asked students in the four classes she co-taught with Steve to write two-page weekly journal entries. Jeanne's interest in examining how students interpreted themselves in journal writing stemmed from one of the larger themes of the class: that is, to get students to think about the process of how history is written and whose history gets preserved. She was also interested in helping students develop their personal writing skills, since such skills are important in writing college admission essays.

Jeanne explained to students that each of them would have to decide what topics to write about—what was important enough in his or her life to warrant reflection. Each week, students decided what issues to write about and how to frame the discussion of those issues. Topics students covered in their journals ranged from recollections of early memories to the trials and tribulations of dating, catalogs of what they had done the previous weekend, fears associated with learning to dance for a *quinceañera* party, and the pain of dealing with the death of a friend or family member. They also wrote about their favorite books, the school subjects they enjoyed studying, their fears of not doing well in school, and their concerns regarding the future. After some students asked for guidance in identifying topics to write about, Jeanne provided her classes with a list of twenty or so topics that students had already written on. Some students, especially those struggling up to that point, began to write on those topics, while others continued to come up with their own topics.

Students were required to do the journal assignments every week. To ensure that they felt free to express themselves in their own terms, students received credit for turning in the journals but did not receive a letter grade. Censorship and bias in the content of the journals were self-imposed by students' decisions regarding what was appropriate to share with someone in the authority position of Jeanne and Steve and what was best to hold back. Students' writing ability also influenced journal content. For example, recent English-language learners often had more difficulty completing two pages of reflective writing than native speakers did. Jeanne marked up each assignment, correcting grammar and spelling, writing comments in the margins, and asking follow-up questions. Her comments let students know that she took the assignment seriously and appreciated their efforts. Because the journals were written to be read by two teachers, they certainly might be different in tone and content from a personal diary. As Jeanne notes in her chapter, it is telling that despite the prevalent view of young people as disrespectful of authority figures and uninterested in education, most of them chose to write in great detail and quantity about their goals and aspirations. Such efforts—whether done solely to impress or gain the respect of their teachers or not—suggest that these young people valued education and cared about how teachers perceived them in ways that are not reflected in the portrayals of young people of color advanced by the "culture of failure" narrative.

Noel Anderson's original engagement with the Upward Bound program that is the subject of chapter 3 came at the invitation of the program's director. As a PhD candidate at the time, Noel was interested in understanding the underlying assumptions about educational opportunity and equity that inform the intended goals and outcomes of such a program, as well as how such a program is or is not aligned with the lived experiences of the young men attending it. In preparation for his field research, Noel analyzed Upward Bound curricula and evaluations as well as strategic plans and annual reports from the organization. The purpose was to glean the goals and intended outcomes of the program. From to 2003 to 2004, Noel spent four afternoons a week at the program. In addition to hanging out with students, he led workshops on the representations of males and females in hip-hop culture. Noel was both an insider and an outsider at the program. There were no white participants; all students and staff members were African American—like himself—or Latino. The workshop leaders included college students, both male and female, as well as veteran educators and community leaders.

In addition to document analysis and participant observation, Noel's data collection process included interviews with students in the program. As Fontana and Frey point out, "There is a growing realization that interviewers are not mythical neutral tools envisioned by survey research. Interviewers are increasingly seen as active participants in an interaction with respondents, and interviews are seen as negotiated accomplishments of both interviewers and respondents that are shaped by the contexts and situations in which they take place."[21] As discussed in the case study, Noel's interactions with the students were clearly shaped by "the context and situations" in which they took place as well as by the "negotiated" interactions between them. Through a dialogical interview process, Noel learned a great deal about both the young men and himself. The "collective sense making" involved in his conversations with these young men allowed Noel to reflect on his own experiences growing up as an African American male in Crown Heights, Brooklyn, and on how those experiences converged with and diverged from the students' experiences, generationally and culturally.

Qualitative researchers must acknowledge that, in Best's words, "gaining acceptance, establishing trust, and developing rapport are central to the ability to embed oneself within the lives and social worlds of those they study and that this in turn yields richer and more complete understanding."[22] To gain students' trust and build a meaningful rapport with them, Noel spent three months hanging out at the program before approaching students regarding setting up interviews. He left the decision to be interviewed up to the students. Many students did not have time to participate in extended interviews. They had to complete homework, take care of siblings, and/or attend after-school jobs. Thus Noel ended up interviewing a dozen young male students out of the total of 150 students participating in the program.[23]

Prior to conducting the interviews, Noel had developed some idea about the initial questions that he was interested in asking students. However, he did not conduct "structured" interviews, in which the researcher asks each participant an exact set of questions developed beforehand, or "semistructured" interviews, in which the researcher asks each participant a dozen or so open-ended questions developed beforehand as a way to begin the interview process. Rather, Noel and the students engaged in long—often rambling—dialogues, sometimes over multiple afternoons. Such an "open-ended conversational interviewing style" can, as Douglas Foley and Angela Valenzuela suggest, "generate more engaged personal narratives and more candid opinions . . . and tend[s] to humanize the interviewer and diminish her [or his] power and control of the interview process."[24] By making the interviews informal, Noel encouraged sharing—of one's own stories of childhood, as well as one's feelings, fears, and aspirations—in his conversations with students. In this manner, Noel allowed each informant to set the agenda for their dialogue, to identify the topics worth discussing, and to frame the discussion of those topics and the language used according to their own self-interpretations.

Celina Su came to the study of Sistas and Brothas United (SBU) presented in chapter 4 as part of a larger project that sought to understand why grassroots groups facing the same political context and structural constraints pursue widely different strategies. As part of that project, she studied four community-based organizations pursuing school reform in the South Bronx: ACORN Bronx, Mothers on the Move, Northwest Bronx, and SBU. Celina was drawn to the South Bronx as a research site because of the high concentration of community-based organizations in the borough and because of its place in the national consciousness as a symbol of racial and economic inequality. By focusing on organizations that were located in the same borough, worked with poor families of color, and were involved with the same reform issues, Celina held constant the local political context, the kind of organization, and the campaign issues.

Celina's original research consisted of a three-pronged plan of data collection: archival research and documentary analysis, participant observation, and interviews. She studied documents such as meeting minutes, newsletters, flyers, Web sites, official mission statements, memoranda, public correspondence, and relevant legislation or reforms enacted, and she gathered quantitative data on funding and personnel aspects of each organization's capacity. She also gathered data on the public school system—for example, school-, district-, and new regional-level dropout rates, achievement test scores, and reduced or free lunch eligibility, as well as basic demographic data on race, gender, and income in the Bronx and New York City. The bulk of the research, however, took the form of participant observation. She attended education committee meetings, accountability sessions, and rallies and spent time, over repeated visits, at each organization. As part of her research into the organizations' cultural norms, Celina paid particular attention to formal and informal rules and routines in their decision-making processes and to protocols during meetings, trainings, and other events or conversations.

Because many organization members did not trust outsiders and because she wanted to ensure that all questions stemmed from the data, Celina waited to begin interviewing informants until the latter third of her fieldwork period. This decision adheres to an "evolving theory" process in qualitative studies, where beginning stages of data collection are designed to be open to all observations and discovery and later stages place gradually greater emphasis on theoretical relevance.[25] She talked with organizing directors, leaders, and parents and with public officials and other third parties. In contrast to Noel's method of unstructured interviews, Celina conducted semistructured interviews. Each interview took place over one to three hours and followed a protocol of ten questions that served as starting points for in-depth discussions on the informant's role in the organization as well as the organization's activities, norms, and political strategies. As explored in the case study, Celina's interactions with the informants were influenced by their respective social positions. Not wanting to take the participants' observations for granted, she tried to disentangle ways in which the positions of different actors (including herself) might affect informants' observations and dialogue.

In all, Celina attended approximately 150 events, ranging from two-hour-long meetings to three-day retreats. These events took place primarily over the fifteen-month period from May 2003 to July 2004. She interviewed approximately fifty informants, some several times. After reviewing the data, she verified and reviewed her analysis, sharing some of the analysis with participants and receiving their feedback, sharing her data to check for bias, and employing a "cross-site analysis" suggested by Matthew Miles and Michael Huberman.[26] In such an analysis, the researcher looks for emerging patterns among data from multiple, comparable cases. She concluded the data collection and analysis stages when new data confirmed, rather than added to, previously obtained data, thus signaling "saturation."[27]

To gain access to students, all three researchers had to get the consent of adult "gatekeepers." These are individuals who, as Robert Burgess explains, "have the power to grant or withhold access to people or situations for the purposes of research."[28] While the consent of such adults—school principals, teachers, program coordinators, and parents—was crucial in allowing each researcher access to his or her informants, the ultimate gatekeepers in each case were the students themselves.[29] They decided how much of their lives and self-interpretation to share either in written form with their teacher (Jeanne) or verbally with researchers interested in their experiences (Noel and Celina). "We do not have direct access, but only that small part of it which our informants can lead us into understanding," Geertz writes. "This is not as fatal as it sounds, for, in fact, not all Cretans are liars, and it is not necessary to know everything in order to understand something."[30]

Writing It

Writers (and readers) of ethnographic work need to pay attention to the methods used not only to gather data in the field but also to write up the findings. All ethnographic writings are, in Geertz's words, "fictions, in the sense that they are 'something made,' 'something fashioned'—the original meaning of *fictio*—not that they are false, unfactual, or merely 'as if' thought experiments."[31] At the time they conducted their original research in Los Angeles and New York, Jeanne, Noel, and Celina did not have on their minds the "culture of failure" narrative that stimulated the collaboration behind this book. In writing up findings for purposes of this collaborative ethnography, each of them reread his or her original findings in light of our discussions regarding the increased currency that the "culture of failure" narrative was gaining in the public realm.

When Jeanne conducted her research in Los Angeles, she was interested in how young people frame their own history, particularly in how they might tell the history of the city of Los Angeles through their own experiences. When she went back to the journals in the spring of 2006, Jeanne looked for redundancy and difference in students' reflections regarding their education. She was struck with the number of journals students wrote about their goals and aspirations, about how they were doing in school and their fears about their academic performance, and about their thoughts on their classes, teachers, and Fremont as a whole. The preponderance of these journals led to the frame for chapter 2. Her interpretation of students' writing was informed by her participant observation as a teacher at the school. While Steve concentrated on grading class exams, Jeanne read and graded weekly essay assignments on current topics. She was thus able to read the journal entries in light of students' other written expression. In her position as a teacher, Jeanne got to know the students and school staff personally and to observe the conditions and dynamics in the school and surrounding communities. The two months she spent helping the school's counselor also gave her insights into the lack of resources at the school. Thus her rereading and interpretation of the journals were influenced by observations she formed during her research at Fremont and her experiences as a teacher at the school.

In writing up his findings, Noel reread his field notes and interview notes with a new research question in mind. While he had originally focused on assessing the Upward Bound program, he was now interested in understanding the life experiences of the young men of color participating in the program. He was particularly interested in understanding how they negotiated segregated public schools and attempted to access work in the youth labor market. By framing the chapter in the form of four life studies, Noel sought to provide the reader with rich portraits of the complex ways individuals interpret their everyday lives.

When Celina went back to the data from the youth organization case (SBU) in her original study, she examined how young people's experiences helped them tackle school reform issues. As a part of her research at SBU, she had conducted participant observation of at least three dozen SBU-linked events, held informal conversations with close to forty people associated with SBU, and conducted semistructured interviews with fourteen informants. In the process of reviewing this data, Celina reformulated her research questions as: How do students in a youth organizing group exercise collective action for school reform? What cultural norms and resources did they begin with, and what processes, norms, and resources were necessary for them to pursue campaigns? She looked closely at the process of empowerment not just in the context of social movements but in the context of education, pedagogy, and political economy. Ironically, these were the concerns that had driven her to study social movements in the first place but that had receded to the background.

The distinct methodological approaches deployed by each researcher in her or his study allowed her or him to approach young people as social agents, as "experts" in their own right. Through journals, interviews, and observation, Jeanne, Noel, and Celina came to "understand something"—to borrow Geertz's phrase—about how high school students of color interpret their own conditions, aspirations, and fears and how they fashion their sense of self on the basis of those interpretations. In turn, "the combination of multiple methodological practices, empirical materials, perspectives and observers," to borrow Denzin and Lincoln's words, reflected in this collaborative ethnography have added to the "rigor, breadth, and depth" of our collective understanding.[32]

Reframing Theory through the Voice of Students

In this section, we conclude by exploring how our collaborative rereading of the data from the original case studies allowed us to examine prevailing theories regarding the educational achievement of students of color and to suggest policy proposals based on the voices of our informants.

Social scientists wedded to "methodological positivism," to borrow George Steinmetz's term, have suggested that case study qualitative research is—at best—of limited theoretical value.[33] According to these critics, the value of social science research is largely measured by the ability to move from the particular to the general and to make generalizations regarding a wide population of cases.[34] Thus they prefer large-N quantitative analysis to case study research, seeing the findings from the latter as simply too singular and particular to generalize from.

Some researchers have responded to this criticism by making "a case for the case study"[35] and by calling on social scientists to reject the positivist temptation to measure the value of all research in terms of its theory-generating and generalization-producing capability. "No research paradigm has a monopoly on quality," Alan Peshkin noted in his discussion of the "goodness" of qualitative research. "None can deliver promising outcomes with certainty. None have the grounds for saying 'this is it' about their designs, procedures, and anticipated outcomes."[36] Thus Steinmetz has noted that "the case study of a specific social event, process, or community is as important a part of the overall sociological enterprise as comparison or sustained theoretical reflection." Case studies can be used to generate questions for theory building or to question the validity of existing theoretical claims regarding causal relations. They are, in fact, "the indispensable building block" of social scientific research.[37]

Another response to the positivist criticism of case study research has taken the form of comparative ethnographies in which one researcher or, more often, a team of researchers conducts similar studies in a variety of sites. By generating comparable data from a population of similar cases, proponents of this approach argue they are able to overcome the problem of particularity and make generalizations with greater certainty than would be possible from a single case. While such studies might appease the generalization-producing urges of some social scientists, they risk obscuring precisely the value of the case study approach—the ability to provide "thick descriptions" of the particular. "With concentration on the bases for comparison, uniqueness and complexities will be glossed over," Robert Stake warns. "A research design featuring comparison substitutes (a) the *comparison* for (b) the *case* as the focus of the study."[38]

As discussed above, this book did not begin and does not aim to be read as a formally designed and seamless comparative ethnography. Clearly, the findings from each distinct case suggest potential avenues for theory building through future research, including comparative quantitative and qualitative research. However, because of the differences between the cases and between the methods deployed in each study, the data generated from them are not easily comparable. While the broad racial composition of the students (African American and Latino) and the specific time frame of the research (the 2003–4 school year) are constant across the cases, as discussed there are significant differences in the research questions and the methods of data collection originally used.

Instead of seeking to read a comparative element retroactively back into the project, we brought the multiple cases together to illuminate the diverse and complex ways in which African American and Latino students attending segregated inner-city schools interpret their school experience. This book, then, is to be read as a collaborative ethnographic study. It recognizes the value of the rich "thick descriptions" that emerge from the particulars of each case study. At the same time, though, it also recognizes the value of scholarly collaborations that bring together researchers who have diverse social positions and deploy a variety of research methods. The diversity of our social positions and of the case study designs allowed us to scrutinize different slices of these students' academic experiences—their in-school experiences, their experiences in after-school programs, and their activism in behalf of school reform. The findings—in particular, the persistent themes emerging from the three cases and highlighted in the Conclusion— provided us with an avenue to interrogate the conceptual models guiding prevailing theoretical paradigms for studying those experiences.[39]

As we sat down to discuss the data from the case studies, we began to notice that in each case the data—students' voices, our interpretation of those voices, and our observations of their everyday experiences and practices—converged on a similar point: school conditions not only influenced students' self-interpretations and self-fashioning but also acted as structural roadblocks to their academic achievement. We found that regardless of students' varied "cultural outlooks" and work ethic, the lack of resources in their schools, the overcrowded conditions in their classrooms, the limited curricula available to them, and so on, stood in the way of their academic progress. Too often the conditions in schools simply curtailed the possibilities of such progress. This was the case even among many of the students who crafted inspiring narratives of how individual effort would allow them to succeed.

As we discussed these findings in light of Gaston Alonso's examination of the prevailing scholarship on the racial achievement gap—presented in chapter 1—it became clear that the very conditions that our data pointed to were underconsidered in much of the scholarship. Rather than dismissing our cases as insignificant anomalies or twisting what our data told us to fit with prevailing theories regarding the causes of the achievement gap, we submitted the disjuncture between the data gathered through our multiple ethnographic cases and those theories to critical examination. The examination highlighted the culturalist assumptions informing the conceptual frameworks guiding much of the scholarship and influencing public discussions. These assumptions tend to narrow scholars' analytical focus in ways that grant primacy to "community forces" at the expense of "school forces"—to use the language of John Ogbu's typology discussed in Gaston's chapter. The disjuncture between our data and the prevailing scholarship on the racial achievement gap then pointed to the need to reframe the study of students of color and to propose different ways to address the troubled state of their education. Scholars, policy makers, and citizens need to *listen* to young people of color as they tell us about "what life is like for them" and to explore the ways their voices push us to reshape our discussions regarding schooling and to rethink our policy initiatives.

Notes

INTRODUCTION

1. Bill Cosby, "Speech at the 50th Anniversary Commemoration of the *Brown v. Topeka Board of Education* Supreme Court Decision, May 22, 2004," *Black Scholar* 34 (Winter 2004): 2–5.

2. Gary Orfield and Chungmei Lee, *Racial Transformation and the Changing Nature of Segregation* (Cambridge, MA: Civil Rights Project at Harvard University, 2006) and *Why Segregation Matters: Poverty and Educational Inequality* (Cambridge, MA: Civil Rights Project at Harvard University, 2005). The authors note that the shift toward resegregation coincides with the Supreme Court's 1971 decision in the case of *Board of Education of Oklahoma v. Dowell*. Since then, there has been a steady erosion of *Brown's* mandate.

3. For a review of court battles beginning with the landmark 1971 *Serrano* case in California, see James E. Ryan, "Schools, Race, and Money," *Yale Law Journal* 109, no. 2 (1999): 249–316; and Terry N. Whitney, "State School Finance Litigation: A Summary and Analysis," *NCSL Legislative Report* 23 (October 1998): 1–14. On legislative efforts, see U.S. General Accounting Office, "School Finance: State Efforts to Reduce Funding Gaps between Poor and Wealthy Districts," 1997, www.gao.gov/archive/1997/he97031.pdf.

4. Robert F. Arnove and Carlos Alberto Torres, *Comparative Education: The Dialectic of the Global and the Local* (Lanham, MD: Rowman and Littlefield, 2003).

5. Michael A. Rebell, "Fiscal Equity Litigation and the Democratic Imperative," *Journal of Education Finance* 24, no. 1 (1998): 25–30, quoted in Margaret Hadderman, *Equity and Adequacy in Educational Finance*, ERIC Digest 129, August 1999.

6. Linda Darling-Hammond, "From 'Separate but Equal' to 'No Child Left Behind': The Collision of New Standards and Old Inequalities," in *Many Children Left Behind*, ed. Deborah Meier and George Wood (Boston: Beacon Press, 2004), 6.

7. Orfield and Lee, *Why Segregation Matters*, 16. See also Gary Orfield and Chungmei Lee, *Brown at 50: King's Dream or Plessy's Nightmare?* (Cambridge: MA: Civil Rights Project at Harvard University, 2004).

8. The Columbus, Ohio, school district serves more than sixty-five thousand students. African Americans account for 57 percent of students, whites 39 percent, and other racial/ethnic groups 4 percent. The study defines "total per-pupil spending" as "total annual per student spent on all functions combined, expressed in thousand of dollars." See Dennis J. Condron and Vincent J. Roscigno, "Disparities Within: Unequal Spending and Achievement in an Urban School District," *Sociology of Education* 76 (2003): 18–36.

9. Linda Darling-Hammond, "New Standards and Old Inequalities: School Reform and the Education of African American Students," *Journal of Negro Education* 69, no. 4 (2000): 263–87; U.S. General Accounting Office, *School Finance: State Efforts to Equalize Funding between Wealthy and Poor Districts* (Washington, DC: U.S. General Accounting Office, 1998), cited in "The Persisting Myth That Black and White Schools Are Equally Funded," *Journal of Blacks in Higher Education* 22 (Winter 1998–99): 17–18, 20. See also Jean Anyon, *Ghetto Schooling: A Political Economy of Urban Educational Reform* (New York: Teachers College Record, 1997); Gary Orfield and Chungmei Lee, *Racial Transformation and the Changing Nature of Segregation* (Cambridge, MA: Civil Rights Project at Harvard University, 2006); Orfield and Lee, *Why Segregation Matters;* Janet Ward Schofield, "Review of Research on School Desegregation's Impact on Elementary and Secondary School Students," in *Handbook of Research on Multicultural Education,* ed. James A. Banks and Cherry A. McGee Banks (New York: Macmillan, 1995); Marvin P. Dawkins and Jomills Henry Braddock, "The Continuing Significance of Desegregation: School Racial Composition and African American Inclusion in American Society," *Journal of Negro Education* 63 (Summer 1994): 394–405; David Monk and Emil Haller, "Predictors of High School Academic Course Offerings: The Role of School Size," *American Educational Research Journal* 30 (Spring 1993): 3–21; and Gary Natriello, Edward. L. McDill, and Aaron M. Pallas, *Schooling Disadvantaged Children: Racing against Catastrophe* (New York: Teachers College Press, 1990).

10. Lynn Olson, "The Great Divide," *Education Week,* January 9, 2003, 17–18; Jonathan Kozol, *Savage Inequalities: Children in America's Schools* (New York: Crown, 1991).

11. Christopher Jenks and Meredith Phillips, eds., *The Black-White Test Score* (Washington, DC: Brookings Institution, 1998).

12. Orfield and Lee, *Why Segregation Matters,* 6.

13. Juan Williams, *Enough: The Phony Leaders, Dead-End Movements, and Culture of Failure That Are Undermining Black America—and What We Can Do about It* (New York: Crown Books, 2006), 211.

14. Bob Herbert, "A Triumph of Felons and Failure," *New York Times,* August 24, 2006.

15. Herman Badillo, *One Nation, One Standard: An Ex-liberal on How Hispanics Can Succeed Just Like Other Immigrant Groups* (New York: Sentinel, 2006), 50–51, 32.

16. Orlando Patterson, "A Poverty of the Mind," *New York Times*, March 26, 2006.

17. John McWhorter, interview with Suzy Hansen, "Another Shade of Black," *Salon.com*, January 14, 2003. It is unclear whether McWhorter is describing a particular student or the title character of the novel and film *The World of Suzie Wong*.

18. John M. Bridgeland, John M. Dilulio Jr., and Karen Burke Morison, *The Silent Epidemic: Perspectives of High School Dropouts* (Washington, DC: Civic Enterprises, Peter D. Hart Research Associates, and Bill and Melinda Gates Foundation, 2006).

19. Ibid.

20. Daniel J. Losen, "Behind the Dropout Rate," *Gotham Gazette*, March 20, 2006.

21. Inside Schools, Advocates for Children of New York, "HS. 440, Dewitt Clinton High School" (forum), May 5, 2008, https://insideschools.org/index12.php?fso=1000&page=2&all=y).

22. Ibid.

23. Elora Mukherjee, *Criminalizing the Classroom: The Over-policing of New York City Schools* (New York: New York Civil Liberties Union, 2007).

24. Some scholars argue that public schools in inner cities often structure their curricula and pedagogical techniques to discourage critical analysis, thus reinforcing class differences in the sort of education attained by primary and secondary school students. See Anyon, *Ghetto Schooling;* and Samuel Bowles and Herbert Gintis, *Schooling in Capitalist America: Educational Reform and the Contradictions of Economic Life* (New York: Basic Books, 1977).

25. New York City Department of Education School Construction Authority, "Enrollment—Capacity—Utilization, Report, 2005–2006 School Year," November 2006, http://source.nycsca.org/pdf/bluebook05-06.pdf.

26. Inside Schools, "H.S. 440"; Elissa Gootman, "Lunch at 9:21, and the Students Are the Sardines," *New York Times*, October 15, 2003.

27. Mukherjee, *Criminalizing the Classroom*, 18.

28. Ibid., 16–19.

29. Patterson, "Poverty of the Mind."

30. The examples of these critiques that come from the *New York Times* constitute a public discourse very different from the ways the *Times* writes about young people of color.

31. Jane Gross, "In Fight against Prom Night Drinking, Schools Try Prohibition on Limousines," *New York Times*, June 6, 2003; Amy L. Best, *Prom Night: Youth, Schools, and Popular Culture* (New York: Routledge, 2000).

32. Peter Applebome, "A Plea to Let the Punishment Fit the Prank," *New York Times*, June 21, 2007.

33. Ralph Gardner Jr., "Spring Break, on a Leash," *New York Times*, November 12, 2006.

34. Sara Rimer, "AMAZING +: Driven to Excel; For Girls, It's Be Yourself, and Be Perfect, Too," *New York Times*, April 1, 2007.

35. Shaquesha Alequin et al., *In Between the Lines: How the New York Times Frames Youth* (New York: Youth Force, 2001).

36. Lori Dorfman and Vincent Schiraldi, *Off Balance: Youth, Crime and Race in the News* (Washington, DC: Building Blocks for Youth, Youth Law Center, April 2001).

37. Alequin et al., *In Between the Lines*, 2.

38. Cited in Robin Templeton, "Superscapegoating: Teen 'Superpredators' Hype Set Stage for Draconian Legislation," *Fairness and Accuracy in Reporting Extra!*, January–February 1998, 13–14.

39. Adam McGourney, "Pataki Says That Root of Crime Is Criminals, Not Society," *New York Times*, January 24, 1998.

40. Alequin et al., *In Between the Lines*, 1.

41. Wanda Mohr, Richard J. Gelles, and Ira M. Schwartz, "Shackled in the Land of Liberty: No Rights for Children," *Annals of the American Academy of Political and Social Science* 564 (1999): 37–55.

42. Daniel HoSang, *Youth and Community Organizing Today* (New York: Funders' Collaborative on Youth Organizing, 2003), 4–5.

43. Henry A. Giroux, "Public Intellectuals and the Challenge of Children's Culture: Youth and the Politics of Innocence," *Review of Education, Pedagogy, and Cultural Studies* 21, no. 3 (1999): 193–224.

44. Eileen Poe-Yamagata and Michael A. Jones, *And Justice for Some* (Washington, DC: National Council on Crime and Delinquency, 2000).

45. McGourney, "Pataki Says."

46. Robert J. Sampson, Jeffrey D. Morenoff, and Thomas Gannon-Rowley, "Assessing 'Neighborhood Effects': Social Processes and New Directions in Research," *Annual Review of Sociology* 28 (2002): 443–78.

47. Robert J. Sampson, Stephen Raudenbush, and Felton Earls, "Neighborhoods and Violent Crime: A Multilevel Study of Collective Efficacy," *Science* 277 (1997): 918–24.

48. Cosby, "Speech."

49. John McManus and Lori Dorfman, *Youth and Violence in California Newspapers* (Berkeley, CA: Media Studies Group, 1999).

50. Quoted in Joel Spring, *Political Agendas for Education: From the Religious Right to the Green Party* (New York: Routledge, 2005), 54.

51. Inside Schools, "H.S. 440."

52. See Daniel Patrick Moynihan, "The Negro Family: The Case for National Action," in *The Moynihan Report and the Politics of Controversy*, ed. Lee Rainwater and William C. Yancey (Cambridge, MA: MIT Press, 1965); Winthrop D. Jordan, *White over Black: American Attitudes toward the Negro, 1550–1812* (Chapel Hill: University of North Carolina Press, 1968); and the documentary *Ethnic Notions: Black Images in the White Mind* (directed and produced by Marlon Riggs, 1987).

53. James Baldwin, "In Search of a Majority," in *Nobody Knows My Name: More Notes on a Native Son* (New York: Delta Books, 1962).

54. Steve Burghardt, *The Other Side of Organizing: Resolving the Personal Dilemmas and Political Demands of Daily Practice* (Cambridge, MA: Schenkman, 1982).

55. Celina Su, "Cracking Silent Codes: Critical Race Theory and Education Organizing," *Discourse: Studies in the Cultural Politics of Education* 28, no. 4 (2007): 531–48, and *Reading, Writing, and Reform in the South Bronx: Lessons for Family-School Partnerships* (Cambridge, MA: Harvard Family Research Project, 2005).

56. Later, when I thought about whose story I could highlight in the Introduction, I asked Jorman whether I could conduct follow-up interviews with him. I did not know anything about his school experiences, as our previous conversations had focused on his relationship to SBU. I had approached him, rather than other SBU leaders I had interviewed in 2003–4, because I knew that he was still in New York City and that he had once dropped out. I suspect that if I took the time to follow other dropouts as closely as I did Jorman I would hear similarly rich and nuanced stories about personal challenges and aspirations, cruel circumstances, and feelings of frustration and hope.

57. Jill Jonnes, *South Bronx Rising* (New York: Fordham University Press, 2002).

58. David Halle, ed., *New York and Los Angeles: Politics, Society, and Culture—A Comparative View* (Chicago: University of Chicago Press, 2003).

59. Gertrude Stein, *Lectures in America* (New York: Vintage Books, 1975), 169.

60. See, for example, Project STAR (Student Teacher Achievement Ratio) in Tennessee, a rare experimental design study in education policy, where almost twelve thousand students were randomly placed in classes of different sizes in kindergarten through third grade. The positive impact of small class size on achievement tests remained even after students returned to larger classes in later grades, and the effects were larger for minority and poor students, as discussed in Alan Krueger, "Experimental Estimates of Education Production Functions," *Quarterly Journal of Economics*, 114, no. 2 (1999): 497–532. These data suggest that for each low-income student who attends small classes and graduates from high school as a result, the government saves almost $200,000

over the student's lifetime—by collecting more in tax revenues, paying less in public assistance, etc. See Peter Muennig and Steven H. Woolf, "Health and Economic Benefits of Reducing the Number of Students per Classroom in US Primary Schools," *American Journal of Public Health* 97, no. 11 (2007): 2020–27. A study in Ypsilanti, Michigan, followed 123 African Americans from similarly low-income households for over forty years. Approximately half of them were placed in comprehensive preschool, and the remaining half constituted a control group. Those who attended preschool reported higher incomes, lower crime rates, and educational attainment. Overall, studies have found $17 in returns for every tax dollar used for the program. These results are presented in Lawrence J. Schweinhart et al., *Lifetime Effects: The High/Scope Perry Preschool Study through Age 40* (Ypsilanti, MI: High/Scope Press, 2004). A similar study followed 1,539 children from high-poverty Chicago neighborhoods for two decades. Those who attended day care and received family and health services until age nine reported higher employment rates, higher marriage rates, higher incomes, and higher rates of high school completion at age twenty. To the researchers, these studies show conclusive proof that "established programs administered through public schools can promote children's long-term success." See Arthur J. Reynolds et al., "Long-Term Effects of an Early Childhood Intervention on Educational Achievement and Juvenile Arrest: A 15-Year Follow-up of Low-Income Children in Public Schools," *Journal of the American Medical Association* 285, no. 18 (2001): 2339–46. Further, high school graduates live about 9.2 years longer than high school dropouts. Much of this increase in life expectancy is due to increases in the skills and cognitive abilities conferred by education, as well as preventive care, income, occupational safety, and access to health insurance, as analyzed in Peter Muennig, "The Health Consequences of Inadequate Education," in *The Price We Pay: Economic and Social Consequences of Inadequate Education,* ed. Henry Levin and Clive Belfield (Washington, DC: Brookings Institution Press, 2007).

CHAPTER 1

1. Orlando Patterson, "A Poverty of the Mind," *New York Times,* March 26, 2006.

2. Peter Edelman, Harry Olzer, and Paul Offner, *Reconnecting Disadvantaged Young Men* (Washington, DC: Urban Institute, 2006); Ronald Mincy, ed., *Black Males Left Behind* (Washington, DC: Urban Institute, 2006).

3. Patterson, "Poverty of the Mind."

4. Juan Williams, *Enough: The Phony Leaders, Dead-End Movements, and Culture of Failure That Are Undermining Black America—And What We Can Do about It* (New York: Crown Books, 2006), 234.

5. Bill Cosby, "Speech at the 50th Anniversary Commemoration of the *Brown v. Topeka Board of Education* Supreme Court Decision, May 22, 2004," *Black Scholar* 34 (Winter 2004): 2–5. In this volume the *Black Scholar* also published a forum among leading experts on issues raised by Cosby's speech.

6. Williams, *Enough*, 232, 211.

7. Bob Herbert, "A Triumph of Felons and Failure," *New York Times*, August 24, 2006.

8. Herman Badillo, *One Nation, One Standard: An Ex-liberal on How Hispanics Can Succeed Just Like Other Immigrant Groups* (New York: Sentinel, 2006), 27 (emphasis added), 32, 25, 30. From 1970 to 1977, Badillo represented the Twenty-first Congressional District of New York (South Bronx).

9. Ibid., 8, 31, 28.

10. Williams, *Enough*, 25.

11. Patterson, "Poverty of the Mind."

12. Herbert, "Triumph of Felons."

13. I borrow the concept of "ideological blackening" from Aihwa Ong. She has argued that while the contemporary celebration of some Asian Americans as "model minorities" that I discuss in this chapter has operated as a form of "ideological whitening," Cambodian refugees are currently undergoing a process of "ideological blackening" (86). Aihwa Ong, *Buddha Is Hiding: Refugees, Citizenship, the New America* (Berkeley: University of California Press, 2003). A number of scholars have noted that a similar process of "ideological blackening"—or what they refer to a "negroization"—targeted Chinese immigrants during the second half of the nineteenth century. See Dan Caldwell, "The Negroization of the Chinese Stereotype in California," *Southern California Quarterly* 53 (June 1971): 123–31; and Najia Aarim-Heriot, *Chinese Immigrants, African Americans, and Racial Anxiety in the United States, 1848–1882* (Urbana: University of Illinois Press, 2003).

14. Mary S. Strine, "Critical Theory and 'Organic' Intellectuals: Reframing the Work of Cultural Critique," *Communication Monographs* 58, no. 2 (1991): 195–201, quoted in D. Soyini Madison, *Critical Ethnography: Methods, Ethics, Performance* (Thousand Oaks, CA: Sage Publications, 2005), 16.

15. These are clearly not the only scholarly explanations for the achievement gap. In fact, in reviewing them I refer to other important scholarship. I focus on them, however, because they have received the most attention outside the academy and serve as the intellectual scaffolding of the "culture of failure" narrative.

16. Richard Majors and Janet Mancini Billson, *Cool Pose: The Dilemmas of Black Manhood in America* (New York: Lexington Books, 1992), 4, 105, 1.

17. Robert Kelley has suggested that Majors and Billson's thesis "recycles" the arguments advanced by earlier work on African American culture and "soul," such as Lee Rainwater, ed., *Soul* (New Brunswick, NJ: Transaction Books, 1970);

Ulf Hannerz, "The Significance of Soul," in Rainwater, *Soul*, 15–30, and *Soulside: Inquiries into Ghetto Culture and Community* (New York: Columbia University Press, 1966); Eliot Liebow, *Tally's Corner: A Study of Negro Streetcorner Men* (Boston: Little, Brown, 1971); and Daniel Schulz, *Coming Up Black: Patterns of Ghetto Socialization* (Englewood Cliffs, NJ: Prentice-Hall, 1969). See Robin D. G. Kelley, *Yo' Mama's Disfunktional!* (Boston: Beacon Press, 1997), 23–24. I find that the "cool pose" literature also "recycles" notions of African American masculinity found in Norman Mailer's classic essay "The White Negro," *Dissent,* Summer 1957, 276–93. Also see James Baldwin's critical response to Mailer in his essay "The Black Boy Looks at the White Boy," in *Nobody Knows My Name: More Notes of a Native Son* (New York: Dial, 1961).

18. Elijah Anderson, *Code of the Street: Decency, Violence, and the Moral Life of the Inner City* (New York: W. W. Norton, 1999), and "The Code of the Streets," *Atlantic Monthly,* May 1994, 80–94. Anderson's work here "grows out of the ethnographic work" (10) that he conducted for his book *Streetwise: Race, Class, and Change in an Urban Community* (Chicago: University of Chicago Press, 1990).

19. Anderson, *Code of the Street,* 9.

20. Editor's introduction to Anderson, "The Code of the Streets," 81 (emphasis added).

21. Anderson, *Code of the Street,* 15–26.

22. Ibid., 9–10.

23. Ibid., 34, 323 (emphasis added).

24. See Winthrop D. Jordan, *White over Black: American Attitudes toward the Negro, 1550–1812* (Chapel Hill: University of North Carolina Press, 1968); George M. Fredrickson, *The Black Image in the White Mind: The Debate on Afro-American Character and Destiny, 1817–1914* (Middletown, CT: Wesleyan University Press, 1987); Michael P. Rogin, "'The Sword Became a Flashing Vision': D. W. Griffith's *The Birth of a Nation,*" in *Ronald Reagan, the Movie and Other Episodes in Political Demonology* (Berkeley: University of California Press, 1987), 190–235; Daryl Scott, *Contempt and Pity: Social Policy and the Image of the Damaged Black Psyche, 1880–1996* (Chapel Hill: University of North Carolina Press, 1999); Ronald Takaki, *Iron Cages: Race and Culture in Nineteenth-Century America,* rev. ed. (New York: Oxford University Press, 2000); and the documentary *Ethnic Notions: Black Images in the White Mind* (directed and produced by Marlon Riggs, 1987).

25. Anderson, *Code of the Street,* 35–36, 105, 287. In his response to Loic Wacquant's accusation in the pages of *American Journal of Sociology* that in *Code of the Street* he had engaged in the "reification of cultural orientations into groups," Anderson argues that the terms *decent* and *street,* as used in the book, are "not categorical but fluid" (1544). "The terms 'decent' and 'street,'" he explains, "are quite fluid in their operation, for residents are routinely engage in code-switching" (1543). However, I find that in the book the terms operate less fluidly than suggested by Anderson. In a passage from *Code of the Street* (35) quoted

in his *AJS* response to Wacquant, he writes, "Moreover, decent residents may judge themselves to be so while judging others to be of the street, and street individuals often present themselves as decent, while drawing distinctions between themselves and still other people" (1543). Thus while *decent* and *street* are labels used by individuals to judge and identify themselves and others, Anderson uses the labels to describe types of individuals. As a result, readers encounter in his writing plenty of references to "decent residents" and "street individuals." In fact, even in his response to Wacquant, Anderson describes the central argument of his book as focusing on "the interplay of decent and street families" (1547). See Elijah Anderson, "The Ideologically Driven Critique," *American Journal of Sociology* 107 (May 2002): 1533–50. For Wacquant's critique of *Code of the Street,* see Loic Wacquant, "Scrutinizing the Street: Poverty, Morality, and the Pitfalls of Urban Ethnography," *American Journal of Sociology* 107 (May 2002): 1468–1532. The other books reviewed by Wacquant are Mitchell Duneier's *Sidewalk* and Katherine Newman's *No Shame in My Game.* I am indebted to the anonymous reviewers from NYU Press for the Wacquant/Anderson reference.

26. Anderson, *Code of the Street,* 32–33, 38–9, 45–47.

27. Ibid., 93.

28. Ibid., 93–96 (emphasis added).

29. Ibid., 54–63.

30. Ibid., 32, 325, 324, 180, 218.

31. Ibid., 315, 324.

32. Michael Eric Dyson, *Is Bill Cosby Right? Or Has the Black Middle Class Lost Its Mind?* (New York: Basic Civitas Books, 2005), 110. On the role African American social scientists have played in advancing this critique of working-class and poor African Americans and its accompanying ideology of "racial uplift," see Adolph Reed, "The Study of Black Politics and the Practice of Black Politics: Their Historical Relation and Evolution," in *Problems and Methods in the Study of Politics,* ed. Ian Shapiro, Rogers M. Smith, and Tarek E. Masoud (Cambridge: Cambridge University Press, 2004), 106–43.

33. Cosby, "Speech."

34. Bill Cosby, quoted in Williams, *Enough,* 19.

35. Anderson, *Code of the Street,* 93. Importantly, Yvette, the one student Anderson quotes directly, reports being teased for "being 'a nerd,'" not for "acting white."

36. In *Eminent Educators,* Maurice Berube identifies Ogbu as one of the four most significant intellectuals in the development of American education. The other intellectuals he identifies are John Dewey, Howard Gardiner, and Carol Gilligan. See Maurice R. Berube, *Eminent Educators: Studies in Intellectual Influence* (Westport, CT: Greenwood Press, 2000).

37. John U. Ogbu, "Understanding Cultural Diversity and Learning," *Educational Researcher* 21, no. 8 (1992): 9.

38. Douglas Foley refers to Ogbu's theory as "an eclectic blend of history, ecology and psychology." Douglas Foley, "Ogbu's Theory of Academic Disengagement: Its Evolution and Its Critics," *Intercultural Education* 15, no. 4 (2004): 385.

39. Ogbu notes that "Puerto Ricans may qualify for membership in this category if they consider themselves 'a colonized people'" (8). In early formulations of his typology, Ogbu also included a separate category for "autonomous minorities," or groups such as Jews and Mormons who are minorities in "a primarily numerical sense" (8). See Ogbu, "Understanding Cultural Diversity." For a critique of Ogbu's typology, see Margaret A. Gibson, "Complicating the Immigrant/ Involuntary Minority Typology," *Anthropology and Educational Quarterly* 28, no. 3 (1997): 431–54.

40. As one reads the passage, one wonders how a minority could interpret "social, political, and economic barriers erected against them" as anything other than "undeserved oppression."

41. John Ogbu, "Minority Education in Comparative Perspective," *Journal of Negro Education* 59 (1990): 45–57.

42. Signithia Fordham and John Ogbu, "Black Students' School Success: Coping with the Burden of 'Acting White,'" *Urban Review* 18 (1986): 176–206. As a sign of the intellectual influence of this article, in a 2004 article Ogbu notes that "the joint article has generated responses from the academic community beyond what we anticipated. It is the subject of dissertation studies (Carter, 1999; O'Connor, 1996; Taylor, 2001), several publications (Ainsworth-Darnell and Downey, 1998; Bergin and Cooks, 2002; Cook and Ludwig, 1997) and organized sessions at professional meetings (Epstein, 2003; Horvat and O'Connor, 2001). During the past 2 years, I have reviewed more than a dozen book and journal manuscripts on oppositional culture and schooling from publishers." John U. Ogbu, "Collective Identity and the Burden of 'Acting White' in Black History, Community, and Education," *Urban Review* 36, no. 1 (2004): 2. It is worth noting that the majority of the texts referenced by Ogbu present explicit refutations of his and Fordham's thesis. An Editor's Note remarks that the article, published posthumously, "serves as a powerful reminder of the work that remains to be done 50 years after the *Brown* desegregation decision" (1).

43. John Ogbu, *Black Americans in an Affluent Suburb: A Study of Academic Disengagement* (Mahwah, NJ: Lawrence Erlbaum, 2003).

44. Ogbu, "Understanding Cultural Diversity," 12.

45. John Ogbu, quoted in Felicia Lee, "Why Are Black Students Lagging?" *New York Times,* November 30, 2002.

46. Daniel Solarzano, "Mobility Aspirations among Racial Minorities: Controlling for SES," *Sociology and Social Research* 75 (1991): 182–88; Amanda A. Datnow and Robert Cooper, "Peer Networks of African American Students in Independent Schools: Affirming Academic Success and Racial Identity," *Journal of Negro Education* 65 (1996): 56–72; Carla O'Connor, "Dispositions towards (Collective)

Struggle and Educational Resilience in the Inner City: A Case Analysis of Six African American High Schools," *American Educational Research Journal* 24 (1997): 593–629; James W. Ainsworth-Darnell and Douglas B. Downey, "Assessing the Oppositional Culture Explanation for Racial/Ethnic Differences in School Performance," *American Sociological Review* 63 (1998): 536–53; Phillip J. Cook and Jens Ludwig, "Weighing the 'Burden of Acting White': Are There Race Differences in Attitudes towards Education" *Journal of Policy Analysis and Management* 16, no. 2 (1997): 256–78; Margaret Beale Spencer et al., "Identity and School Adjustment: Questioning the 'Acting White' Assumption," *Educational Psychologist* 36 (2001): 21–30; David A. Bergin and Helen C. Cooks, "High School Students of Color Talk about Accusations of 'Acting White,'" *Urban Review* 34, no. 2 (2002): 113–34; Vinay Harpalani, "What Does 'Acting White' Really Mean? Racial Identity Formation and Academic Achievement among Black Youth," *Penn GSE Perspectives on Urban Education* 1 (Spring 2002), www.urbanedjournal.org/commentaries/c0001. html; Margaret Beale Spencer, "Historical and Development Perspectives on Black Academic Achievement: Debunking the 'Acting White' Myth and Posing New Directions for Research," in *Surmounting All Odds: Education, Opportunity, and Society in the New Millennium,* ed. Carol C. Yeakey and Ronald D. Henderson (Greenwich, CT: Information Age, 2003); and Prudence Carter, *Keepin' It Real: School Success beyond Black and White* (Oxford: Oxford University Press, 2005).

47. See James Anderson, *The Education of Blacks in the South* (Chapel Hill: University of North Carolina Press, 1988) and "Crosses to Bear and Promises to Keep: The Jubilee Anniversary of *Brown v. Board of Education,*" *Urban Education* 39, no. 4 (2004): 359–73; David Cecelski, *Along Freedom Road: Hyde County, North Carolina and the Fate of Black Schools in the South* (Chapel Hill: University of North Carolina Press, 1994); Clarence Taylor, *Knocking at Our Own Door: Milton A. Galamison and the Struggle to Integrate New York City Schools* (New York: Columbia University Press, 1997); James Patterson, *Brown v. Board of Education: A Civil Rights Milestone and Its Troubled Legacy* (New York: Oxford University Press, 2002); Jeanne Theoharis and Komozi Woodard, eds., *Freedom North: The Black Freedom Struggle Outside of the South, 1940–1980* (New York: Palgrave Macmillan, 2002) and *Groundwork: Local Black Freedom Movements in America* (New York: NYU Press, 2003); Wendell Pritchett, *Brownsville, Brooklyn* (Chicago: University of Chicago Press, 2002); Jack Dougherty, *More Than One Struggle: The Evolution of Black School Reform in Milwaukee* (Chapel Hill: University of North Carolina Press, 2004).

48. Scholars have dated the birth of the contemporary "model minority" discourse to the publication of William Peterson's "Success Story, Japanese-American Style," *New York Times Magazine,* January 9, 1966. See Keith Osajima, "Asian Americans as the Model Minority: An Analysis of the Popular Press in the 1960s and 1980s," in *Contemporary Asian America,* ed. Min Zhou and James V. Gatewood (New York: NYU Press, 2000), 449–58; and Ronald Takaki, *Strangers*

from a Different Shore: A History of Asian America (Boston: Little, Brown, 1989). Pointing to Ogbu's Nigerian roots, Kevin Michael Foster has argued that Ogbu's narrative "is consistent with an ethnic immigrant narrative that has long held motivational value among African, Asian, and European immigrant students in the United States—quite possibly including John Ogbu—who came to the US as an immigrant student himself." See Kevin M. Foster, "Narratives of the Social Scientist: Understanding the Work of John Ogbu," *International Journal of Qualitative Studies in Education* 18 (September–October 2005): 565. A number of studies have shown how such narratives hold sway among immigrant students themselves. See Stacey J. Lee, *Unraveling the "Model Minority" Stereotype: Listening to Asian American Youth* (New York: Teachers College Press, 1996); Paul Wong et al., "Asian Americans as a Model Minority: Self-Perceptions and Perceptions by Other Groups," *Sociological Perspectives* 41, no. 1 (1998): 95–148; and Mary Waters, *Black Identities: West Indian Immigrant Dreams and American Realities* (Cambridge, MA: Harvard University Press, 2001).

49. Patterson, "Poverty of the Mind."

50. See Stacey J. Lee, "Behind the Model Minority Stereotype: Voices of High- and Low-Achieving Asian America Students," *Anthropology and Education Quarterly* 25, no. 4 (1994): 413–29, *Unraveling the "Model Minority" Stereotype,* and *Up against Whiteness: Race, School, and Immigrant Youth* (New York: Teachers College Press, 2005); Lucie Cheng and Philip Q. Yang, "The 'Model Minority' Deconstructed," in Zhou and Gatewood, *Contemporary Asian America,* 459–82; Ruben G. Rumbaut, "Vietnamese, Laotian, and Cambodian Americans," in Zhou and Gatewood, *Contemporary Asian America,* 175–206; Frank H. Wu, *Yellow: Race in America beyond White and Black* (New York: Basic Books, 2003), 39–78; Ka Ying Yang, "Southeast Asian American Children: Not the 'Model Minority,'" *Future of Children* 14, no. 2 (2004): 127–33.

51. Karolyn Tyson, "Weighing In: Elementary-Age Students and the Debate on Attitudes towards School among Black Students," *Social Forces* 80, no. 4 (2002): 1163.

52. Lawrence Steinberg, B. Bradford Brown, and Sanford M. Dornbusch, *Beyond the Classroom: Why School Reform Has Failed and What Parents Need to Do* (New York: Simon and Schuster, 1996), 19, quoted in Tyson, "Weighing In," 1162.

53. Tyson, "Weighing In," 1163. The findings from her own study of middle-class African American elementary school children, Tyson reports, "indicate that the origins of a 'burden,' where found, are often less cultural than school-based."

54. Ogbu, *Black Americans,* 46, quoted in Margaret A. Gibson, "Promoting Academic Engagement among Minority Youths: Implications from John Ogbu's Shaker Heights Ethnography," *International Journal of Qualitative Studies in Education* 18 (2005): 588 (emphasis added by Gibson). For critiques of Ogbu's work on this count, see Gibson's "Promoting Academic Engagement," and Foster, "Narratives of the Social Scientist."

55. See Alejandro Portes, "Children of Immigrants: Segmented Assimilation and Its Variants," in *The Economic Sociology of Immigration: Essays on Networks, Ethnicity,* and *Entrepreneurship,* ed. Alejandro Portes (New York: Russell Sage Foundation, 1995), 1–41, and "Divergent Destinies: Immigration, the Second Generation, and the Rise of Transnational Communities," in *Paths to Inclusion: The Integration of Migrants in the United States and Germany,* ed. Peter Schuck and Rainer Munz (New York: Berghahn Books, 1998); Alejandro Portes and Min Zhou, "The New Second Generation: Segmented Assimilation and Its Variants among Post-1965 Immigrant Youth," *Annals of the Academy of Political and Social Sciences* 530 (1993): 74–98; Ruben G. Rumbaut, "The Crucible Within: Ethnic Identities, Self-Esteem, and Segmented Assimilation among Children of Immigrants," *International Migration Review* 28 (1994): 748–94; Alejandro Portes and Ruben G. Rumbaut, *Legacies: The Story of the Immigrant Second Generation* (Berkeley: University of California Press, 2001); and Ruben G. Rumbaut and Alejandro Portes, eds., *Ethnicities: Children of Immigrants in America* (Berkeley: University of California Press, 2001).

56. The CILS study was funded by grants from the Andrew W. Mellon Foundation, the Spencer Foundation, the National Science Foundation, and the Russell Sage Foundation. A follow-up study funded by the Russell Sage Foundation was conducted from 2001 to 2003. It tracked the CILS sample through early adulthood (ages twenty-three to twenty-seven). The findings of this survey are reported in a 2005 special issue of *Ethnic and Racial Studies* coedited by Portes and Rumbaut as well as in the third edition of their coauthored book *Immigrant America.* See Alejandro Portes and Ruben Rumbaut, eds., "The New Second Generation in Early Adulthood," special issue, *Racial and Ethnic Studies* 28 (November 2005), and *Immigrant America: A Portrait,* 3rd ed. (Berkeley: University of California Press, 2006), ch. 8. For CILS results, see Center for Migration and Development, "The Children of Immigrants Longitudinal Study," n.d., http://cmd.princeton.edu/cils.shtml.

57. Alejandro Portes and Ruben Rumbaut, *Immigrant America,* 2nd ed. (Berkeley: University of California Press, 1996), 248–50.

58. Ibid., 247–53. Portes and Rumbaut acknowledge their debt to Ogbu's scholarship in the endnotes to ch. 7 of the second edition of *Immigrant America* (317).

59. James Baldwin, "In Search of a Majority," in *Nobody Knows My Name: More Notes on a Native Son* (New York: Delta Books, 1962), 133.

60. Lee, *Up against Whiteness,* 124. Lee's findings echo L. Janelle Dance's findings in *Tough Fronts.* Dance's four-year ethnographic study of the "poses" and "fronts" assumed by urban teenagers in a variety of settings led her to conclude that "beneath the surface of hard postures are student critique of a mechanism of schooling, namely uncaring teachers, that facilitate educational inequality" (148). L. Janelle Dance, *Tough Fronts: The Impact of Street Culture on Schooling* (New York: Routledge Falmer, 2002).

61. Karl L. Alexander, Doris R. Entwisle, and Maxine S. Thompson, "School Performance, Status Relations, and the Structure of Sentiment: Bringing the Teacher Back In," *American Sociological Review* 52 (1987): 665–82; George Farkas et al., "Cultural Resources and School Success: Gender, Ethnicity, and Poverty Groups within an Urban School District," *American Sociological Review* 55 (1990): 127–42; Cynthia Ballanger, "Because You Like Us: The Language of Control," *Harvard Educational Review* 62 (1992): 199–208; Jomills Braddock II and Robert E. Slavin, "Why Ability Grouping Must End: Achieving Excellence and Equity in American Education," *Journal of Intergroup Relations* 20 (1993): 51–64; Larry V. Hedges, Richard Laine, and Rob Greenwald, "Does Money Matter? A Meta-Analysis of Studies of the Effects of Differential Inputs on Students Outcomes," *Educational Researcher* 23 (1994): 5–14; Larry V. Hedges and Rob Greenwald, "Have Times Changed? The Relation between School Resources and Student Performance," in *Does Money Matter? The Effects of School Resources on Student Achievement and Adult Success*, ed. Gary Burtless (Washington, DC: Brookings Institution Press, 1996); Rob Greenwald, Larry V. Hedges, and Richard Laine, "The Effects of School Resources on Student Achievement," *Review of Educational Research* 66 (1996): 361–96; Daniel Solomon et al., "Teacher Practices Associated with Students' Sense of the Classroom as a Community," *Social Psychology of Education* 1 (1997): 235–67; Harold Wenglinsky, "How Money Matters: The Effect of School District Spending on Academic Achievement," *Sociology of Education* 70 (1997): 221–37; Michelle Fine, Lois Weis, and Linda C. Powell, "Communities of Difference: A Critical Look at Desegregated Spaces Created for and by Youth," *Harvard Educational Review* 67 (1997): 247–83; Marta Elliott, "School Finance and Opportunities to Learn: Does Money Well Spent Enhance Students' Achievement?" *Sociology of Education* 71 (1998): 223–45; Ronald Ferguson, "Teachers' Perceptions and Expectations and the Black-White Test Score Gap" and "Can Schools Narrow the Test Score Gap?" both in *The Black-White Test Score Gap*, ed. Christopher Jenks and Meredith Phillips (Washington, DC: Brookings Institution Press, 1998), 273–317 and 318–74 respectively; Angela Valenzuela, *Subtractive Schooling: U.S.-Mexican Youth and the Politics of Caring* (Albany: State University of New York Press, 1999); Deborah A. Verstegen and Richard A. King, "The Relationship between School Spending and Student Achievement: A Review and Analysis of 35 Years of Production Function Research," *Journal of Education Finance* 24 (1998): 243–62; Karen Osterman and Stephanie Freese, "Nurturing the Mind to Improve Learning: Teacher Caring and Student Engagement," in *The Academic Achievement of Minority Students*, ed. Sheila T. Gregory (Lanham, MD: University of America Press, 2000), 287–305; Dennis J. Condron and Vincent J. Roscigno, "Disparities Within: Unequal Spending and Achievement in an Urban School District," *Sociology of Education* 76 (2003): 18–36; and Gibson, "Promoting Academic Engagement."

62. *Legacies* received the 2002 Distinguished Scholarship Award of the American Sociological Association and the 2002 W. I. Thomas and Florian Znaniecki Award for best book from the International Migration Section of the American Sociological Association.

63. Portes and Rumbaut, *Legacies*, 242.

64. In a 2004 article Portes and Lingxin Hao acknowledged that "the potential effects of school contextual variables on academic achievement and school retention were not examined exhaustively" in *Legacies* or the series of articles that led to the publication of the book (Portes, "Children of Immigrants" and "Divergent Destinies". Drawing on CILS data, they analyze "the effect of the class and ethnic composition of schools attended in early adolescence on the probability of graduation and on levels of educational attainment." Ethnic composition and average school SES levels are important contextual factors but, as suggested above, they are not the only school-level factors identified in the relevant literature as influencing educational outcomes. Alejandro Portes and Lingxin Hao, "The Schooling of Children of Immigrants: Contextual Effects on the Educational Attainment of the Second Generation," *Proceedings of the National Academy of Sciences of the United States of America* 101, no. 3 (2004): 119–27.

65. Alejandro Portes and Ruben Rumbaut, "Conclusion: Mainstream Ideologies and the Long-Term Prospects of Immigrant Communities," in *Legacies*, 269–86, and "Conclusion—The Forging of a New America: Lessons for Theory and Policy," in Rumbaut and Portes, eds. *Ethnicities*, 301–15.

66. See Oscar Lewis, *Five Families: Mexican Case Studies in the Culture of Poverty* (New York: Basic Books, 1959), *The Children of Sanchez* (New York: Random House, 1961), *La Vida: A Puerto Rican Family in the Culture of Poverty—San Juan and Puerto Rico* (New York: Random House, 1966), and "The Culture of Poverty," in *On Understanding Poverty*, ed. Daniel P. Moynihan (New York: Basic Books, 1969); Michael Harrington, *The Other America* (New York: Macmillan, 1962); Daniel Patrick Moynihan, "The Negro Family: The Case for National Action," in *The Moynihan Report and the Politics of Controversy*, ed. Lee Rainwater and William C. Yancey (Cambridge, MA: MIT Press, 1965); and Edward Banfield, *The Unheavenly City*, 2nd ed. (Boston: Little, Brown, 1970). Alford Young has argued that the intellectual foundations of the "culture of poverty" studies of the 1960s was laid by the pioneering pre–World War II work of W. E. B. Du Bois in *The Philadelphia Negro* and St. Clare Drake and Horace Clayton in *Black Metropolis*. This work, as Young puts it, asserted that "the culture of low income African Americans was a source of their problems in attaining social mobility" (21). Alford A. Young Jr., *The Minds of Marginalized Black Men: Making Sense of Mobility, Opportunity, and Future Life Chances* (Princeton: Princeton University Press, 2004).

67. Etienne Balibar, "Is There a 'Neo-racism'?" in *Race, Nation, Class: Ambiguous Identities*, ed. Etienne Balibar and Immanuel Wallerstein (London: Verso, 1992), 22, quoted in Lee, *Up against Whiteness*, 7.

68. For useful discussions of the place of the "culture of poverty" thesis in U.S. social science and public policy discussions, see Michael B. Katz, *The Undeserving Poor: From the War on Poverty to the War on Welfare* (New York: Pantheon Books, 1989), 9–35; and Alice O'Connor, *Poverty Knowledge: Social Science, Social Policy, and the Poor in Twentieth-Century U.S. History* (Princeton: Princeton University Press, 2001), 99–123. Katz argues that the "culture of poverty" thesis underlies the concept of "cultural deprivation" found in the literature of the times on the education of nonwhite children (20–22). See Frank Riessman, *The Culturally Deprived Child* (New York: Harper, 1962).

69. Dyson, *Is Bill Cosby Right?* 84.

70. John McWhorter, *Losing the Race: Self-Sabotage in Black America* (New York: Harper Perennial, 2001), front cover. The Free Press originally published the hardback edition of the book in 2000.

71. John McWhorter, *Winning the Race: Beyond the Crisis in Black America* (New York: Gotham Books, 2005), inside cover.

72. For example, the editor's blurb on the back cover of *Losing the Race* refers to McWhorter as a "Berkeley linguistics professor," and the promotional blurb on the back cover of his 2004 *Authentically Black* proclaims him "Bill O'Reilly with a Ph.D." *Black Issues Book Review* provided the blurb. See John McWhorter, *Authentically Black: Essays for the Black Silent Majority* (New York: Gotham Books, 2004), back cover.

73. McWhorter, *Losing the Race*, x. In the Afterword to the 2001 edition of the book, McWhorter defends himself against critics who argued that he "claimed that there is 'no' racism in the United States" by explaining, "My claims are rather that 1) racism is quickly receding, and (2) to the extent that it still exists today, it is no longer a significant obstacle to black advancement or well-being" (266).

74. Ibid., 83.

75. Ibid., 150–51. McWhorter also refers to African Americans' supposed anti-intellectualism as "a culture-internal legacy" (84).

76. Ibid., 129.

77. Ibid., 125 (emphasis in the original).

78. Ibid., 123–24.

79. While Ogbu argues that African Americans' fear of "acting white" is rooted in the oppositional identities developed as a result of their historical experiences as involuntary minorities, McWhorter asserts that its emergence dates to 1966 (*Losing the Race*, 270, and *Winning the Race*, 262). By locating the genesis of the fear of "acting white" in 1966, McWhorter characterizes it as a post–civil rights phenomenon—one that emerged as the result of *Brown* bringing Black students into contact with white students in ways that taught them that academic achievement is "white."

80. McWhorter, *Losing the Race*, 129. Tellingly, in this passage, McWhorter slips from a discussion of how Black students consider themselves to how others—perhaps he—consider them.

81. Ibid., 144, 269–70. McWhorter (p. 130) references no evidence for any of the passages cited in this paragraph. Earlier in the book, he does reference Lawrence Steinberg's study of teenagers on the differences in levels of schoolwork done by white, Asian, Black, and Latino students (Steinberg, Brown, and Dornbusch, *Beyond the Classroom*). He cites two publications by Nathan Caplan, Marcella H. Choy, and John K. Whitmore to support his claims regarding the academic drive of Asian students (281). He cites no evidence, beyond his own observations, for his claims regarding the academic drive of Black Caribbean students. See Nathan Caplan, Marcella H. Choy, and John K. Whitmore, *The Boat People and Achievement in America: A Study of Family Life, Hard Work, and Cultural Values* (Ann Arbor: University of Michigan Press, 1989) and "Indochinese Refugee Families and Academic Achievement," *Scientific American*, February 1992.

82. McWhorter, *Losing the Race*, 89. On this point, he notes that "none of this is to suggest that there are no excellent black students—I have had those too. . . . But existence of these people does not belie my sad point about the culture as a whole, because as the very cream of the crop, they are exceptions, not the rule. At Berkeley, I have found it impossible to avoid nothing less than fearing that a black student in my class is likely a problem case" (84, emphasis in the original). Again, "The sad but simple fact is that while there are some excellent black students, on the average, black students do not try as hard as other students" (100).

83. Ibid., 265.

84. Ainsworth-Darnell and Downey, "Assessing the Oppositional Culture Explanation"; Cook and Ludwig, "Weighing the 'Burden.'"

85. McWhorter, *Winning the Race*, 278.

86. Ibid., 276.

87. Ibid., 280.

88. Ibid., 277.

89. Ibid., 281.

90. Ibid., 282 (emphasis added).

91. Ibid., 270. He writes: "A new 'culture matters' meme is getting out there. . . . An emblematic moment was when, at the 2004 Democratic Convention, Barack Obama called on us to 'eradicate the slander that says that a black youth with a book is acting white' and the audience went nuts."

92. Barack Obama, keynote address at the 2004 Democratic Party National Convention, Boston, July 27, 2004, www.pbs.org/newshour/vote2004/demconvention/speeches/obama.html.

93. Clarence Page, "Acting White," Essay for PBS Newshour, September 27, 2004, www.pbs.org/newhour/essays/july-dec04/page_9-27.html.

94. On his campaign Web site, Obama, like other presidential candidates, highlights a variety of policy proposals that address the issue of education (see Barack Obama, "Education," 2008, www.barackobama.com/issues/education). However, these proposals have not received the same attention on the stump or in the media as what the *Washington Post* refers to as Obama's message of "tough love."

95. Perry Bacon Jr., "Obama Reaches Out with Tough Love: Candidate Criticism of Black America Reflects Its Private Concerns," *Washington Post,* May 3, 2007, A01. Though praising Obama for raising issues like "the concept of 'acting white,'" the story notes that "some scholars assert that even if black kids do say that other black students who excel in school are 'acting white,' it is hardly a sufficient explanation for the achievement gap between black and white students, which remains vast."

96. On the role of social scientists as "cultural brokers" whose work has a significant impact on the way people understand what phenomena constitute "social problems," what precisely is problematic about such problems, and how such problems should be addressed through public policies, see O'Connor, *Poverty Knowledge.*

97. Jonah Goldberg, "The Cos Takes on Benign Neglect," *National Review Online,* July 12, 2004.

98. Dyson, *Is Bill Cosby Right?* 61.

99. Williams, *Enough,* 205.

100. Ibid., 89. While Ogbu views African Americans' oppositional identities as rooted in their historical experiences, Williams, like McWhorter, views such identities as the result of the community only recently turning its back on African Americans' historical valuing of education. Despite this difference, readers of either author are left with the impression that in the present moment African Americans are immersed in a dysfunctional culture that explains their unwillingness to succeed academically.

101. Williams reports that the phrase was told to Ogbu by a student interviewed as part of his Shaker Heights study. However, Williams fails to provide the reader with a proper citation. Williams, *Enough,* 100.

102. Ibid.

103. Bill Cosby, quoted in Williams, *Enough,* 169.

104. Badillo, *One Nation, One Standard,* 32, 42, 37, 3. Badillo gives only anecdotal evidence for the first claim, cites no evidence for the second, and cites only that "in the 2004 presidential election, 18 percent of Hispanics voted, compared with 39 percent of blacks and 51 percent of whites" (3) as evidence for the third. The book provides no source for these data.

105. Badillo, *One Nation, One Standard,* 108.

106. Williams, *Enough,* 91–92, 92, 103, 103.

107. Badillo, *One Nation, One Standard,* 44, 4, 4, 51.

108. Public Law 107-110. The act was a six-year reauthorization of the 1965 Elementary and Secondary Education Act (ESEA), which directed federal money to schools with large populations of economically disadvantaged students. See U.S. Department of Education, "No Child Left Behind," n.d., www.ed.gov/nclb/landing.jhtml?src=ln. At the time of this writing, the reauthorization of NCLB is stalled in the U.S. Congress.

109. Schools must also continue to administer the federal National Assessment Education Program (NAEP) tests.

110. Deborah Meier, "NCLB and Democracy," in *Many Children Left Behind,* ed. Deborah Meier and George Wood (Boston: Beacon, 2004), 67.

111. George Bush, quoted in Williams, *Enough,* 45.

112. Badillo, *One Nation, One Standard,* 104.

113. Rudolph W. Giuliani, foreword to Badillo, *One Nation, One Standard,* ix.

114. George Bush, foreword to White House, "No Child Left Behind," January 2002, www.whitehouse.gov/news/reports/no-child-left-behind.html, quoted in Katheryne Mitchell, "Educating the National Citizen in Neoliberal Times: From Multicultural Self to the Strategic Cosmopolitan," *Transactions of the Institute of British Geographers* 28 (2003): 399.

115. Mitchell, "Educating the National Citizen," 399.

116. The original NCLB act provided slight increases in federal funding to Title I schools.

117. In *Talking Back,* bell hooks explains that "moving from silence into speech is for the oppressed, the colonized, the exploited . . . a gesture of defiance that heals, that makes new life and new growth possible. It is that act of speech, of 'talking back,' that is no mere gesture of empty words, that is the expression of our movement from object to subject—the liberated voice." bell hooks, *Talking Back: Thinking Feminist, Thinking Black* (Boston: South End Press, 1989).

CHAPTER 2

1. Because of severe overcrowding and because the district ignored community calls to build another high school in South L.A., the school was changed to a year-round schedule.

2. Students on A Track go to school from September to December, are off January and February, and then go back on from March to June; students on B Track are on from November through February (interrupted to change semesters at the beginning of January), are off through April, then go back on from May through August, with the new school year for B Track starting in July. In essence, B-Track students finish their year on the last Friday of June and then return the following Monday to begin their new year. C-Track students go to school from January through April and July through October.

3. IDEA's publications can be downloaded from their Web site at www.idea.
gseis.ucla.edu/publications/index.html. For the purposes of this chapter, see "Report on the Education Gap in Los Angeles County" (2004) and "Separate and Unequal 50 Years after Brown: California's Racial 'Opportunity Gap'" (2004). I am indebted to John Rogers for his help and perspective on these issues.

4. Beverly Hills High School is a smaller high school than Fremont, with only 2,370 students in 2006. The average class size was 27.5:1, but in the ninth and tenth grades the school reduced the class size to 20:1. Ninety-six percent of the graduating class of 2006 planned to attend two- or four-year colleges.

5. Math teacher Joel Vaca testified in his declaration for the *Williams* case, "I have seen live rats and their droppings in my classroom. Since the beginning of the 2001–2 school year, I have had to clean up rat feces in my classroom about once a week. I have also had to play what I call 'roach hockey' already twice this school year." His declaration and those of others quoted in this chapter have been taken from www.decentschools.org, which has put all the case's declarations and legal briefs online.

6. Fremont has a complicated racial history. Built in the 1920s as a haven for white students as the demographics of South L.A. were beginning to change, it remained all white until the late 1940s. Two white riots and fairly persistent racial harassment occurred in the school in the 1940s and early 1950s as Black students began to enroll in small numbers. By the 1960s, white students had left the school altogether, and Fremont became a nearly all-Black school, though the top administration remained white. Like their Chicano counterparts in East L.A., Black students walked out of Fremont in 1968 and 1969 to protest racially biased curricula and staff and the lack of college courses and preparation, in hopes of creating a school more responsive to the community and more committed to diversity. That student body began to change in the 1980s, and by the early 1990s the student body was predominantly Latino.

7. Jonathan Kozol provides a damning summary of conditions at Fremont in *The Shame of the Nation: The Restoration of Apartheid Schooling in America* (New York: Crown, 2005).

8. After this case was filed, the state sued each of the eighteen school districts where the ninety-seven student plaintiffs attended school. The state claimed that the deplorable school conditions were a problem for the local school districts to resolve on their own and not the responsibility for the state. The judge put this case on hold till *Williams* was decided.

9. The state committed $188 million in 2007–8 for new textbooks and repairing buildings at 2,400 of the lowest-performing schools across California.

10. 2000 U.S. Census population data for census tracts 2395, 2396, 2397, and 2398, which border the school, downloaded from www.census.gov; Susannah Rosenblatt, "More L.A. County Children Live in Poverty," *Los Angeles Times,* October 19, 2006.

11. At the end of the school year, I talked with students about my using their journals in my research. Students were given a form to fill out to give consent to having their journals used in my research and writing. A handful of students did not want their journals used and indicated their lack of consent on the forms. Most were eager and gave back all their previous journals so they could be included. All names have been changed to protect their identities.

12. I came to Fremont almost accidentally. I had been awarded a Rockefeller Humanities Fellowship and wanted to spend the year in L.A. working in a high school. I met with the superintendent of District I, responsible for the South L.A. high schools, to talk about my idea of doing an intensive writing/ethnic studies project in an L.A. high school. While I expressed an interest in working with African American students, she referred me to Fremont, in part because it was year-round and I could go visit the school in early July (which is when I was in L.A. to set this program up) and in part because she was excited about the work of the new principal, LaVerne Brunt. Ms. Brunt was happy at the possibility of having a (free) college professor part time at Fremont for a year and gave me access and her blessing to set up the program I wanted at the school. Through the advice of the UCLA resource person working at the school, I paired with Steve Lang and Sarah Knopp, two A-Track U.S. history teachers recommended for their teaching talents and receptivity to an ethnic studies focus.

13. While students were required to do journals, they were just given credit each week for having done them, rather than being graded on their work. We checked them off, wrote comments on them, and turned them back. Some students would respond in later journals to questions we had asked, and many were eager to read our remarks when they got their journal back.

14. The original assignment included the following suggestion: "You can write about your family, your plans for the weekend or things that have happened to you in the past, your ideas about Fremont High School or music or politics, your thoughts about Los Angeles or who should be president of the United States or the war in Iraq." Later in the semester we passed out a list of additional topics that included childhood memories and where you grew up, your favorite place in L.A., your plans and dreams for the future, and descriptions of your family or best friend.

15. Nearly twenty-five thousand eighth graders were first surveyed as part of the 1988 National Educational Longitudinal Survey along with these students' teachers, parents, and school administrators. Coursework and grades from their high school and postsecondary transcripts were also available. A sample of these respondents were then resurveyed in 1990, 1992, 1994, and 2000 on a range of topics, including school, work, and home experiences; educational resources and support; the role in education of their parents and peers; neighborhood characteristics; and educational and occupational aspirations. Philip Cook and Jens Ludwig, "Weighing the Burden of 'Acting White': Are There Race Differences in

Attitudes toward Education?" and "'Acting White': Is It the Silent Killer of the Educational Aspirations of Inner-City Blacks?" *Journal of Blacks in Higher Education*, no. 17 (Autumn 1997): 93–95.

16. Quoted in Michael Eric Dyson, *Is Bill Cosby Right? Or Has the Black Middle-Class Lost Its Mind?* (New York: Basic Civitas Books, 2005), 87–88.

17. In these journal excerpts, I have corrected most spelling and some grammar. Given that most writers have access to spell and grammar check but that these writers did not, it did not seem fair to keep their spelling mistakes when I was correcting mine. Many of their errors were made in haste and certainly would have been corrected if their papers had been returned to them for revision or if they had typed them on the computer. However, in choosing to correct the spelling, I also have likely corrected some mistakes that were made because the student had more limited writing skills. A large number of students were not writing at the eleventh-grade level—and many had significant difficulty with writing.

18. Ronald Ferguson at Harvard's Kennedy School of Government has found that high- and low-achieving young men report pressure coming from outside of their peer groups, from strangers, storekeepers, and teachers. These negative attitudes were the ones felt most strongly by these young men surveyed. Cited in Deborah Prothrow-Stith, *Deadly Consequences* (New York: Harper Collins, 1991), 93.

19. Studies like Sharon Thompson's *Going All the Way: Teenage Girls' Tales of Sex, Romance, and Pregnancy* (New York: Hill and Wang, 1995) and Penelope Eckert's *Jocks and Burnouts: Social Categories and Identity in the High School* (New York: Teachers College Press, 1989) demonstrate how anti-intellectualism is by no means limited to nonwhite high schools. Cook and Ludwig's studies ("Weighing the Burden" and "Acting White") also found that Black students do not report any less popularity as the result of school success than whites; in fact, if anything, their findings suggest that Black students get a larger popularity boost from academic successes than white students.

20. Our philosophy—which not all teachers share—was that there was a pedagogical value in reading out loud: students would improve through the act of doing it, and ultimately it was important for them to get to a place of comfort with their reading. While we sought to create a supportive environment for this (making clear that laughing or interrupting the student to tell him or her how to read the word was not appropriate), we did not have access to extra reading specialists when we identified students with difficulties. We worked with them in class, particularly on the days when students were doing bookwork because it was easier to call a student over for extra work without making him or her feel singled out. But our ability to remediate significant difficulties with reading was limited—and we recognized the courage it took for some students to read publicly.

21. Part of what seems mystifying about commentaries such as Williams's and Cosby's is that they seem to forget what teenagers are actually like. Teenage attitude is often a good signal that you have hit upon something important. While such attitude is often infuriating (I certainly left class on a number of occasions fed up and despairing), it rarely signals actual indifference or disdain. More often than not, apathy is a costume put on to protect the young person from being disappointed by something or someone he or she actually considers quite valuable.

22. W. E. B. Du Bois writes, "Between me and the other world there is ever an unasked question: . . . How does it feel to be a problem? . . . It is a peculiar sensation, this double-consciousness, this sense of always looking at one's self through the eyes of others, of measuring one's soul by the tape of a world that looks on in amused contempt and pity." W. E. B. Du Bois, *Souls of Black Folk* (New York: Signet, 1969), 213, 215.

23. Michelle Fine, in *Framing Dropouts: Notes on the Politics of an Urban Public High School* (Albany: State University of New York Press, 1991), has shown how quickly students who drop out possessing larger critiques of school and society lose these and blame themselves for their failure (136–37).

24. Alexander Donnell and Bobbi Murray, "L.A. High School Confidential," *Los Angeles City Beat*, September 15, 2005.

25. Nearly one-fifth (19.9 percent) of the teachers at Fremont were emergency certified and another 14.7 percent were in a preinternship program, compared to 4.9 percent emergency certified and 2.0 percent preinternship throughout the state.

26. For 2003–4, on the basis of scores from the California Standards Test, 7 percent of students met or achieved the state standard in English, 1 percent in math, 2 percent in science, and 7 percent in social studies (as compared with districtwide percentages of 24 percent, 26 percent, 12 percent, and 18 percent respectively).

CHAPTER 3

1. Pseudonyms are being used for persons and places in this study.

2. Upward Bound Programs were created in 1965. As part of the "War on Poverty" initiatives in the 1960s, President Lyndon Johnson signed legislation such as the Economic Opportunity Act, which gave rise to the Office of Economic Opportunity and special programs targeting students from disadvantaged backgrounds. Upward Bound was part of the TRIO initiative and was supported by the Higher Education Act of 1965. Among the goals of Upward Bound are to target youth between the ages of thirteen and nineteen years (grades nine through twelve) who have experienced low academic success. For students to be admitted into the program they must be low-income and first-generation college-bound students. The program can then support students for four years of

high school by providing supplementary educational services after school and in the summer to increase the college-going rate of this population. Currently, there are several types of Upward Bound programs: traditional Upward Bound programs and Upward Bound Math/Science. Each program targets the same populations, but traditional Upward Bound programs provide a liberal arts–based curriculum, whereas Upward Bound Math/Science emphasizes math and science skills enhancement. For more on the history of Upward Bound, see Edward J. McElroy and Maria Armesto, "TRIO and Upward Bound: History, Programs, and Issues—Past, Present and Future," *Journal of Negro Education* 67 (Autumn 1998): 373–80.

3. Royster has observed that society's gendered perceptions of less affluent Black boys and men, coupled with their own gendered patterns of resistance, tend to preclude any further examination of the ways in which institutional practices curtail Black males' opportunities, such as the educational inequities that underprepare and stigmatize black boys and delay Black men's transitions from school to work and Black men's severe networking disadvantages during the job search, hiring, and early job entry stages. Hence CAI staff's explanation for the decline of Black male participation in CAI tends to reinforce false notions that young men value making money more than school and that girls are more disciplined toward school than boys, without delving into whether these young men actually left the program for a job or subsequently received one. Deirdre A. Royster, "What Happens to Potential Discouraged? Masculinity Norms and the Contrasting Institutional and Labor Market Experiences of Less Affluent Black and White Men," *Annals of the American Academy of Political and Social Science* 609 (January 2007): 153.

4. In a Triangle Research Institute study of Upward Bound programs in the United States, Cahalan and Curtin found that the programs were disproportionately female and that one of the biggest reason for students leaving before completing the program was to "seek part-time work." Margaret W. Cahalan and Thomas R. Curtin, *A Profile of the Upward Bound Program: 2000–2001* (Washington, DC: U.S. Department of Education, 2004), www.ed.gov/programs/trioupbound/ubprofile-00-01.pdf.

5. For more on young men's experiences in the CAI program, see Noel Anderson, "A Good Student, Trapped: Urban Minority Males and Constructions of Academic Achievement," *Perspectives in Education* 22 (December 2004): 71–82.

6. Pedro A. Noguera, *City Schools and the American Dream: Reclaiming the Promise of Public Education* (New York: Teachers College Press, 2003).

7. Royster, "What Happens to Potential?"

8. According to information from the New York City Department for Youth and Community Development, summer youth employment jobs declined approximately 20 percent from 1999 to 2006. See Center for an Urban Future, "Summer Help," June 2007, www.nycfuture.org/images_pdfs/pdfs/Summer%20Help.pdf.

9. Mark Levitan, "Out of School, Out of Work . . . Out of Luck? New York City's Disconnected Youth," Community Service Society of New York, January 2005, www.cssny.org/pubs/special/2005_01_disconnectedyouth/2005_01_disconnectedyouth.pdf.

10. Harry J. Holzer, "Reconnecting Young Black Men: What Policies Would Help?" in National Urban League, *The State of Black America 2007: Portrait of the Black Male* (New York: National Urban League, 2007).

11. Ibid.

12. The term *pushed out* or *discharged* is used to classify public school students who are released from schools by the school administration for a variety of reasons, including but not limited to failing academic performance, excessive absences, truancy, suspensions, or expulsions. Students are often transferred to alternative high schools or to GED programs. It has been common for students to be discharged from a school without proper notice to families and without support in finding an alternative schools or programs.

13. Betsy Gotbaum and Advocates for Children, "Pushing Out At-Risk Students: An Analysis of High School Discharge Figures. A Report by the Public Advocate for the City of New York," Citizens Committee for Children of New York, November 21, 2002, http://pubadvocate.nyc.gov/policy/ pdfs/pushing_out_at-risk_students.pdf.

14. Since this report, several lawsuits have been filed against the New York City Department of Education by parents of students who were discharged. Officials have begun closer investigation of the discharge issue to get a handle on where students go after being released.

15. According to a 2006 report by the Community Service Society of New York, the unemployment rate for teenagers and young adults has increased since the recession period in 2000. See Mark Levitan, "Unemployment and Joblessness in New York City 2006: Recovery Bypasses Youth," February 2006, www.cssny.org/pdfs/LaborMarketReport2006.pdf.

16. Stuart Tannock, "Why Do Working Youth Work Where They Do? A Report from the Young Worker Project," March 2002, http://laborcenter.berkeley.edu/youngworkers/working_youth.pdf.

17. Harry J. Holzer, Keith Ihlanfeldt, and David Sjoquist, "Work, Search and Travel among White and Black Youth," *Journal of Urban Economics* 35 (1994): 320–45; Keith Ihlanfeldt and David Sjoquist, "Intra-urban Job Accessibility and Hispanic Youth Employment Rates," *Journal of Urban Economics* 33 (1993): 254–71.

18. Michael A. Stoll, *Race, Space and Youth Labor Markets* (New York: Routledge, 1999).

19. Ibid., 32.

20. Roberto Fernandez and Celina Su, "Space in the Study of Labor Markets," *Annual Review of Sociology* 30 (April 2004): 545–69.

21. Also see Holzer, "Reconnecting Young Black Men."

22. Michael A. Stoll, "When Jobs Move, Do Black and Latino Men Lose? The Effect of Growth in Job Decentralization on Young Men's Jobless Incidence and Duration," *Urban Studies* 35 (December 1998): 2222.

23. William J. Wilson, *The Declining Significance of Race: Blacks and Changing American Institutions* (Chicago: University of Chicago Press, 1978); William J. Wilson, *The Truly Disadvantaged: The Inner City, the Underclass and Public Policy* (Chicago: University of Chicago Press, 1987); William J. Wilson, *When Work Disappears: The World of the New Urban Poor* (Chicago: University of Chicago Press, 1996).

24. Mwlami Shujaa, *Too Much Schooling, Too Little Education: A Paradox of Black Life in White Societies* (New York: Africa World Press, 1994).

25. Royster, "What Happens to Potential?"

26. Tannock, "Why Do Working Youth Work?"

27. Cornel West, *Race Matters* (New York: Beacon Press, 1994).

28. Rodriguez and Morrobel argue that the "formation of ethnic identity in Latino adolescents is a complex process, complicated by building relationships in mainstream culture while participating in families with various levels of traditions and acculturation. There is some evidence to suggest that bicultural environments can lead to identity crises. However, some youths are able to develop the capacity to handle themselves in various settings, negotiate the demands of each situation, and maintain pride in their various roles." Michael C. Rodriguez and Diana Morrobel, "A Review of Latino Youth Development Research and a Call for an Asset Orientation," *Hispanic Journal of Behavioral Sciences* 26 (May 2004): 11.

29. Gilbert N. Garcia, "The Factors That Place Latino Children and Youth at Risk of Educational Failure," in *Effective Programs for Latino Students*, ed. Robert Slavin and Margarita Calderon (Mahwah, NJ: Lawrence Erlbaum, 2001), 307–30.

30. Marcelo Suarez-Orozco and Carola Suarez-Orozco, *Transformations: Immigration, Family Life, and Achievement Motivation among Latino Adolescents* (Stanford: Stanford University Press, 1995).

31. The National Employment Law Project has done extensive research highlighting the discriminatory labor practices and working conditions of immigrants. See their list of publications at their Web site, www.nelp.org.

32. Stuart Tannock, *Youth at Work: The Unionized Fast Food and Grocery Workplace* (Philadelphia: Temple University Press, 2001).

33. Michael A. Stoll, "When Jobs Move."

34. Alice O'Connor, *Poverty Knowledge: Social Science, Social Policy, and the Poor in Twentieth-Century U.S. History* (Princeton: Princeton University Press, 2001).

35. Richard Majors and Janet Mancini Billson, *Cool Pose: The Dilemmas of Black Manhood in America* (New York: Lexington Books, 1992).

36. In "What Happens to Potential?" Royster argues that "though less affluent Black and white boys and men adhere to similar gendered norms and aspirations and begin with similar labor market potential, they are often sorted into very different and unequal educational and labor market trajectories" (153).

CHAPTER 4

1. The alliance was originally going to "better" schools, but that would have given the group the unfortunate acronym of STABS.

2. Orlando Patterson, "A Poverty of the Mind," *New York Times*, March 26, 2006.

3. Herman Badillo, *One Nation, One Standard: An Ex-Liberal on How Hispanics Can Succeed Just Like Other Immigrant Groups* (New York: Sentinel, 2006).

4. Bill Cosby, "Speech at the 50th Anniversary Commemoration of the *Brown v. Topeka Board of Education* Supreme Court Decision, May 22, 2004," *Black Scholar* 34 (Winter 2004): 2–5.

5. John Ogbu, quoted in Felicia Lee, "Why Are Black Students Lagging?" *New York Times*, November 30, 2002.

6. For more information, visit the UYC Web site at www.urbanyouthcollaborative.org/.

7. In 2003, the city dissolved the thirty-two community districts that organized schools since the late 1960s, replacing them with ten large, geographically defined elementary/middle school regions, each composed of several old districts, along with citywide regions for high schools and special education. In 2007, the mayor announced that these regions, too, would be dissolved. Instead, schools would be organized into four Learning Support Organizations, plus an Empowerment Zone for schools who were allowed to purchase support services on their own.

8. Kavitha Mediratta, Norm Fruchter, and Anne Lewis, *Organizing for School Reform: How Communities Are Finding Their Voices and Reclaiming Their Public Schools* (New York: Institute for Education and Social Policy, 2002).

9. Kavitha Mediratta, "A Rising Movement," *National Civic Review* (Spring 2006), 15–22; Daniel HoSang, *Youth and Community Organizing Today* (New York: Funders' Collaborative on Youth Organizing, 2003).

10. HoSang, *Youth and Community Organizing*, 8.

11. Ibid.

12. Kohei Ishihara, *Urban Transformations: Youth Organizing in Boston, New York City, Philadelphia, and Washington, D.C.* (New York: Funders' Collaborative on Youth Organizing, 2003).

13. HoSang, *Youth and Community Organizing*, 15.

14. Ishihara, *Urban Transformations*, 21.

15. See more on Generation Y at the Southwest Youth Collaborative Web site (www.swyc.org) and the Web site of the Funders' Collaborative on Youth Organizing (www.fcyo.org).

16. See the Web site of Make the Road by Walking (www.maketheroad.org/).

17. Kavitha Mediratta, "A Rising Movement," 15, 17.

18. Ibid.; Advocates for Children of New York, "School Profile: H.S. 475 John F. Kennedy High School," 2008, www.insideschools.org/fs/school_profile.php?id=1005.

19. Cosby, "Speech."

20. James Traub, "The Test Mess," *New York Times Magazine,* April 7, 2002; Anemona Hartocollis, "Boycotts and a Bill Protest Mandatory State Tests," *New York Times,* March 6, 2002.

21. Urban Youth Collaborative, "The New York City Students' 'Bill of Rights,'" n.d., www.urbanyouthcollaborative.org/sites/uyc/files/billofrights.pdf.

22. Mediratta, "Rising Movement," 19.

23. Emily Brady, "Knives on the Streets," *New York Times,* May 6, 2007.

24. David Gonzalez, "A Harsh Lesson in Finances for After-School Students," *New York Times,* June 18, 2007.

25. Julie Bosman, "A Plan to Pay for Top Scores on Some Tests Gains Ground," *New York Times,* June 9, 2007; Jennifer Medina, "Schools Plan to Pay Cash for Marks," *New York Times,* June 19, 2007.

26. Kate Stone Lombardi, "High Anxiety of Getting into College," *New York Times,* April 8, 2007.

27. Kate Stone Lombardi, "Ready, or Not," *New York Times,* November 9, 2003.

28. Mary C. Bounds, "Older (but Smarter?)," *New York Times,* April 25, 2004.

29. Abigail Sullivan Moore, "If at First You Don't Succeed," *New York Times,* November 6, 2005.

30. Amy Harmon, "Internet Gives Teenage Bullies Weapons to Wound from Afar," *New York Times,* August 26, 2004.

31. Allison Lee Cowan, "Schools' Deep-Pocketed Partners," *New York Times,* June 3, 2007.

32. Winnie Hu, "Spreadsheets and Power Plays: PTAs Go Way beyond Cookies," *New York Times,* February 23, 2007.

33. Shaquesha Alequin et al., *In between the Lines: How the New York Times Frames Youth* (New York: Youth Force, 2001), 10–11.

34. Ibid., 15 (caps in original).

35. Richard D. Kahlenberg, *Economic School Integration: An Update,* Idea Brief 2 (Washington, DC: Century Foundation, 2002).

36. Jeffrey Rosen, "The Lost Promise of School Integration," *New York Times,* April 3, 2000.

37. Ford Fessenden, "Westchester School Districts among Top Spenders," *New York Times,* June 10, 2007.

38. Eli Moore, "Paying More, Getting Less: A Comparison of NY School District Tax Rates and Expenditure per Pupil," 2006, www.maxwell.syr.edu/geo/community_geography/docs/eilimoore.pdf.

39. Education Trust, "The Funding Gap 2005: Low-Income and Minority Students Shortchanged by Most States," Winter 2005, www2.edtrust.org/NR/rdonlyres/31D276EF-v72E1-458A-8C71-E3D262A4C91E/o/FundingGap2005.pdf.

40. Michelle Fine, Janice Bloom, and Lori Chajet, "Betrayal: Accountability from the Bottom," *Voices in Urban Education,* no. 1 (Spring 2003): 19.

41. According to the U.S. Census, a Hispanic/Latino background is one of ethnicity rather than race per se, and a person can be both if he or she is an African descendant from Puerto Rico, for instance.

42. Michael Jacobson and Philip Kasinitz, "Burning the Bronx for Profit," *Nation,* November 15, 1986.

43. Manny Fernandez, "Memories Fade, as Do Some Bronx Boundary Lines," *New York Times,* September 16, 2006.

44. This point is based on the observations and comments made during meetings associated with the Northwest Bronx Clergy and Community Coalition (www.northwestbronx.org). See also David W. Dunlap, "Bronx Housing Devastation Seen Slowing Substantially," *New York Times,* March 22, 1982, and Edward Lewine, "The South Bronx? It's a State of Mind," *Bronx Beat,* March 13, 1995, for more contemporaneous documentation of the moving "northernmost" boundaries of the South Bronx.

45. Fernando Carlo et al., "Youth Take the Lead on High School Reform Issues," *Rethinking Schools* 19, no. 4 (2005), www.rethinkingschools.org/archive/19_04/yout194.shtml.

46. The program is administered by New Visions, a private intermediary organization formed to support the small schools and funded by the Carnegie Corporation of New York, the Open Society Institute, the Bill and Melinda Gates Foundation.

47. Carlo et al., "Youth Take the Lead."

48. For example, their Bronx Schools Strike Back campaign attempts to ensure that neither "small schools" housed on half of one floor in a large building nor the comprehensive high school students left behind are disadvantaged as the Gates Foundation pours money into creating small schools as the latest big educational trend.

49. Carlo et al., "Youth Take the Lead."

CONCLUSION

1. For a more detailed analysis of Barbara Johns's and the NAACP's case in *Brown,* see Bob Smith, *They Closed Their Schools: Prince Edward County, Virginia, 1951–1964* (Greensboro: University of North Carolina Press, 1965); Richard Kluger, *Simple Justice: The History of Brown v. Board of Education* (New York:

Vintage Books, 1975); Juan Williams, *Eyes on the Prize: America's Civil Rights Years, 1954–1965* (New York: Penguin, 1988).

2. Smith, *They Closed Their Schools*, 27–35.

3. The schools that the students in this book attend represent the norm for millions of poor and minority students in this country. In its report *Fifty Years after Brown v. Board of Education,* the National Commission on Teaching and America's Future concluded, "As we mark the fiftieth anniversary of *Brown v. Board of Education,* millions of low income students and children of color are concentrated in separate and unequal schools. Many are being taught by unqualified teachers, with insufficient instructional materials and a limited supply of textbooks and inadequate technology, in crumbling buildings—with vermin and broken bathrooms. These substandard teaching and learning conditions are rarely found in schools where the majority of students come from more affluent backgrounds and have a low risk of school failure. . . . As a nation we say that our goal is to leave no child behind, but the schools we provide for some children say otherwise." *National Commission on Teaching and America's Future, Fifty Years after Brown v. Board of Education: A Two-Tiered Education System* (Washington, DC: National Commission on Teaching and America's Future, May 2004), www.nctaf.org/documents/Brown_Full_Report_Final.pdf.

4. According to Justice Tom Clark, *Brown,* the Kansas case, was chosen to head the list "so that the whole question would not smack of being a purely Southern one." Williams, Eyes on the Prize, 31.

5. *Brown v. Board of Education of Topeka,* 347 U.S. 483 (1954).

6. *Brown v. Board of Education of Topeka (II),* 349 U.S. 294 (1955).

7. See Adina Back, "Exposing the Whole Segregation Myth," in *Freedom North: The Black Freedom Struggle Outside of the South, 1940–1980,* ed. Jeanne Theoharis and Komozi Woodard (New York: Palgrave Macmillan, 2002); Clarence Taylor, *Knocking at Our Own Door: Milton A. Galamison and the Struggle to Integrate New York City Schools* (New York: Columbia University Press, 1997); and Joshua Freeman, *Working-Class New York: Life and Labor since World War II* (New York: New Press, 2000).

8. *New York Times,* February 10, 1957.

9. Quoted in John and LaRee Caughey, *School Segregation on Our Doorstep: The Los Angeles Story* (Los Angeles: Quail Books, 1966), 10.

10. For more on these struggles, see Jeanne Theoharis, "Alabama on Avalon," in *The Black Power Movement,* ed. Peniel Joseph (New York: Routledge, 2006). In 1963, parent activists went to court in *Crawford v. Los Angeles Board of Education.* Originally, the plaintiffs sought to halt the renovation of Jordan High School until desegregation had been accomplished between South Gate and Jordan High Schools, but the case was expanded in 1968 to desegregation of the whole district. In 1970, Judge Alfred Gitelson issued his ruling in *Crawford,* finding both de facto and de jure segregation and ordering a comprehensive plan

for desegregation. His decision was met with vituperative opposition from many political leaders, including President Nixon and Governor Reagan, and Gitelson lost his seat on the bench. Under Judge Paul Egly, a comprehensive desegregation plan was drawn up for September 1978 but was derailed by Proposition 1 when 70 percent of California voters ratified an amendment to prevent school desegregation through court-ordered busing. Superior Court Egly lambasted the Board of Education for not even "meet[ing] the standard of *Plessy v. Ferguson.*" David S. Ettinger, "The Quest to Desegregate Los Angeles Schools," *Los Angeles Lawyer,* March 2003, 55–67.

11. *San Antonio Independent School District v. Rodriguez,* 411 U.S. 35 (1973).

12. In his dissent in the *Rodriguez* case, Thurgood Marshall noted that "the majority's holding can only be seen as a retreat from our historic commitment to equality of educational opportunity and as unsupportable acquiescence in a system which deprives children in their earliest years of the chance to reach their full potential as citizens" (ibid., 71).

13. *Milliken v. Bradley,* 418 U.S. 782 (1974).

14. Linda Greenhouse, "Justices Reject Diversity Plans in Two Districts," *New York Times,* June 28, 2007. Labor historian Nancy MacLean has argued that *Seattle* follows from a history of resistance to *Brown* advanced by the Federalist Society and other conservatives who opposed the 1954 decision and transformed their opposition to school desegregation into new language and tactics. Roberts's decision, MacLean writes, "is replete with quotable phrases from the lexicon conservative strategists honed in their think tanks in the 1970s and then carried into the nation's courtrooms through their various legal societies." Nancy MacLean, "The Scary Origins of Chief Justice Roberts's Decision Opposing the Use of Race to Promote Integration," *History News Network,* August 6, 2007, http://hnn.us/articles/41501.html.

15. He continued, "The districts here invoke the ultimate goal of those who filed *Brown* and subsequent cases to support their argument, but the argument of the plaintiff in *Brown* was that the Equal Protection Clause 'prevents states from according differential treatment to American children on the basis of their color or race,' and that view prevailed—this Court ruled in its remedial opinion that *Brown* required school districts 'to achieve a system of determining admission to the public schools on a nonracial basis.'" *Community Schools v. Seattle,* 127 S. Ct. (2007).

16. Justice Breyer's dissent asserts, "[The decision] distorts precedent, it misapplies the relevant constitutional principles, it announces legal rules that will obstruct efforts by state and local governments to deal effectively with the growing resegregation of public schools. . . . This cannot be justified in the name of the Equal Protection Clause" (ibid., 2797).

17. Jeffrey Rosen, "Can a Law Change Society," *New York Times,* July 1, 2007, sec. 4, 1.

18. Juan Williams, "Don't Mourn Brown v. Board of Education" [op-ed], *New York Times,* June 29, 2007, A29.

19. David Brooks, "The End of Integration," *New York Times,* July 6, 2007, A15.

20. Williams, "Don't Mourn Brown," A29.

21. However, Blacks see the issue somewhat differently from whites and Hispanics. While 80 percent of non-Hispanic whites and 73 percent of Hispanics believe Black children and white children have equal educational opportunities, only 49 percent of Blacks do. Lydia Saad, "Black-White Educational Opportunities Widely Seen as Equal," *Gallup Poll,* July 2, 2007, www.gallup.com /poll/28021/ BlackWhite-Educational-Opportunities-Widely-Seen-Equal.aspx. These widespread attitudes exist even though the United States boasts the greatest inequities between highest- and lowest-scoring students of any industrialized nation. William Mathis, "No Child Left Behind: Costs and Benefits," *Phi Delta Kappan,* April 2003, www.pdkintl.org/kappan/k0305mat.htm#8a.

22. Patricia Williams, "Invisible America," *Nation,* May 28, 2007.

23. For further elaboration of this history, see Theoharis and Woodard, *Freedom North,* and their *Groundwork: Local Black Freedom Movements in America* (New York: New York University Press, 2003).

24. These discourses became popular in the South as well. By the later 1960s and 1970s, increasingly southern public officials had moved from an outright defense of segregation and states' rights to a language of culturally deprived students, law and order, and forced busing.

25. Report of the Ad Hoc Committee, John Caughey Papers, Box 164, Department of Special Collections, UCLA.

26. W. E. B. Du Bois, *The Souls of Black Folk* (New York: Signet, 1969), 215.

27. Rummana Hussain, "Obama Fears 'Big Brother' over Our Shoulders," *Chicago Sun-Times,* June 26, 2005, http://obama.senate.gov/news/050626-obama_fears_big_brother_over_o/.

28. For a transcript of Bush's remarks, see "Press Conference by the President," September 20, 2007, www.whitehouse.gov/news/releases/2007/09/20070920-2.html#.

29. "George W's Love-Hate Affair with Yale," *Time,* May 23, 2001, www.time.com/time/columnist/carney/article/0,9565,127630,00.html.

30. "Obama Offers Hard Truths to Supporters," CBS.com, August 29, 2007. In a Father's Day 2008 speech at a black church in Chicago, he admonished his audience, "Don't get carried away with that eighth-grade graduation. You're supposed to graduate from eighth grade." "Obama Calls for More Responsibility from Black Fathers," *New York Times,* June 16, 2008.

31. Adolph Reed, "The Underclass as Myth and Symbol: The Poverty of Discourse about Poverty," *Radical America* 24, no. 1 (1990): 32.

32. Bill Cosby and Alvin F. Poussaint, *Come On, People: On the Path from Victims to Victors* (Nashville, TN: Thomas Nelson, 2007), 234.

33. Eva Moskowitz, "From the Mouths of Babes: New York City Public School Kids Speak Out," May 9, 2005, www.insideschools.org/nv/KIDS_REPORT.pdf.

34. For a detailed account of the act's legislative history, see Andrew Rudalevige, "No Child Left Behind: Forging a Congressional Compromise," in *No Child Left Behind? The Politics and Practice of School Accountability,* ed. Paul E. Peterson and Martin R. West (Washington, DC: Brookings Institution, 2003), 23–54.

35. Jonathan Kozol, *Shame of the Nation: The Restoration of Apartheid Schooling in America* (New York: Crown, 2005), 209. For arguments in favor of standardized testing, see Lou Gerstner Jr. et al., *Reinventing Education: Entrepreneurship in America's Public Schools* (New York: Dutton, 1994). For arguments critical of standardized testing, see Alfie Kohn, *The Schools Our Children Deserve: Moving beyond the Traditional Classroom and "Tougher Standards"* (Boston: Houghton Mifflin, 1999); and *The Case against Standardized Testing: Raising the Scores, Ruining the Schools* (Portsmouth, NH: Heinemann, 2000); and Kathy Swope and Barbara Miner, eds., *Failing Our Kids: Why the Testing Craze Won't Fix Our Schools* (Milwaukee, WI: Rethinking Schools, 2000).

36. Stan Karp, "Exit Strategy: Finding the Way Out of Iraq and NCLB," *Rethinking Schools,* Summer 2007, 14, www.rethinkingschools.org/archive/21_04/exit214.shtml.

37. In 2004, the Bush administration called for $12 billion as compared to $18 billion authorized by Congress—but light-years away from conservative figure of $84.5 billion that education professor William Mathis estimates it would take to reach NCLB mandates. See Mathis, "No Child Left Behind."

38. John R. Novak and Bruce Fuller, "Penalizing Diverse Schools? Similar Test Scores, but Different Students, Bring Federal Sanctions," Policy Brief 03-4, December 2003, Policy Analysis for California Education, http://pace.berkeley.edu/reports/PB.03-4.pdf.; Claudia Wallis and Sonja Steptoe, "How to Fix No Child Left Behind," *Time,* June 4, 2007, 41.

39. Jonathan Kozol, "The Big Enchilada," *Harper's,* August 2007, 9. Privatization, while often sold as the answer to urban school mismanagement and disrepair, lacks public accountability. Most schools that have been taken over by private enterprises, like those in Philadelphia, do no better academically, but there are even fewer means for parents and students to object.

40. S. Stullich et al., *National Assessment of Title I: Interim Report* (Washington, DC: U.S. Department of Education, Institute of Education Studies, 2006), quoted in Center for Education Policy, "Choices, Changes, and Challenges: Curriculum and Instruction in the NCLB Era," July 2007, www.cep-dc.org/_data/n_0001/resources/live/07107%20Curriculum-WEB%20FINAL%207%2031%2007.pdf.

41. Center for Education Policy, "Choices, Changes."

42. David Price, for example, has noted, "The rituals of standardized testing teach our children: that complex problems have a limited number of solutions; to write, think, and question in specific limited ways; to answer question humorlessly and to the point; that diversity of thought must give way to authoritarianism; to disengage from tangents; that learning is something we do for tests; to suppress their own analysis for that of the testing authority." David H. Price, "Outcome-Based Tyranny: Teaching Compliance While Testing Like a State," *Anthropological Quarterly* 76 (Fall 2003): 727.

43. Stan Karp, "NCLB's Selection Vision of Equality: Some Gaps Count More Than Others," in *Many Children Left Behind,* ed. Deborah Meier and George Wood, (Boston: Beacon Press, 2004), 58. Karp concludes, "NCLB imposes a mandate on schools that is put on no other institution in society: wipe out inequalities while the factors that help produce them stay in place. . . . If this sounds unfair and absurd, that's because it is. Imagine a federal law that declared that 100 percent of all citizens must have adequate health care in twelve years or sanctions will be imposed on doctors and hospitals. Or all crime must be eliminated in twelve years or the local police department will face privatization" (54, 60).

44. The removal of disruptive students from schools was a major grievance in the Black community fifty years ago, crucial to the formation of the Afro-American Teachers Association in New York City and ultimately to the movement for community control in the late 1960s.

45. Drum Major Institute, "A Look at the Impact Schools," June 2005, www.drummajorinstitute.org/library/report.php?ID=18.

46. Elora Mukherjee, *Criminalizing the Classroom: The Over-policing of New York City Schools* (New York: New York Civil Liberties Union, 2007), 21. Jennifer McCormick has written about the "holding tank" setup that now characterizes many New York schools in *Writing in the Asylum: Student Poets in City Schools* (New York: Teachers College Press, 2004).

47. If these officers were considered their own police force, the NYPD's School Safety Division would be the tenth largest police force in the nation. Mukherjee, *Criminalizing the Classroom,* 10.

48. Bloomberg and the Department of Education continue to refuse to reveal statistics on complaints of excessive force within the schools. Beth Furtig reported this information on the radio, obtained from roundabout sources.

49. Roland Fryer has gained attention for his focus on John Ogbu's "acting white" hypothesis. While much of his own evidence discounted the hypothesis, Fryer nonetheless suggested, "Minority communities in the United States have yet to generate a large cadre of high achievers. . . . As long as distressed communities provide minorities with their identities, the social costs of breaking free will remain high." Yet in describing his own cousins who got in trouble with the law, Fryer notes, "If you had put them in the schools that a lot of these people came up in [gesturing toward the apartment buildings that border Central Park,]

they probably would have been fine." Roland Fryer, "Acting White," *Education Next,* Winter 2006, 52–59; Stephen J. Dubner, "Toward a Unified Theory of Black America," *New York Times Magazine,* March 20, 2005.

50. For further description of what has happened with New York's small schools, see Lynnell Hancock, "School's Out," *Nation,* July 9, 2007.

51. See Jeannie Oakes and John Rogers, *Learning Power* (New York: Teachers College Press, 2005).

52. Eric Hanushek, "Who Could Be against 'Adequate' School Funding?" *Daily Report* (Hoover Institution), January 19, 2004, www.hoover.org/pubaffairs/dailyreport/archive/2827251.html.

53. See, for instance, Sol Stern, "New York's Fiscal Equity Follies," *City Journal,* Spring 2004; Charles Upton Sahm, "Education Policy in Wonderland," *City Journal,* Summer 2005; "Testimony of Jay P. Greene on the CFE Lawsuit," January 8, 2005, www.manhattan-institute.org/html/greene01-25-05.htm.

54. For transcript of Mayor Bloomberg's speech, see "Mayor Bloomberg Addresses National Urban League Annual Conference," July 25, 2007,www.nyc.gov:80/portal/site/nycgov/menuitem.c0935b9a57bb4ef3daf-2f1c701c789a0/index.jsp?pageID=mayor_press_release&catID=1194&doc_name=http%3A%2F%2Fwww.nyc.gov%2Fhtml%2Fom%2Fhtml%2F2007b%2Fpr256-07.html&cc=unused1978&rc=1194&ndi=1.

55. Moreover, as of spring 2007, this was not even true. Many Brooklyn high school students in a free SAT preparation program at Brooklyn College reported not ever taking the PSATs. If students attending an after-school SAT preparation program had not been given the PSAT, one can only imagine how many other New York public school students had not as well.

56. Paul Tough, "What It Takes to Make a Student," *New York Times Magazine,* November 26, 2006. What characterizes the KIPP approach, Tough claims, is "the specific types and amounts of instruction, both in academics and attitude, to compensate for everything they did not receive in their first decade of life."

57. Paul Tough, "The Class Consciousness Raiser," *New York Times Magazine,* June 10, 2007.

58. Tough reduces Payne's lack of substantive data to a frivolous concern of academics unduly concerned with approval of their academic peers. "Her talks are nothing like university lectures. They're a blend of cracker-barrel wisdom, Tony Robbins-style motivational speaking and a Chris Rock comedy routine. And that means that among academics in good standing, saying something nice about Ruby Payne is a good way to invite the disapproval of your peers" (ibid.).

59. Cosby and Poussaint, *Come On, People,* 104, 224.

60. James Baldwin, "A Talk to Teachers," in *The Price of the Ticket: Collected Nonfiction, 1948–1985* (New York: Macmillan, 1985), 326.

61. For useful reviews of school finance litigation, see Molly S. McUsic, "The Future of Brown v. Board of Education: Economic Integration of the Public

Schools," *Harvard Law Review* 117, no. 5 (2004); 1334–77, and "The Law's Role in the Distribution of Education: The Promises and Pitfalls of School Finance Litigation," in *Law and School Reform: Six Strategies for Promoting Educational Equity,* ed. Jay P. Heubert (New Haven: Yale University Press, 1999); Douglas S. Reed, "Twenty-Five Years after Rodriguez: School Finance Litigation and the Impact of the New Judicial Federalism," *Law and Society Review* 32, no. 1 (1998): 175–220; James E. Ryan, "Schools, Race, and Money," *Yale Law Review* 109, no. 2 (1999): 249–316, and "The Influence of Race in School Finance Reform," *Michigan Law Review* 98, no. 2 (1999): 432–81.

62. *Campaign for Fiscal Equity v. State of New York,* 719 N.Y.S.2d 475 (2001).

63. Foundation aid is the single classroom operating aid category that replaces over thirty different categories of school aid—and was the focus of the lawsuit and years of advocacy by the Campaign for Fiscal Equity. The adopted budget includes $1.1 billion in new foundation aid for schools across the state.

64. Jonathan Glater, "Fight over California Schools Raises New Issue of Priorities," *New York Times,* April 18, 2003.

65. The *Williams* settlement has at least four gaps, according to UCLA professor John Rogers: "There was not enough capacity in County Offices (let alone district offices) to do meaningful oversight. The power of the complaint process lies in transparency and empowered community organizations. People need to know about their rights of complaint and they need organizations to support them in the complaint process and to help them strategize about how to use the complaint process. A meaningful reform would have provided state funding to community-based non-profits to play this role. *Williams* deferred the issues of teachers to NCLB compliance. Hence, the most critical factor is not really in play in *Williams*'s implementation (aside from reporting). The number of unqualified teachers has dropped in the last couple years, but this is largely due to budgetary changes and demographic changes. New and acute shortages are likely in the next five-ten years unless new policies are put in place. And even now, many schools serving low-income students cannot maintain stable faculties. Fundamentally, what is needed is more money." Pers. comm., August 23, 2007.

66. California's constitution has even more vague language. Two provisions were used to establish the legal claims of educational adequacy. Article IX, Section 1, says: "A general diffusion of knowledge and intelligence being essential to the preservation of the rights and liberties of the people, the Legislature shall encourage by all suitable means the promotion of intellectual, scientific, moral, and agricultural improvement." Article IX, Section 5, says: "The Legislature shall provide for a system of common schools by which a free school shall be kept up and supported in each district at least six months in every year, after the first year in which a school has been established."

67. For arguments in favor of the shift from "equity" to "adequacy" claims in school finance litigation, see William H. Clune, "The Shift from Equity to Adequacy in School Finance," *Education Policy* 8, no. 4 (1994): 376–94; Peter Enrich, "Leaving Equality Behind: New Directions in School Finance Reform," *Vanderbilt Law Review* 101 (1995): 122–28; and Michael Heise, "State Constitutions, School Finance Litigation, and the 'Third Wave': From Equity to Adequacy," *Temple Law Review* 68, no. 3 (1995): 1152–76. Enrich notes that "adequacy" claims are politically appealing for "elites who derive the greatest benefits from existing inequalities, because adequacy does not threaten their ability to retain a superior position." It is precisely because "adequacy" cases do not threaten the "supreme position" of elites that they are limited as tools to bring about a more equitable and just distribution of resources and power. Quoted in James E. Ryan, "Schools, Race, and Money," *Yale Law Journal* 109, no. 2 (1999): 270. In thinking about the limitations of "adequacy" claims, it is important to consider Marshall's observation in his dissent in *Rodriguez* that "the Equal Protection Clause is not addressed to the minimal sufficiency but rather to the unjustifiable inequalities of state action. It mandates nothing less that that 'all persons similarly circumscribed shall be treated alike.'"

68. John Dewey, *The School and Society* (Chicago: University of Chicago Press, 1907).

69. Daniel Aloi, "Educator-Activist Robert Moses Calls for Federal Education Reform at Ithaca Community Forum," *Cornell University News Service*, June 10, 2005, www.news.cornell.edu/stories/June05/Moses_talk.dea.html.

70. To meet A-G requirements, districts would have to require two years of foreign language and one year of visual/performing arts; three years of math, including geometry, algebra I, and algebra II; and two years of high school science that would have to be lab-based biology and chemistry.

71. Smith, *They Closed Their Schools*, 34.

72. Ibid., 48.

73. On the ways "money matters" in improving student achievement, see sources cited in chapter 1, note 61. For a critique of the conclusion that "money matters," see Eric A. Hanushek, "Money Might Matter Somewhere: A Response to Hedges, Laine, and Greenwald," *Educational Researcher* 23, no. 4 (1994): 5–8.

74. Samuel Freedman, "A Queens High School with 3,600 Students, and Room for Just 1, 800," *New York Times*, January 16, 2008; Rudalevige, "No Child Left Behind," 35.

75. One of the curious aspects of NCLB is that it moved the federal government from having oversight and a role in the education of poor children (established in EASA in 1965) to having this oversight and role in the education of all children. While it undermined the overall intent of EASA and Title I, its very insertion of federal authority over education policy and standards may actually

provide a platform for equity. Andrew Rudalevige writes, "NCLB makes an important extension of federal authority of state and local schools" ("No Child Left Behind," 24). Indeed, by weakening the federalist system of education in crucial ways and by asserting the national interest in education, it demonstrates the ways equity issues can no longer be reserved just for the states.

76. We agree with scholars and educators who are calling for different measures to assess student proficiency—and their considered objections that standardized testing does not do this reliably or substantively. Our purpose here is to augment these criticisms with a more far-reaching reimagination of NCLB.

77. Establishing the right to a quality education moves us beyond the post–civil rights position of having to prove that these young people deserve such an education. The idea of right to a quality education is that one gets to have it regardless of whether one deserves it or uses it well; as with the right to free speech, a person may speak recklessly, poorly, or not very often, but the person still has the constitutional right to free speech.

78. The goal of amending the Constitution to establish every child's right to a quality education would face resistance, given public fears that such "nationalization" of public education might erode local controls of schools. In fact, the Court's decision in *Rodriguez* reflected such fears. On how the *Rodriguez* decision was shaped by Justice Lewis Powell Jr.'s Cold War–influenced opposition to centralized control of public education, see Paul Sracic, "The Brown Decision's Other Legacy: Civic Education and the Rodriguez Case," *PS: Political Science and Politics* 37, no. 2 (2004): 215–18.

79. Several states are experimenting with having student representatives on school governance councils. Students are a part of the interview process for teachers, curriculum matters, and the review of the quality of learning in a number of charter and New Vision Schools in New York, such as Bushwick High School for Social Justice. Relatedly, in 2003, students in REAL HARD (Representing Educated Active Leaders—Having A Righteous Dream), a community youth leadership organization, designed and collected one thousand report card surveys evaluating teaching, counseling, school safety, and facilities at three Oakland, California, high schools. The students compiled their findings, analyzed the results, and made concrete recommendations to improve the schools in a comprehensive report.

METHODOLOGICAL APPENDIX

1. Andrea Fontana and James H. Frey, "The Interview: From Neutral Stance to Political Involvement," in *The Sage Handbook of Qualitative Research*, ed. Norman K. Denzin and Yvonna S. Lincoln, 3rd ed. (Thousand Oaks, CA: Sage Publications, 2005), 722.

2. Rebecca Raby, "Across a Great Gulf? Conducting Research with Adolescents," in *Representing Youth: Methodological Issues in Critical Youth Studies,* ed. Amy L. Best (New York: New York University Press, 2007), 39–60.

3. G. Stanley Hall, "Child Study and Its Relation to Education," *Forum* 29 (1900): 688–702, and *Adolescence: Its Psychology and Its Relation to Physiology, Anthropology, Sociology, Sex, Crime, Religion, and Education* (New York: Appleton, 1904).

4. For critiques of the developmental psychology model, see Virginia Caputo, "Anthropology's Silent 'Others': A Consideration of Some Conceptual and Methodological Issues for the Study of Youth and Children Cultures," in *Youth Cultures: A Cross-Cultural Perspective,* ed. Vered Amit-Talai and Helena Wulff (New York: Routledge, 1995); Allison James, Chris Jenks, and Alan Prout, *Theorizing Childhood* (Cambridge: Polity Press, 1998); Jan Nespor, "The Meaning of Research: Kids as Subjects and Kids as Inquirers," *Qualitative Inquiry* 3, no. 4 (1998): 368–88; Nancy Lesko, *Act Your Age: The Cultural Construction of Adolescence* (New York: Routledge, 2001); Sandy Fraser et al., eds., *Doing Research with Children and Young People* (Thousand Oaks, CA: Sage Publications, 2004); Diane Hogan, "Researching 'the Child' in Developmental Psychology," in *Researching Children's Experience: Methods and Approaches,* ed. Sheila Green and Diane Hogan (Thousand Oaks, CA: Sage Publications, 2005), 22–41.

5. Nancy Lesko, "Denaturalizing Adolescence: The Politics of Contemporary Representations," *Youth and Society* 28 (1998): 156.

6. Ibid., 140.

7. On the discourse on the state of "crisis" among young people and its relation to racialized discourses regarding teenagers of color, see Henry Giroux, *Fugitive Cultures: Race, Violence, and Youth* (New York: Routledge, 1996).

8. Lesko, "Denaturalizing Adolescence," 156.

9. See Paul Willis, *Learning to Labour: How Working Class Kids Get Working Class Jobs* (Farnborough, UK: Saxon House, 1977); Stuart Hall and Tony Jefferson, eds., *Resistance through Rituals: Youth Subcultures in Post-war Britain* (Milton Keynes, UK: Open University Press, 1975); Nadine Dolby, "Review: Youth, Culture, and Identity: Ethnographic Explorations," *Educational Researcher* 31, no. 8 (2002): 37–42; Best, *Representing Youth;* and James et al., *Theorizing Childhood.*

10. Sari Knopp Bilken, "Trouble in Memory Lane," in Best, *Representing Youth,* 265.

11. Norman K. Denzin and Yvonna S. Lincoln, "Entering the Field of Qualitative Research," in *The Landscape of Qualitative Research: Theories and Issues,* ed. Norman K. Denzin and Yvonna S. Lincoln (Thousand Oaks, CA: Sage Publications, 1998), 8.

12. Norman K. Denzin, *The Research Act: A Theoretical Introduction to Sociological Methods,* 3rd ed. (Englewood Cliffs, NJ: Prentice Hall, 1989), 116, quoted in Fontana and Frey, "Interview," 720. On how social positions "filter knowledge,"

see Cherríe Moraga and Gloria Anzaldúa, *This Bridge Called My Back: Writings by Radical Women of Color* (New York: Kitchen Table/Women of Color Press, 1983); Gloria Anzaldúa, *Borderlands/La Frontera: The New Mestiza* (San Francisco: Aunt Lute Books, 1999); bell hooks, *Feminist Theory from Margin to Center* (Boston: South End Press, 1984); Patricia Hill Collins, *Black Feminist Thought: Knowledge, Consciousness, and the Politics of Empowerment* (New York: Routledge, 1990); and Sandra Harding, ed., *Feminism and Methodology* (Bloomington: Indiana University Press, 1987).

13. Donna Haraway, "Situated Knowledges: The Science Question in Feminism and the Privilege of Partial Perspective," in *Simians, Cyborgs, and Women: The Reinvention of Nature* (New York: Routledge, 1991), 191.

14. Sandra Harding, "Introduction: Is There a Feminist Method?" in Harding, *Feminism and Methodology*, 9.

15. Lesko, "Denaturalizing Adolescence," 149.

16. Amy L. Best, introduction to *Representing Youth*, 12.

17. Raby, "Across a Great Gulf," 50.

18. For a consideration of how memories influence field relations between young research participants and adult researchers as well as the gathering and analyzing of data, see Bilken, "Trouble on Memory Lane."

19. Clifford Geertz, "Thick Description: Toward an Interpretive Theory of Culture," in *The Interpretation of Cultures* (New York: Basic Books, 2000), 13.

20. James P. Spradley, *The Ethnographic Interview* (New York: Holt, Rinehart and Winston, 1979), 25.

21. Fontana and Frey, "Interview," 716.

22. Best, introduction to *Representing Youth*, 21. Building trust and rapport with young research participants can be complicated by the age differences between them and the researchers. Nancy Mandell has suggested that researchers conducting fieldwork among children can reduce the social distance between research participants and themselves by adopting a "least-adult" role in which the researcher minimizes her or his "adult-like characteristics" by engaging in rather than simply observing the everyday practices of children—playing games, for example. Nancy Mandell, "The Least-Adult Role in Studying Children," *Journal of Contemporary Ethnography* 16 (1988): 435. Neither Jeanne, Noel, nor Celina attempted to adopt such a role in the course of their fieldwork. As Best notes, in research with teenagers, the researcher who adopts such a role "runs the risk of being defined a 'wannabe,' a most undesirable label within adolescent peer groups." Best, introduction to *Representing Youth*, 23.

23. In chapter 3, Noel explains his focus on the stories of male students.

24. Douglas Foley and Angela Valenzuela, "Critical Ethnography: The Politics of Collaboration," in Denzin and Lincoln, *Sage Handbook*, 223. On unstructured interview techniques, see James P. Spradley, *The Ethnographic Interview* (New

York: Holt, Rinehart, and Winston, 1979); Denzin, *Research Act;* and John Lofland et al., *Analyzing Social Settings: A Guide to Qualitative Observations and Analysis,* 4th ed. (Belmont, CA: Wadsworth, 2005).

25. Anselm Strauss and Juliet Corbin, *Basics of Qualitative Research: Techniques and Procedures for Developing Grounded Theory,* 2nd ed. (Thousand Oaks, CA: Sage Publications, 1998).

26. Matthew B. Miles and Michael Huberman, *Qualitative Data Analysis: An Expanded Sourcebook* (Thousand Oaks, CA: Sage Publications, 1994).

27. Janice M. Morse et al., "Verification Strategies for Establishing Reliability and Validity in Qualitative Research," *International Journal of Qualitative Methods* 1 (2002): 1–19.

28. Robert G. Burgess, *In the Field* (London: Routledge, 1993), 48, quoted in Madeline Leonard, "With a Capital 'G': Gatekeepers and Gatekeeping in Researching Children," in Best, *Representing Youth,* 135.

29. On youth as gatekeepers, see Leonard, "With a Capital 'G'," and Gary A. Fine and Kent L. Sandstrom, *Knowing Children: Participant Observation with Minors* (Newbury Park, CA: Sage Publications, 1988).

30. Geertz, "Thick Description," 20.

31. Ibid., 15 (emphasis in the original).

32. Denzin and Lincoln, "Entering the Field," 4.

33. See George Steinmetz, "Odious Comparisons: Incommensurability, the Case Study, and 'Small N's' in Sociology," *Sociological Theory* 22, no. 3 (2004): 371–400. Also see Sophia Mihic, Stephen G. Engelmann, and Elizabeth Rose Wingrove, "Facts, Values, and 'Real' Numbers: Making Sense in and of Political Science," in *The Politics of Method in the Human Sciences: Positivism and its Epistemological Others,* ed. George Steinmetz (Durham: Duke University Press, 2005); and Ian Shapiro, Rogers Smith, and Tarek E. Masoud, *Problems and Methods in the Study of Politics* (New York: Cambridge University Press, 2004).

34. Stanley Lieberson, "Small Ns and Big Conclusions: An Examination of the Reasoning Based on Small Number of Cases," *Social Forces* 20 (1991): 307–20, and "More on the Uneasy Case for Using Mill-Type in Small-N Comparative Studies," *Social Forces* 72 (1994): 1225–37, both quoted in Steinmetz, "Odious Comparisons," 397.

35. Joe R. Feagin, Anthony M. Orun, and Gideon Sjoberg, *A Case for the Case Study* (Chapel Hill: University of North Carolina Press, 1991).

36. Alan Peshkin, "The Goodness of Qualitative Research," *Educational Researcher* 22 (March 1993): 23.

37. Steinmetz, "Odious Comparisons," 383.

38. Robert E. Stake, "Qualitative Case Studies," in Denzin and Lincoln, *Sage Handbook,* 457 (emphasis in the original).

39. In this manner, our approach echoes Michael Burawoy's methodological concept of the extended case method in which anomalies are problematized rather than dismissed (279) in order to reconstruct theory "out of data collected through participant observation" (271). Michael Burawoy, "The Extended Case Method," in *Ethnography Unbound: Power and Resistance in the Modern Metropolis,* ed. Michael Burawoy et al. (Berkeley: University of California Press, 1991), 271–87.

Index

About the Authors

GASTON ALONSO is Assistant Professor of Political Science at Brooklyn College, City University of New York. His research interests lie in understanding the incorporation of contemporary immigrants into the United States in light of the experiences of past immigrants as well as exploring how changing understandings of race, ethnicity, and national belonging have shaped the models that social scientists have used to understand those experiences.

NOEL S. ANDERSON is Assistant Professor of Political Science at Brooklyn College, City University of New York. His scholarly research focuses on urban politics and education, education policy, and comparative issues in education policy (in South Africa and the United States). Along with Haroon Kharem, he is coeditor of *Education as Freedom: African American Thought and Activism* (2009).

CELINA SU is Assistant Professor of Political Science at Brooklyn College, City University of New York. Her research interests lie in the role of civil society in social policy making, especially in the intersection of cultural practices and discourse, grassroots groups, and education and health care policy. She is the author of *Streetwise for Book Smarts: Grassroots Organizing and Education Reform in the Bronx* (forthcoming).

JEANNE THEOHARIS is Associate Professor of Political Science and Endowed Chair in Women's Studies at Brooklyn College of the City University of New York. She is the coauthor with Alejandra Marchevsky of *Not Working: Latina Immigrants, Low-Wage Jobs, and the Failure of Welfare Reform* (2006); coeditor with Komozi Woodard of *Freedom North: Black Freedom Struggles Outside of the South, 1940–1980* (2003) and *Groundwork: Local Black Freedom Movements in America* (2005); and coauthor with Athan Theoharis of *These Yet to Be United States: Civil Rights and Civil Liberties in America since 1945* (2003).

Photo of Sistas and Brothas United, 2008.